Learning
Styles
in Action

Barbara Prashnig

Published by Network Continuum Education
The Tower Building, 11 York Road, London SE1 7NX

www.continuumbooks.com

An imprint of the Continuum International Publishing Group Ltd

First published 2006
© Barbara Prashnig, 2006
Reprinted 2006

ISBN-13:   978 1 85539 208 3
ISBN-10:   1 85539 208 9

Managing editor: Janice Baiton – Janice Baiton Editorial Services
Design by: Neil Hawkins
Cover design by: Marc Maynard

Printed in Great Britain by MPG Books Ltd, Bodmin, Cornwall

Contents

To obtain more information and to access the Learning Style Analysis and Teaching Style Analysis discussed in this book, visit

www.networkcontinuum.co.uk/lsa

Preface

The solutions we need for our most pressing problems are not always found near at hand. Sometimes we have to hunt for exciting possibilities, scanning the horizon to see if answers can be spotted there. When we find them, and eventually we do find them no matter how many obstacles stand in our way, dark places are illuminated, the impossible becomes possible and what was previously thought to be 'wackiland' becomes just what we need to solve the seemingly unsolvable.

Of the many ways Network Continuum Education helps teachers to solve their pressing problems, one that requires considerable care is the role of identifying new possibilities from other countries to bring to their attention. Over the years, the company has supported Gordon Dryden in spreading his vision of how ICT can underpin effective learning. The Critical Skills Programme originally developed at Antioch Graduate School, New Hampshire, was brought to the attention of UK teachers and has become hugely successful in changing classroom practice. Sitting prominently among these influential programmes is the work of Barbara Prashnig. *Learning Styles in Action*, Barbara's second book for Network Continuum Education, could not be more timely.

Many teachers around the world are now familiar with VAK. Deriving from Richard Bandler's and John Grinder's analysis of successful therapists' Neuro-Linguistic Programming, the framework for VAK is having some repercussions in schools that may be counterproductive. Children are being labelled on the basis of a handful of ill-researched and unvalidated questions. In some places they literally do carry labels that they place on their desks so their teachers supposedly know the learning styles of the children they are teaching. Having been so labelled, learners are then confined to their preference. The claims that children are turning to their teachers and saying, 'Don't talk to me I'm kinesthetic', may be apocryphal, but this kind of urban myth does illustrate the danger of simplistic stereotyping. Finally, teachers are rejecting the whole notion of learning styles, not from any theoretical or carefully researched standpoint, but because they cannot envisage how the content can be taught to a class in at least three different ways. This book is timely, therefore, because it guides educators out of the blind alley of crude typology.

When learners leave home to go to school, college or university, they don't leave as visual, auditory or kinesthetic learners. They leave as unique individuals with a bundle of different preferences. Yes, some of these do relate to VAK, but not exclusively. Barbara draws our attention to T (tactile) and haven't we all been irritated by learners who have to fiddle with something while they are concentrating. For me the light bulb moment, however, the point at which the dark place was illuminated, came when Barbara drew my attention to the fact that what affects your learning isn't just what is inside your head, it's equally important in which physical environment students learn.

Parents know that some children like to work lying on the floor with music on. Indeed they often try to battle against it. Barbara shows us that some children do need to move around or fiddle while they learn. They may need to have music on or be on the floor or be in a dimly lit space or be nibbling and, by and large, schools can't cope with them so they may get a new label – it might say ADHD or 'problem student'.

This book is now of the utmost importance for teachers who wish to address the learning needs of students who are currently failing in education systems around the world. It shows us that learning styles is a complex phenomenon not subject to crude stereotyping. It shows us how learners can be helped to work with their preferences and when they should stretch their flexibilities. It shows us how we work with group profiles rather than asking us to struggle with 30 or more individual profiles. This is, in my experience, the unique feature of LSA and the case studies and testimonies gathered here will gladden the hearts of all those who are looking for answers to the pressing problem of underachievement.

Chris Dickinson
January 2006

Introduction

After my second book, *The Power of Diversity*, had brought the concept of style diversity at school, at home and at work to people's attention, it became clear to me that classroom practitioners needed and wanted more information about implementing learning styles (LS) in their daily teaching practice. Teachers kept asking how to do this and how to change that and I learned more and more about the practical aspects of using LS through my work with teachers in many different countries. I saw first hand how, after only two days of professional development, these progressive and committed educators used the LS concept in their classes, changing the dynamics of whole student groups, turning schools around and achieving results unthinkable without the knowledge of students' true learning needs.

Despite the many enlightened teachers who are doing amazing work with young people, often under incredibly difficult conditions, there are too many educators, particularly administrators and decision makers, in every country who believe learning should not be fun, it isn't play and it can't be made to look like play; it's hard, hard work that can be made interesting. With such beliefs it is no wonder that many students fail in education systems that do not cater for diverse learning needs. I know that many people will be challenged by the thought that school learning in future will not be as they know it, but in many countries education systems are in crisis, they are not delivering the expected outcomes for society and something has to be done to help students to learn and to keep them off the streets, drug free and motivated for learning. In times of crisis we must avoid both ignorant change and ignorant opposition to change and maybe today what was already true in Confucius' times is still true: '*He teaches best that he needs most to learn.*'

What I admire most in teachers who are open to new and better ways of teaching is that they have the courage to take their new knowledge about LS to the classroom and implement, experiment, learn as they go, overcome obstacles, stand up to ridicule and still keep going to make a difference to their students' learning. The experiences of these practising educators are the main content of this book and I am extremely grateful for their contributions, which I know will help many other educators coming to terms with a concept so natural and yet so foreign because we have all been trained in teaching practices that follow the 'one-size-fits-all' approach, disregarding individual learning needs.

My contribution is to elaborate on these reports, creating a framework, bringing them into a certain order, as well as answering most of the questions I have encountered over the past 12 years.

These questions could actually be called FAQs (frequently asked questions) because I myself had asked these questions ever since I began studying the area of learning styles, and thousands of teachers have asked and are still asking the same questions to this day. During my LS training seminars most of these questions are being answered and discussed, but as many teachers will unfortunately never have a chance of participating, I have collated these FAQs for the readers of this book. Each chapter gives answers to different areas, ranging from how to start a learning styles programme, to multisensory teaching, to the do's and don'ts with learning styles.

I have made sure that there is something for everyone, no matter in which educational context or organization they work. Special care has been given to the application of LS in different age groups because despite the same underlying concept and philosophy, teaching strategies, classroom set-ups and interaction with students vary profoundly from pre-school to university level.

The book also attempts, albeit briefly, to explain the integration of LS with other pedagogic concepts such as learning cycles, multiple intelligences (MI), information communication technology (ICT) and suggests strategies for problem students.

With all these reports from practising teachers, I also want to give evidence that learning styles DO exist, that knowledge of students' learning needs based on an accurate assessment instrument DO provide significant advantages for teaching and learning, and that finding out more about one's style combination is immensely valuable and has even been a life-changing experience for many.

Quite different from my previous book, there will be fewer provocations, hardly any hair-raising suggestions or off-the-wall teaching methods because what readers will find are descriptions of real experiences at the chalk face of education, in the classroom. Even for the staunchest sceptic it is quite difficult to disregard the results of the work these teachers have been and are still doing, in all sorts of educational settings, to brush it aside as irrelevant or to discredit the whole style diversity thing. Since the publication of *The Power of Diversity* seven years ago a lot has changed in the educational world (still not enough for my taste) but even very conservative educators are slowly coming to terms with the fact that style diversity and personalized learning is not going to go away. The diversity concept is actually growing rapidly worldwide, mainly because of the desperation of people in non-functioning education systems but also because Creative Learning Centre instruments are available on the internet. This makes access very easy for schools and our simplified system makes it easy for students to get their profiles and for teachers to manage them.

Our assessment instruments (LSA, TSA and WSA) are now available in English, Swedish, Finnish, Danish, Norwegian, German, Spanish and Mandarin, mainly via the internet from our website www.creativelearningcentre.com or from the foreign language websites of our licence holders who are offering the software in their countries.

As we are constantly improving these instruments, they are still in the international field study phase and have not yet been validated. However, they have pragmatic validity and their successful use by thousands of teachers disproves questionable research findings in the UK from 2004 claiming that LS have no practical value. With this 'How to' book I also wanted to help repair the damage such negative reports have done and give decision makers and classroom teachers the confidence to use LS. Practitioners are the ones who need them most, together with their students and parents. It is encouraging that the DfES in the UK is now recommending the use of learning styles because this concept supports and enhances personalized learning.

The newspaper-column style should help make the book faster to read and the layout allows dipping into the content at any point, gathering the desired information and enhancing it with the content supplied on the left-hand pages. These pages partly elaborate the content of the right-hand pages and partly illustrate and explain the concepts discussed on opposite pages.

I now invite you to find the best possible environment for yourself while reading – maybe you want to sit in a comfortable chair or upright at a desk, maybe lie back on a couch or bed, put on background music, switch on the light you feel most comfortable with, or take the book outside if this is what you want to do – and enjoy a journey into the fascinating world of education. It is truly a glimpse into the future; a future that has arrived in many places where learning and teaching are now enjoyable and successful. And you might like to dream how it would be if you were to use learning styles and personalized learning for all.

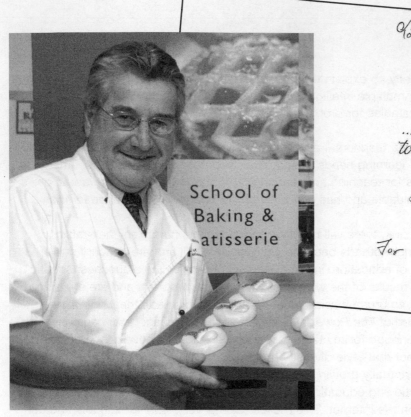

School of Baking & Patisserie

'Come to the edge' he said.
'We are afraid'
'Come to the edge' he said.
They came, he pushed them
And they flew...

Thank you
thank you
thank you

To my skillful master chef.
I can't find any word
to express my appreciation
for your teaching for the
past year but thank you
from the bottom heart ♡

Best regards
Mickey Mi

Dedication and thanks

This book is dedicated to my late husband, Armin Praschnig, who has been taken from us far too early, with too many plans unfinished and goals unreached. A week before his 63rd birthday a brain tumour was diagnosed, just when he was preparing to start his new school year after the summer holidays. There were no signs whatsoever and the illness set in with frightening ferocity. He had a successful operation but after three weeks the tumour grew back bigger than before, and after another three weeks of nearly unbearable suffering he passed away, leaving a legacy to education and the baking trade that will be felt for a long time in New Zealand. Since he went into vocational training over ten years ago, he dedicated himself to help his students achieve successful learning outcomes, something he had always struggled with himself because he was not an academic learner whose learning style was never met during his own schooling. He understood those hands-on learners who wanted to further their education but could not sit still in class and were bored stiff listening to lectures because he had experienced the same – school failure. As he was not a trained teacher, he was spared all the theoretical knowledge about teaching and learning and fully embraced creative learning methods and LS, often to the ridicule of his colleagues and the harsh critique of his supervisors. But he was undeterred, implementing style diversity in all his classes and achieving incredible learning outcomes, particularly for those who had little school success before, often giving them a fresh outlook on life and new-found self-esteem. (See also his contribution in Chapter 21.)

Although he was not always easy to be with and our marriage had many ups and downs, he was the one who supported me through thick and thin in my effort to bring the diversity concept to educators worldwide because he passionately believed in me and my ability to make a difference. He was also my staunchest critic and challenged me to do better, to search for new ways of helping teachers and students achieve their best. Even when he was very ill, he urged me to continue with my seminars because he said they were too important and I had to promise him to continue with my work, which I am certainly doing, probably with more intensity than before. But I miss him and his passion for teaching and our often heated discussions about how far a teacher should go in caring for his students' learning without suffering too much stress. There is one saying he always quoted to illustrate why a teacher must always bring out the best in his students and it will stay with me as I am also using it for my situation when I work with educators who are less than enthusiastic about style diversity and creative learning: 'You can't MAKE a horse drink but you can make it so thirsty that it WANTS to drink.'

And this is the intention with this book. If it makes you so keen on LS and personalized learning that you cannot wait to have your students assessed and the diversity concept applied, then I have fulfilled my promise to Armin: to make you thirsty for new knowledge, not in your subject area but in the many ways that you can reach and teach your students.

My special thanks go to all the educators who have contributed to this book, making it highly practical and who are pioneering the diversity concept around the world. I know your work will be an inspiration to many others who are equally enthusiastic about helping their students learn better.

A big thank you also to the editorial staff at Network Continuum Education who believe in my work and who had the patience to wait for this manuscript, delayed by events out of my control.

Thank you also to all my friends, family and co-workers for their support during these very difficult past few months – I couldn't have done it without your help when I needed it most.

How to use this book

Like my previous books, this one has been written more like a reference book, in a user-friendly style for easy reading with a brain-friendly layout: mainly text columns on the right-hand pages and graphs, pictures and reports on the left-hand pages to illustrate and elaborate on the content of the right-hand pages.

The whole book is also answering frequently asked questions (FAQs) about learning styles. These have been accumulated over the years, posed by educators who have been using learning styles and who are often grappling with practical applications in the classroom.

Although the chapters have been compiled to follow a learning cycle in itself (see Chapter 18), readers can still dip into the book anywhere they like because each chapter deals with different aspects of style diversity and its use in the learning process.

As I have collected so much valuable materials from educators around the world and would really like to share this, I have come up with a novel idea: an online appendix accessible on the two websites below that will be updated as and when more information becomes available. To indicate that an online resource is offered on the websites below, this computer icon 🖥 is shown in the text. Useful websites are also suggested throughout the book and are indicated by this mouse icon 🖱 in the text.

For best outcomes, I would recommend to readers that you get to know your learning style by going to the websites 🖱 www.networkcontinuum.com or to www.creativelearningcentre.com and obtaining your personal learning style analysis (LSA) profile to understand how you learn best. After all, this is not just for pleasure reading, it is more like a textbook. Once you know your best way of learning, I strongly recommend you do your reading in an environment conducive to your personal style in a manner where you can most easily achieve the most benefit.

If you already have LSA results from your students, you can use different chapters in the book to help you find information about the best possible applications in your daily teaching practice. But, above all, have fun and enjoy learning all you can about style diversity and making learning more personal and more successful.

As applications of LS are ever-evolving, I am still keen to hear from practitioners about their own experiences with learning styles. The best reports will be selected and added to our online appendix to keep it current. Please send your contributions and updates to my personal email address: 🖱 barbara.prashnig@clc.co.nz

To those who understand,
No explanation is necessary.

To those who do not understand,
No explanation is possible.

Chapter 1

Personalized learning through learning styles

Most education systems are struggling to meet education targets, academic achievement is going down in many Western countries, discipline is deteriorating and high schools particularly are no longer the safe places they once were.

David Hood has been involved in education in New Zealand for over 38 years, as a secondary school teacher, principal, Department of Education official, regional manager at the Education Review Office and foundation chief executive of the New Zealand Qualifications Authority. He is author of the fascinating book *Our Secondary Schools Don't Work Anymore* (1998) and I am grateful that he has allowed me to include his contribution right at the beginning.

His essay below describes the reasons why we must personalize learning through learning styles.

In my book *Our Secondary Schools Don't Work Anymore*, I refer to Charles Handy's analogy of the workplace in which the employee is required to move from office to office five or six times a day, working with different supervisors with different expectations, and with no attempt to make any connections from one work situation to the other. As adults we would find it extremely difficult to cope with that environment, let alone be productive learners, or producers of quality work.

Why is it that we assume that 13 to 18 year olds in our secondary schools can cope, and be successful in their learning? Some do have the coping skills, even though they might feel less than positive about the learning environment. Others do not; as a result they become the victims of the system, the non-learners, the truants, the suspended or expelled students, the dropouts. It does not take much intelligence to realize that those from more 'advantaged' backgrounds are more likely to have the coping skills, those from less advantaged backgrounds are more likely to appear in all the negative statistics.

If we are serious about wanting to make schooling a successful experience for all students, we need to do something about how we organize learning in schools. However, before deciding what it is we should be doing we need to:

a) be clear as to what should be the main purposes of schooling in the twenty-first century;

b) understand what research and experience is telling us about what makes for quality learning; and

c) examine how we currently organize learning in our schools.

In the twenty-first century the prime purpose of secondary schooling should be to develop independent, self-managing learners with the basic knowledge and skills which adequately prepare them for the challenges they will face in their futures. Students leaving our schools should know how to learn, and have confidence in their ability to go on learning. They should be knowledgeable about their own individual talents and how to use them effectively.

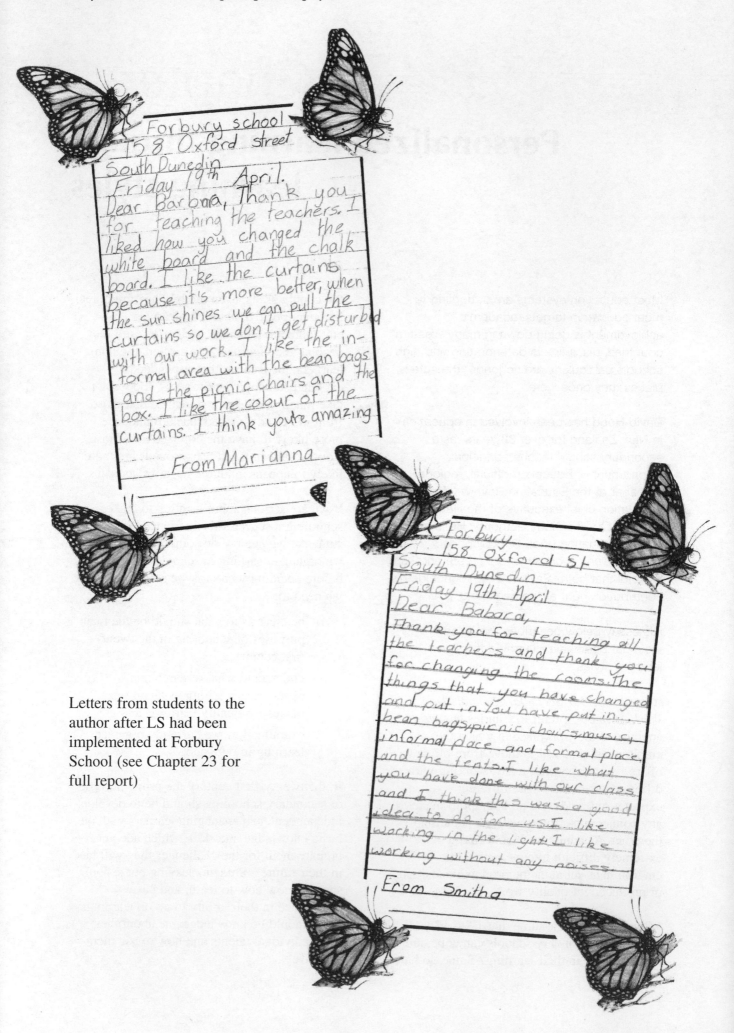

Forbury school
158 Oxford street
South Dunedin
Friday 19th April.
Dear Barbra, Thank you
for teaching the teachers. I
liked how you changed the
white board and the chalk
board. I like the curtains
because it's more better, when
the sun shines we can pull the
curtains so we don't get disturbed
with our work. I like the informal area with the bean bags
and the picnic chairs and the
box. I like the colour of the
curtains. I think you're amazing

From Marianna

Forbury
158 Oxford St
South Dunedin
Friday 19th April
Dear Babara,
Thank you for teaching all
the teachers and thank you
for changing the rooms. The
things that you have changed
and put in. You have put in
bean bags, picnic chairs, music,
informal place and formal place
and the tents. I like what
you have done with our class
and I think this was a good
idea to do for us. I like
working in the light. I like
working without any noises.

From Smitha

Letters from students to the author after LS had been implemented at Forbury School (see Chapter 23 for full report)

That means schools should be places where students enjoy learning, where the curriculum is relevant to their needs, where students receive recognition for their learning. Schools need to be focused on individuals not classes, need to be firmly rooted in the future not in the past, and concentrate on success not failure.

Schools should not be about every student knowing the same stuff, determined by bunches of subject 'experts'. It would be a dull world if we as adults knew only the same material. If we want to create a diverse and creative society, we need to allow our students to choose where they want to go, and to give them the proper guidance to do that successfully. Schools should also not be about preparing students for one-shot examinations where they regurgitate the stuff, and then begin to forget it as soon as they leave the exam room.

There is a wealth of international literature, readily available from bookstores and on the internet, on how to ensure quality learning in our schools.

I would suggest we don't need research to tell us this; it is common sense. As adults we recognize that the two key motivations to our own success and job satisfaction are interesting work and being involved. Change the language and you can establish close parallels with how successful enterprises ensure their employees are happy and productive in their work. We need to ask why we treat young people so differently in our schools, why we continue to organize learning so that many of those young people are not happy and not productive in their work. William Glasser (1986) is right when he comments that 'we are mistaken if we believe that discipline, dropouts and drugs are what is wrong with today's schools. Serious as they are, they are symptoms of a much larger underlying problem which is that far too many capable students make little or no effort to learn.'

Because schools operate with individual teachers working with separate groups of students in classroom boxes and teaching different subjects, they need to have numerous staff – APs, DPs, HODs, deans, counsellors, careers advisers etc. – who have the task of trying to administer and support the system. All of them need non-contact time to discharge their responsibilities. Numerous meetings are also required – management meetings, HODs' meetings, deans' meetings, staff meetings etc. – to try to provide some cohesion and co-ordination to this disjointed structure. As a result, in many schools there are more chiefs than indians. It is Taylorism gone mad! More importantly it is stressful for both teachers and students, it is not conducive to good learning, and it is grossly inefficient.

So what is the alternative to achieving the prime purpose? To illustrate let me take a specific example of a secondary school with a roll of 570. It has a staffing entitlement of about 37 teachers. Although there are some variations, these staffing/student ratios are about the same for all schools. I suggest dividing the students into groups of about 80 students with a team of five teachers allocated to each. That leaves two teachers, in addition to the principal, whose prime responsibility would be to provide teaching and learning support to the teams. Each teaching team will be responsible for the learning and welfare of their students. The focus of everyone, including the students, will be on producing quality work. That means teachers and students will need to be knowledgeable about, and frequently discuss, what quality means.

Each team of teachers will be responsible collectively for curriculum, its 'delivery', organization, discipline, their own non-contact time and professional development etc. Under this kind of arrangement:

- the team can plan together, rather than separately plan for a range of different classes, and can negotiate the use of teachers with special expertise from other teams;
- grouping of students can be flexible, rather than fixed;
- quality time on tasks will not be continually disrupted by bells;
- students can work to negotiated Individual Action Plans based on their learning styles with clear personal, including learning, goals;

From one extreme ... to another

- students can much more easily work individually or collaboratively with others;
- community experts, parents and community volunteers can be regular and welcome visitors to the classroom to act as role models, mentors and tutors;
- students will be able to do much more learning out in the community simply because it will be so much easier to organize.

The only reason we group students together by age is because of now outdated beliefs about how children learn; we believed learning needed to be both linear and progressive, and that all students should be able to learn in the same way and at the same pace. If students didn't learn by these 'rules', it was assumed it was their fault rather than that of the system. We now know differently. There is no reason why students in these groups need to be of the same age; we don't divide people by age in any other learning situation and a few minutes thinking about it would suggest groups of students of different ages would lead to better learning for all.

The potential benefits to teachers are also considerable. Working in such a learning environment would be demanding and challenging but it would be considerably less stressful and a lot more professionally satisfying. We are, for example, talking about five teachers working with 80 students, not one teacher with up to 150, which is the current model. The multitudinous layers of 'support' will not be required, teachers can focus and get on with what their jobs should be about – helping students to learn.

At the national level, of course, we will need to recognize the importance of professional development. And it is about time we did. So many reforms have consistently ignored the obvious: what teachers know and can do makes the crucial difference in what children learn. Student learning will only improve when we focus our efforts on improving teachers' knowledge and skills. Too much professional development is still focused on

schooling as it is, rather than what it can and should be.

Working in this alternative structure will require teachers to know how to act as facilitator, coach and mentor, rather than as a knowledge expert; to know how to develop learning strategies based on the concepts of partnership and mutual respect; to know how people learn best so that they have high expectations of success and quality work from all students; and to know how to actively involve parents and the community in children's learning. It will also require teachers who are able to demonstrate to their students that they are passionate about learning and are themselves learners. All of these are identified through research and experience as critical factors in ensuring quality learning. That has implications for pre-service and in-service training.

There are those who would argue that it would be impossible to embark on such radical change without totally redesigning school buildings, and the way we assess and report on student learning. Although I agree that schools should be progressively redesigned, opening up access between classroom boxes will do much to create the more flexible teaching and learning environment required by such approaches. That is not expensive; it has already been done in several secondary schools.

Learning styles (LS) are now extensively used by the Department for Education and Skills (DfES) in the UK. In part, this reflects the new emphasis on choice, but underpinning it is the theory that everyone has an individual style of learning and that working with that style, rather than against it, will benefit both pupil and teacher.

One recent DfES pamphlet on this subject states that 'Through an understanding of learning styles, teachers can exploit pupils' strengths and build their capacity to learn', but sadly the media have picked up on that negatively, discrediting the notion of style diversity in learning because some academics deny in so-called 'research reports' that students have different learning

The following letter demonstrates in a very personal way how knowledge of learning styles AND an understanding teacher can profoundly change school and home life for a student. It was sent to me by the teacher of this adult student at an Australian Technical and Further Education (TAFE) institute (with permission for publication) and it speaks for itself. Since then, Kim has gone on to study at university. Bob, you made a difference and I thank you for that!

Dear Bob,

Whilst the LSA was a light bulb experience for me, you as a teacher were just as much so. You were our salvation; you kept so many of us hanging in there and if it had not been for you many wouldn't have stayed till the end of the year, me inclusive!!!! You have had such a profound impact on our lives and our self-confidence as students. This impact is still resounding this year and the reverberations are being felt through this household as everything you ever taught me with LSA is being utilized as much as possible here.

How I envy my children to be students at a time when this program is being picked up by their school and practised to some degree within the classroom. This gives me hope that they won't slip through the system and become disillusioned with learning. How exciting it is for me as a mature age student to finally understand my own learning style and put into practice everything that my analysis revealed to me. This has been an enormous boost for my self-confidence, as I now realize that it is nothing to do with my intelligence, but how to take information in and then bring it back out.

I have tried to separate the LSA and your teaching methods but the two are so intertwined I am unable to do so. Not only did you believe in the program, you practised it as well. You were one of the teachers we all performed well with - our work was completed and we all had fun doing it. You gave us assignments to suit our learning styles and you were amazingly flexible in the way you let us present these assignments. You brought out the best in us. You allowed us to be creative and dared us to think outside the square. Your class was the one place we were able - and encouraged - to put our LSA into practice.

There are not many teachers who can come away saying that they have made meaningful friendships with their students, but you have. Thank you for being the only teacher in my life who treated me as a person and as a peer. As you say we are all just people. We're all supposed to be equal!! How refreshing it was to actually be treated with compassion, dignity, equality and integrity by a teacher. This really enriched my experience as a student last year. You had an uncanny ability to make each and everyone of us feel so special, so important and make learning for us sooo worthwhile.

Kim

Today's date is 23rd March 04

styles and that through matched instructions better results can be achieved.

Some articles have misrepresented the concept of LS, even denied that they exist (see *Teaching Thinking*, Spring 2004), and I consider it my duty to disprove these faulty theories created by academics who are far removed from daily classroom practice and are actually not interested in helping teachers to cope with difficult students and their related problems (see *Teaching Thinking*, Summer 2004). All they do is look at some theories, deny the practical value of style diversity and demand more research until a concept is 'researched to death'.

In contrast to these negative academic viewpoints, the contributions from practitioners throughout this book are ample proof that learning styles DO exist and that students DO HAVE different learning preferences; the many reports about improvements in discipline, learning motivation and academic performance from schools in various countries are clear evidence for these facts. We also know this from our work with our various learning style analysis (LSA) assessments instruments around the world and I can only hope that classroom teachers will not be discouraged by misleading reports about LS from using this valuable concept to help students learn better and improve their own teaching practice.

In response to this damning article about LS, one of the past teachers at a Technical and Further Education (TAFE) institute in Australia, Bob Ayliffe, sent me this encouraging letter:

Dear Barbara,

If you'll pardon some basic Aussie expression, I don't give a bugger what a heap of lofty British academics think of learning styles. I have seen it work miracles with REAL people: those with nil self-esteem or confidence in their ability to learn. I saw last year how it turned around at least a dozen lost souls and made their lives worthwhile again, gave them confidence and hope. To my dying day I will remain proud of my achievements there (achievements you made possible).

Perhaps we should bundle up Kim and her boys and send them to England as living proof that LSA is no red herring!

Good luck with the fight. You simply MUST win this one Barbara – please.

Cheers, Bob

(see Kim's 'Dear Bob' letter opposite)

The following passage by Dave, a New Zealand high school teacher, is one of the many reports I received from practitioners worldwide, all with the same conclusion: LS has helped their students learn better.

The class had a 22 per cent average improvement between pre and post test for this unit. The results of the maths pre test average were 55 per cent and post test averages were 77 per cent which was a very pleasing result with two-thirds of the class scoring into the 80–100 per cent range. From a teaching perspective this indicates that these students have grasped most of the concepts that were taught in this unit.

All students were assessed with the LSA and the result showed that this class is highly holistic in its learning style make-up; I attempted to provide a balance of learning experiences that would cater to their needs. If I was to do anything differently in planning learning experiences for this particular class, I think I would allow greater time on problem-solving activities using games and learning tools. As a whole the class responded really well to these kinds of activities. Children

Consensogramme used by Mary Brell to create a tactile gap analysis before and after LS training

seem to learn better when they are having fun and challenging each other with practical problems to solve.

Having said that, I do believe that these particular students are flexible in adapting to the learning experiences, even if they don't suit their particular LS all the time. The test results demonstrate most students have grasped what was taught in this unit.

As time was taken to actually make the learning tools, games and so on, it cut short our own time that we had available to experiment with them. Next time around this won't be an issue as the tools and games are already made and reusable.

Perhaps another area to focus on doing differently next time around would be to do with personal reflection. Again time constraints have hindered this process; for example, I felt the class needed the time available to focus on learning all concepts presented in this unit. Personal reflection doesn't appear to have much value unless issues are raised that can be addressed next time.

Having to think about the learning styles within my maths class and how individual needs can be addressed through learning experiences has been a valuable experience. It has helped me to broaden my approach to teaching in general and has made me more aware of my own teaching style and how that can assist or even restrict the learning that takes place in my class.

Personalized learning and using LS, however, is not restricted to students in the classroom as the experience of Mary Brell, a Learning and Development specialist from Orange in NSW, Australia shows and she reports:

My work involves working with organizations and schools in various areas such as leadership, team development and communication. It is during my workshops I am presenting to various groups that I model the work of Barbara Prashnig.

Some of the strategies I utilize during my training sessions include: lights dimmed in one part of the room; different types of seating available around the room – formal and comfortable; koosh balls placed on tables for tactile stimulation; visuals for further stimulation on walls; learning games used when appropriate; movement exercises introduced at various times throughout the day; activities involve manipulating objects, such as Post-It® Notes, coloured dots, some learning tools; and music played at various intervals.

Participants are debriefed about the purpose of this modelling and it's fun and interesting to watch as people move from the upright seating to the more informal seating, as they move from the dim area to the brightly lit area or the reverse. I find that the learning environment becomes more effective and meaningful and my participants benefit.

They often talk about their own learning or the learning styles of their own children and how they might be more tolerant of their children and their learning requirements, particularly as they do their homework.

I will continue to use these techniques in my work as I believe that there is no point coming to a workshop or learning activity if learning does not occur. The learning requirements of participants are critical and I always try to ensure that their individual needs are being met.

Mary uses an exercise that classroom teachers can use for any age group or kind of content. A Consensogramme is created (see page 18) that gives the teacher an instant overview of students' level of knowledge or their opinions about a topic. Students receive two small stickers of a different colour at the start of a lesson and a question is posed. As an answer, they put their first sticker on the Consensogramme matrix between 1 and 10. At the end of the lesson, another related question is posed and students put their second response sticker into the matrix. The result shows clearly how far students have moved in their knowledge about a topic. They have created a visual/tactile/kinesthetic gap analysis that can be discussed later.

LS training in New Zealand

LS training in Finland

LS training in Cyprus

LS training in Chile

LS training in Denmark

Chapter 2

Learning styles around the world

Over the past 12 years I have been working with educators in many different countries, conducting seminars about learning styles and their practical application in teachers' daily work. Many of these professional development sessions are conducted away from schools in conference centres and I often wondered if and how teachers would be using what I had presented because sometimes the 'Diversity Concept' met with resistance, disbelief and often discomfort. Even when I did in-service training (called INSET days in the UK) and we went through classrooms to see and discuss what was available and how learning environments could be better utilized for improving learning outcomes for students, I always asked myself if I had given teachers enough practical tips and often worried how classroom practitioners would actually do it to everyone's satisfaction. I need not have been concerned. The reports I have been collecting for this book over the past few months are proof that this concept works, is sustainable and brings about positive changes not even I had dared to hope for. Even in places where I did not have a chance of training teachers, the work they are doing with LS is incredible. It is heart-warming and very humbling to read about the efforts these pioneers of education have put into their daily work, and every single one is inspirational. Throughout this book I want to share these experiences with readers to encourage them in finding out their students' learning styles, in applying and accepting learning diversity in each and every classroom and in beginning to apply new teaching methods, even on a very small scale initially.

Charles Davies, Moulsecoomb Primary, Brighton, UK

Why did we become interested in developing learning styles?
When I became headteacher five years ago, behaviour was poor in and around the school. Children would regularly run out of school; physical disagreements were common at breaktimes and lunchtimes; attendance was well below the local and national average; children's attitudes to learning needed to be improved urgently.

There was great pressure on teachers to deliver national programmes in all areas of the curriculum without any regard to the child's emotional state. Many children were not ready to learn when expected and consequently emotional issues were commonplace in classes. With such high levels of children with special needs and very little in the national programmes to help teachers meet the needs of schools such as ours, we consequently had to look at developing our own programmes to meet the needs of the children.

How we started
We began by looking at accelerated learning and having four INSET days where the whole staff (teachers and teaching assistants)

LSA and adult learning

Bob Ayliffe, teacher, Australian TAFE Institute

As a teacher of 30+ years' standing, and with a somewhat eclectic career, I found that Barbara's work gave me the answers to many of the questions I have asked in those years. Initially I was a secondary school teacher; then a careers adviser; and later an adult educator in learning environments as diverse as 'second-chance education'; an indigenous education unit; a corrections centre; teacher of adults with intellectual disability – but I was always wondering WHY different things came easily to some students while others struggled to grasp the concepts. Jack of all trades, and master of none is probably an adequate summation of my diverse skills (all learned 'on the job').

Seeking answers, and in an attempt to improve my teaching skills, I availed myself of many training courses: Learning to Learn; 4-MAT Learning; accelerated learning among them. I also trained as an Irlen (scotopic sensitivity) Senior Screener. Each of these inputs provided me with answers, but also with more questions. It became my habit, no matter what course I was teaching, to spend the first few weeks dealing with 'Learning' – familiarizing students with the concepts of brain hemisphericity, learning styles and multiple intelligences. For the past ten years I found this very rewarding, for teacher as well as students. I got to know what made students tick, and they came to realize just why things had gone wrong for them in earlier educational experiences. It worked well, with many benefits, but never could I find an accurate assessment instrument that went into sufficient detail.

Enter Barbara Prashnig. Almost by accident (or fate?), I was lucky enough to attend training courses run by Barbara in Wagga Wagga and Tumbarumba. Like many of my own students before me, the lights went on! At last, here it was – the LSA; the instrument I'd been anxious to find for the past decade. For what LSA, along with Barbara's other teachings, provides is the bringing together of all the elements of modern learning theory in one accurate, user-friendly instrument. A godsend to those seeking to know the individuality of each student.

As chance would have it, my first Prashnig course coincided with the beginning of the academic year. A major part of my brief was to teach a humanities programme to a group of 30 post-school learners. This afforded me great flexibility: humanities courses lend themselves well to both analytic and holistic learners, and by good fortune the syllabus stipulated a progression from Personal Identity to Community Identity, and finally National Identity. The perfect opportunity to use LSA at the start of the course, so demonstrating to each student her/his own individual learning profile, and, by running a group profile, giving them an understanding of the diversity within the class.

All learners were 'second-chancers'. The group was divided into two classes of 15: one, a group of 15 to 16 year olds who had either left school early, or had been 'encouraged' to do so by their schools. Most were school-phobic, had changed schools frequently, or had 'issues' with authority. Almost all students in this group were strong kinesthetic/tactile learners: a very tiny minority rated more than 'flexible' in visual modalities. The second group was composed of mature adult learners, each of whom had left school at the minimum age (no formal qualifications), had very unpleasant memories of formal schooling and the consequent poor self-belief that accompanies negative learning experiences. In fact, most were petrified of beginning again, and scared of making fools of themselves in front of their peers. Interestingly, almost all students in the cohort rated strong on the kinesthetic internal (intuitive) modality.

The plan of attack on the course was therefore patently obvious. It was quite clear that traditional, chalk-and-talk/teacher-centred learning would have small chance of success. We therefore negotiated an alternative approach: we agreed that as long as the syllabus requirements were met, each student would essentially be in control of her/his own route to the destination. This progress took a diverse range of forms: some worked individually, some in pairs, others in small groups. Those needing a formal learning environment worked in the campus library (minimal noise, formal tables); those needing informality did much work outdoors (under a tree on the lawn, or on a verandah during inclement weather). Others preferred the classroom with background music. Students who excelled in cyber-learning used internet facilities in the library (and don't some of our younger students run rings around us oldies in this field!

continued on page 24

received training on how the brain works, chunking lessons down, brain breaks, self-esteem, learning styles, multiple intelligences and so on. This was very important to lay the foundation of what was to follow later. For the vast majority of the staff it was the first in-depth training they had received on the brain and how it works and certainly the first training outside the rigid structures of national strategies training. For example, one of the biggest difficulties our teachers had was from the initial training to deliver the National Literacy Strategy in 'rigid' time slots. For most of our children sitting for 20 minutes, concentrating, was too long a block. Using accelerated learning techniques, teachers started to plan by 'chunking' down lessons, including brain breaks, and consequently improving attention span. However, when we began to look at learning styles and how to implement them in a practical, useful way, we found the original accelerated learning training wasn't in-depth enough.

I then went on a two-day training course with Barbara Prashnig in London on how to implement learning styles effectively and felt that this was what I had been looking for. I then arranged for her to deliver the same two days to all our staff. What effect has this had on our school?

Learning style analysis (LSA)

All our children during the academic year 2003–2004 in Years 4, 5 and 6 undertook the LSA, either in groups or one-to-one with the class teacher. Many of our children have reading difficulties and, although we had to finance a supply teacher while the class teacher was working with a child/children, we felt this was worth it. There were added dividends to this approach in that it allowed the class teacher to find out things about their children that they wouldn't necessarily have ever found out about. We decided not to introduce the LSA to Year 3 children at this stage.

Learning style environment

We began to look at our classroom layouts. In the main, most classes had children sitting in groups around tables. After the training and a period of reflection, we began to look at how our classes could begin to cater for the many different style combinations. We are working on a two-year cycle to gradually transform our classes. Although we are only at the beginning of the fifth term in this cycle, most classes now have areas of light and shade, tables and chairs arranged in such a way to allow children to work on their own, in pairs or groups, near music or in a quiet area, soft seating, cushions on the floor and screens acting as dividing spaces. The children have been fully involved in all aspects of this development and choose which area most suits their learning style needs. There have been no issues of children abusing this choice. Rooms have been repainted in more appropriate colours for learning.

We are continually trying to improve the classroom learning environment, in particular at the moment soft cushions are being made up for the hard plastic chairs we expect children to sit on for hours every day. The increasing use of ICT, in particular SMART boards, is of particular use for kinesthetic learners.

– a very positive thing I feel, because it does such students a power of good to see the teacher struggling to keep up with them, thus dispelling the myth of teacher as all-round expert). I feel sure that by the end of the year I was more physically fit than at the start, so there's another 'hidden' benefit! Essentially, we adopted a learning styles input approach to the course.

Assessment was achieved through a multiple intelligences approach, using portfolios as the assessment device. This allowed – encouraged – each student to utilize strong modalities, and thus gain confidence. All presented work of high quality. However, to encourage diversity and increase the challenge, restrictions were placed on the number of items of identical format (for example, no more than 3/10 pieces to be, say artworks, or poems, raps etc.). (A very worthwhile book here is *Multiple Intelligences Approach to Assessment* by David Luzear. It is packed with great ideas!) Some of the portfolio work was of astounding quality, which surprised the students submitting it, and reinforced the whole concept.

As a senior Irlen screener (scotopic sensitivity/visual dyslexia), I discovered some interesting, though not surprising facts. Over the years, I have found that IS runs at about 25–50 per cent of students enrolling in second-chance education, depending on the specific course (Adult Literacy being at the higher end). By running Irlen screening in conjunction with LSA, I deduced that many Irlen students have strong kinesthetic/tactile modalities (all three), strong auditory (internal), and often strong visual (external). Clearly, I have not yet carried out enough comparisons for a statistically valid result, but a theory is developing.

An interesting by-line: Barbara recommends experimenting with low-light areas in the classroom. When I tried this with the younger group, I was amazed at the instant decrease in the level of 'angst' – bickering, complaining, resistance to task etc. Lights out produced a major upsurge in work output, at a much more peaceful level. It also provided an element of comedy, as the aged teacher stumbled into desks and chairs in his perambulations around the room in the dim light!

What was the outcome of this brave experiment?

From the students' perspective, it was a great success. They learned – very quickly – that their beliefs that their intellectual abilities were low were indeed false. They recognized – and embraced – their strengths, and used these to achieve success, and build self-esteem. Some surprised themselves with their marks and results. They became more tolerant of others' needs in a classroom environment, and indeed as fellow human beings. Co-operation improved dramatically and intolerance declined.

Overall, the retention rate/pass rate in the modules which were LS taught/MI assessed was close to double that in modules where it was eschewed by the teachers. Some students in fact completed the course/year in ONLY the humanities subjects, voting with their feet. To me, this was the proof of the pudding, so to speak.

However, there was a downside. Although I firmly believe that the approach was right for the students (and teacher), we need to acknowledge that we will meet resistance from colleagues. Sadly, this became extreme. New ideas are often threatening to traditional teacher-centred practitioners. Ultimately, the total embrace of the LS/MI approach to learning involves the transfer of power from the teacher to the learner. Some organizations and individuals find this very hard, if not impossible, to accept. While I no longer work for the organization concerned, I realize that the students who had the benefit of LSA have a healthy empowerment over their own learning: something that will be invaluable to them in life.

This is a teacher's story, and thus shows a teacher's perspective. For an altenative insight into the impact of the power of LSA, please read Kim's story (see pages 50 and 52): the perspective of a student, the ultimate beneficiary of Barbara Prashnig's work. Since she wrote her article, Kim has achieved her lifelong ambition: to attend university – an ambition which she thought an impossible dream, until she embraced the concept of learning through her strong modalities.

Gillian Anton, Marulan Primary School, Australia

I first became aware of learning styles when I visited New Zealand in 2002 and saw them in practice in several of the schools I visited. At that time I was new to my current school and was struggling with various issues which affected my students both socially and academically; they had difficulty in getting on with one another and showed little interest or enthusiasm for learning. Upon finally being able to purchase one of the last copies of Barbara's book in Wellington (NZ), I soon found myself absolutely enthralled as everything I was reading was helping me to understand where my children were at and where they were coming from.

After several meetings with staff and parents we were ready to begin a total overhaul of the way in which our school was run and the way in which I was running my classroom. The changes that were to be introduced were negotiated with the students and we began by looking at the various roles and responsibilities each of us had within the school and how these impacted on their learning. I wanted to ensure the children understood why we were looking at school in a different way and how the changes would best support their learning and help to enhance their learning environment. This involvement was the first step in empowering the children to be part of the decision-making process that was to have a direct effect on their learning.

The next step was to look at how they learned and how they liked to learn. This was probably the most exciting step as the children really started to think about the way in which they went about their learning and why some ways were more effective than others. We changed the room around, removed the teacher's desk, bought in cushions and created learning centres around the room. We covered our walls with information, turned on 'learning music' and became daily practitioners of Brain Gym®! Our room buzzed and hummed, the children were hooked into learning as each child found the learning style (or combination) that worked best for them. There were many days where I started to feel somewhat superfluous as the children just knew what it was they needed to do and were into it!

As this was a senior class their behaviour and attitude had considerable influence on the rest of the school . . . and what an influence! The changes occurred not only in the classroom but in the playground as well. The children were excited about their new roles and responsibilities both in and out of the classroom and they willingly undertook many jobs around the school. It was so exciting to see a change in the culture of the school and the example this first group of students set has continued to be built upon. Learning styles have played and continue to play an important role in our school as 70 per cent of our 115 students are boys.

Juan Carlos Lopez, Funwork Learning Centre, Santiago, Chile

In Chile the learning styles are practically unknown as well as accelerated learning. We start our programmes with a learning profile that includes LSA, MI, a cognitive abilities evaluation and finally an academic abilities assessment; with these tests we gather enough information about the child's learning process. That is knowledge about information input (how the kid prefers to learn), output, his abilities to actually process and memorize information and finally how he is doing in school considering also the social side (relationship with his school). For us information input is crucial, because that is where the learning process starts. Problems or difficulties in this

In memory of another dedicated teacher

I know that Pani would have loved to have contributed to your request but unfortunately she passed away at the end of June 2004.

I can give you feedback on learning styles from her point of view.

As a private training establishment we deal predominantly with second-chance learners whom the education system has failed. Our area of expertise has been the delivery of Level 2 subjects in tourism, retail and hospitality subjects.

Pani as a facilitator found through doing the teaching style analysis that she was initially heading off down a wrong career path. She was training to become a secondary teacher. Dealing with adults was more to her liking as she had a passion for learning styles because of the huge difference it made to the students she came in contact with.

Being analytical, Pani found it extremely difficult initially to comprehend that people learned differently. I still remember her saying: 'I hated having students on the floor and behind me; they should be sitting up straight at a desk.'

Having delivered learning styles, Pani could see a correlation between the way her own child best learned and the way he was being taught. Certainly a huge mismatch hence her son being expelled from two schools because of his behavioural problems.

She felt extremely frustrated particularly as she had been a board member at both schools. Pani advocated strongly as a board member to introduce learning styles. Unfortunately she was unsuccessful. She was encouraging the school where he is at currently, to explore the learning style concepts. What she did notice was the difference between the European schools and the Kura Kaupapa, where he is now. There is more flexibility in that her son was able to lie on the floor. Subtle differences has impacted on his behaviour in such a short period of time. This is a school that knows very little about learning styles so imagine the difference it could make to their students.

Empowering students to take responsibility for their learning has been the best thing since sliced bread. We get comments from students like 'I wish I knew all this before. It would have made a huge difference to my attitude to learning', 'I'm not dumb after all, I can learn', 'Why isn't this stuff being taught in the schools?'

One of our students had a literacy problem and was quick tempered. He was declared bankrupt at 20 and had been turned down by a polytechnic because of his circumstances. This boy enrolled with us, then progressed onto the Pacific International Institute of Management. He entered a national competition and beat students from the institute who refused to accept him.

James is now in Australia managing a tourist resort. That was over two and a half years ago. On hearing of Pani's death he rang with his condolences. James found that he wasn't a freak, gained a huge amount of self-confidence and has gone on to realize his dream. The contributing factors were the difference learning styles made and having a facilitator who had a respect and passion for 'Learning Styles' and believed in empowering her students.

Sorry Barbara I'm not the best story writer. I would like you to consider this contribution as a eulogy to Pani. I know that learning styles has made a difference to her students and I know that she believed 100 per cent in the difference it made to her students' achievement.

Regards
Lei Graham

area are often mistakenly identified and therefore treated as problems of the cognitive and intelligence abilities.

We talk about the LSA profile report in separate sessions with the child and their parents, putting special emphasis on their personal learning needs. I have been amazed by the reaction about the LSA results of both parents and children, because the parents recognize their child in the report and understand that there is nothing wrong with their kids when they like to study lying on the floor or eating something. And the kids feel that they are being listened to and considered as a person.

Only with the permission of the parents do we go to the child´s school with his LSA profile and talk to the teacher about the results. Here we have had opposite reactions; some teachers believe that LS is nonsense and that they know how students learn and what is good for them, based on

their own experience. Others show great interest and are even prepared to compromise to try to respect LS in their classes. We know that sometimes it is not possible, because the classroom layouts are not prepared yet for LS. Fortunately, teachers being interested have been the majority, which encourages us to keep going.

The advice to teachers starting with LS that we frequently give, is that they have to sharpen their observation on their students and compare it with the results in the LSA, and they will be amazed on their findings! How they could easily explain common things such as doodling, fiddling, not liking to read, etc. of their students and how to take advantage of these 'signs' in order to use the proper learning material to teach them. Also, we advise that the more teachers know about LS, the less they would label a student as 'flojo' (lazy), a preferred Chilean label for kids that for one reason or another do not get good grades.

LS in Santiago, Chile

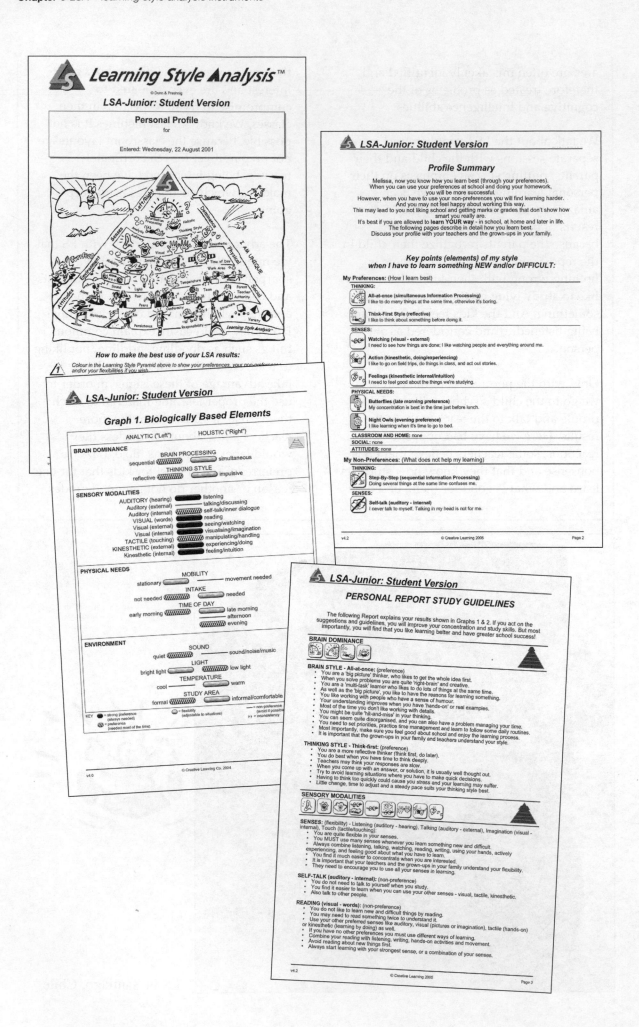

Chapter 3
LSA – learning style analysis instruments

Learning style analysis (LSA) instruments are computerized instruments available on the internet and developed over the past 12 years. They are based on the original Dunn and Dunn learning style model created during the early 1970s in the USA. Expanded and reshaped, the LSA allows students to find out what their preferred learning conditions are and how they function best when they have to learn something new and/or difficult. Research has found and our work with practitioners has proven that every individual prefers to learn and concentrate in a different way, and information intake and understanding is greatly enhanced when students can think, learn or concentrate through their preferences.

The LSA model consists of 49 individual elements in the following six basic areas that are represented as layers of a pyramid. The elements in the four top layers of the LSA pyramid seem to be biologically determined and remain fairly stable over a lifetime, whereas elements in the two bottom layers seem to be conditioned or learned, can be influenced at will and can change frequently in a person.

The four top layers of the LSA pyramid contain the following style elements:

1 **Left/Right information dominance**
   Showing analytic/holistic information processing strategies; reflective or impulsive thinking styles; and overall analytic or holistic/global learning style tendencies.

2 **Sensory modalities or perception**
   Including Auditory (hearing, talking, inner dialogue), Visual (reading, seeing/watching, visualizing), Tactile (manipulating, touching) and Kinesthetic (doing, feeling) preferences.

3 **Physical needs**
   Identifying needs for mobility (moving or being stationary); intake (eating, nibbling, drinking, chewing); and time of day preferences (personal biorhythm).

4 **Environmental conditions**
   Revealing preferences for sound or quiet, low or bright light, room temperature (needing cool or warm) and formal or informal/comfortable study area).

The remaining two layers define the following style elements.

5 **Social groupings**
   Including preferences for working alone, with a partner, with peers, or in a team; with or without an authority figure.

6 **Attitudes**
   Showing motivation (internally or externally motivated for learning), persistence (high, fluctuating or low), conformity (conforming or non-conforming/rebellious), responsibility (high or low), need for structure (being self-directed or needing guidance from others) and variety (needing routine or wanting change and variety).

The widespread use of LSA in eight different languages and the worldwide successful application of learning styles in different educational institutions has encouraged us to differentiate and constantly improve our instruments so that they are now available in the following versions:

- **LSA-Junior for primary school pupils** between 6 and 14 years of age,

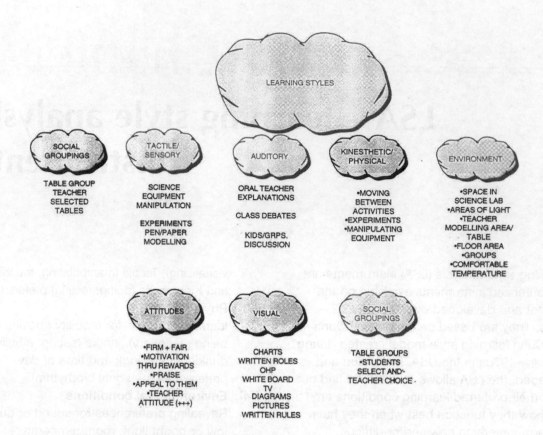

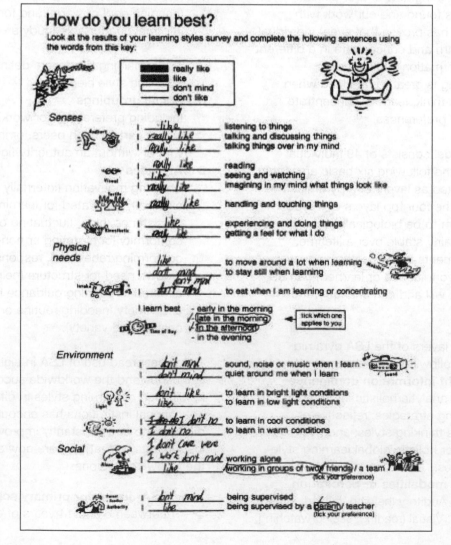

available as student, parent and teacher versions.

- **LSA-Senior for high school students** between 14 and 18 years of age, available as student, parent and teacher versions.
- **LSA-Adult for adult learners** who are in formal education, available as student version.

All instruments have the same look and format, consisting of a cover page, a profile summary, the personal report, graph 1: biologically based elements, graph 2: conditioned/learned elements and graph 3: learning style tendencies.

Profile interpretations

To interpret the graphs in the LSA profile, the personal report gives detailed information about preferences, flexibilities, non-preferences and inconsistencies of a student's learning style. Each report is self-explanatory but for further in-depth explanations and practical applications in the classroom there is also an LSA Interpretation Manual available from the CLC website: www.creativelearningcentre.com

Although it is important to interpret individual elements of a student's profile, it is even more important to understand style combinations because they give insight into a student's behaviour and learning capabilities as well as providing explanations for underachievement or learning success.

There are several options for teachers when interpreting LSA profiles:

a) to find strong preferences and look at the combination of their needs – different combinations result in very different academic performance and behaviour;

b) to look out for non-preferences and see how they clash with existing learning/teaching strategies and classroom conditions;

c) to specifically look at preferences and flexibilities in the sensory modalities – the more strong preferences students have, the easier information intake

becomes, and the more flexibilities students have, the more their learning success will depend on interest in the topic and motivation to learn;

d) to compare their own teaching styles based on the TSA-Ed instrument with the learning style results of their students LSAs and uncover style mismatches – over longer periods of time they always result in learning difficulties;

e) if there are severe problems with a student or concerns for their well-being or school success, a look at question marks in their profile often reveals stress factors that can be found in mismatched teaching situations or traced back to the home environment.

Often teachers will not have time to interpret all individual LSA profiles of their students, particularly in high schools where they have to deal with up to a hundred students at a time. In this case, the guidelines for interpreting individual profiles can be used for interpreting group profiles (see Chapter 6).

Many teachers have been very creative in interpreting students' LSA reports to gain a good overview of their students' true learning needs. Samples of good summaries and observations are below; and overleaf there is a mind map interpreting a student's LSA results in a different way.

Summaries

To complete the Diploma in Holistic Education, participants have to submit LSA interpretations, and here are two very good ones, provided by Darrell Goosen, a New Zealand primary school teacher:
'Summary: My observations of Daniel have out of necessity been intense. He arrived in my class as an 'out-of-control-child', labelled as being behaviourally oppositional in all aspects. His LS is absolutely true and consistent with my knowledge of him. I have found that by seating him on his own in a formal area of the class, on an informal chair has changed his entire outlook towards his learning. He has a fish tank beside him that seems to calm him down, and building cubes abound in containers near his desk. This child

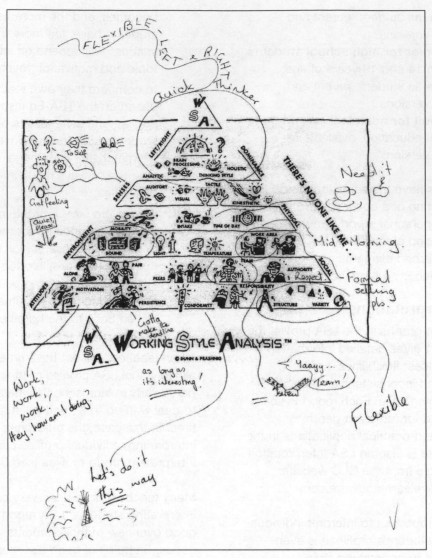

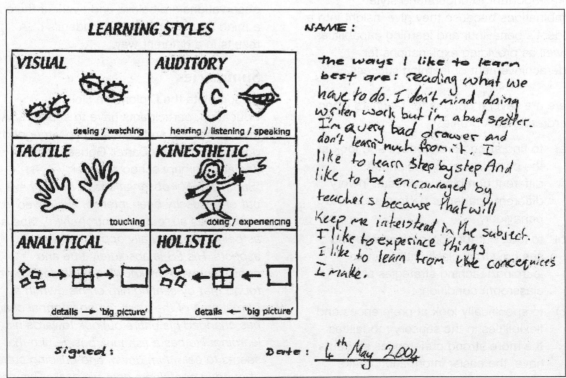

has also been diagnosed with Asperger's syndrome, and in spite of a very tough school career so far he has shown unbelievable progress in a matter of three months due to me teaching to his learning style.'

And in total contrast this description of one other student in Darrell's class:
'Summary: Elaine is a very serious yet a relaxed learner. She is systematic and can on occasion be quite vocal but also extremely quiet. She is highly intelligent and can work in a traditional learning environment just as well as in an 'LS classroom'. She is naturally attuned to her peers as a twin but also prefers to work on her own.'

As a conclusion, this experienced teacher has this advice for educators wanting to use the LSA: 'It would not be wise to attempt an in-depth interpretation of a student's LSA without the Interpretation Manual, and not until one is very familiar with the interpretation of profiles. Undoubtedly, these profiles will confirm observations, guide learning and direct teaching strategies for the students concerned.'

Adult personal profile interpretation

Athol Barlow, tutor at BOP Polytechnic, Tauranga, NZ provided the following results for one of his students.

- **Biological learning style elements**
  The results indicate this student uses a holistic learning style. He is very flexible in his sensory modalities, physical and environmental learning style elements, which is a disadvantage for him because if he is to lose interest with the lesson he will turn off. Although his sensory modalities are flexible, they also show some strong preferences that support a holistic learning style.
- **Conditioned/learned learning style elements**
  The results in these elements indicate clearly this student uses an analytic learning style. He shows clear preferences across both social and attitudes apart from persistence.

The above results shows this student's natural learning styles are holistic and (very flexible) but his conditioned learning styles are analytic. I believe this student to basically use a holistic learning style with some analytic social and attitude tendencies depending on the learning situation.

Teaching advice for this student:

1. Needs supervision
2. Must be kept interested in the subject
3. Suggest he joins a peer group
4. Late morning is best learning time of day
5. Informal study areas are a must for him
6. Needs tactile stimulation
7. Allow to use visualization and intuition

Adult learning styles: general facts

1. Adults possess a unique learning style just as children do.
2. Adults' learning style preferences tend to remain stable over time and task.
3. When the learning style preferences of an adult are accommodated, it is realistic to expect that both achievement and attitude towards learning will be positively impacted.
4. Adults possess, generally speaking, one or more sensory modalities as a strength. Accommodating these during a training programme is important.
5. Adults possess a preference for learning at different time periods during the day. Accommodating these preferences during a training programme is important.

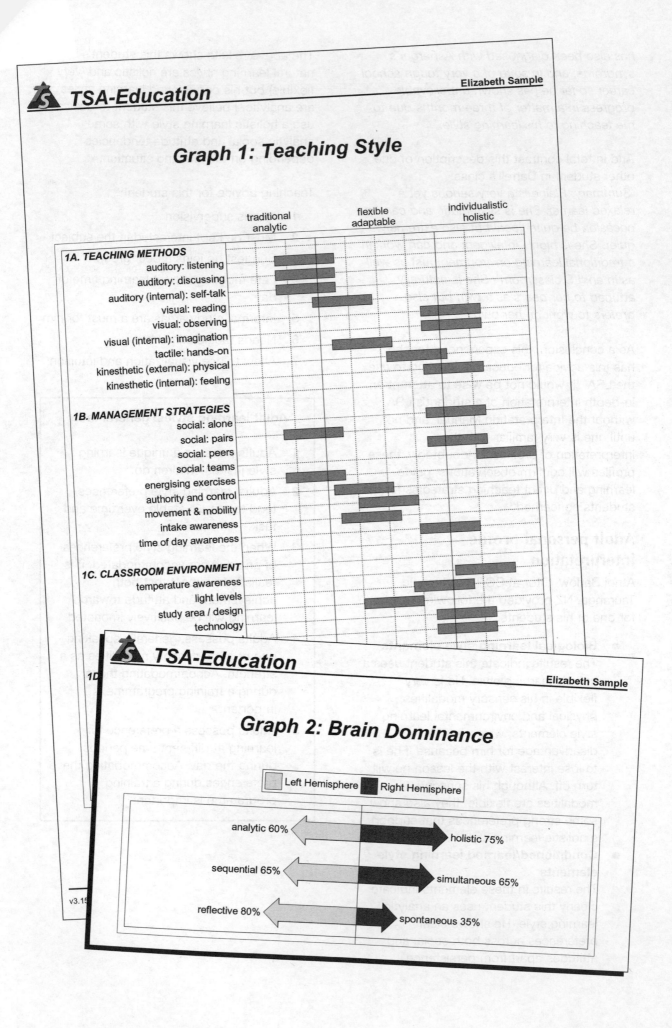

Chapter 4

TSA-Ed – teaching style analysis instrument

As more and more teachers begin to accept style diversity among their students, and many are implementing learning style approaches successfully in their classrooms, it is important to consider how their teaching styles match their students' learning needs. But maybe even more important is an understanding of how teachers and their own teaching styles come across, particularly when under stress.

Since the launch of the TSA-Ed instrument thousands of teachers have gone through the questionnaire and discussed and compared their style features with colleagues and friends. Many have reported that once they became aware of certain techniques they were often (over)using, they endeavoured to learn about new techniques and began to consciously increase the use of different teaching strategies based on the learning needs of their students.

In many cases, teachers were relieved to find that it was actually style differences in student groups that made certain teaching strategies highly successful one year but led to stress, disappointment and frustration the next. They realized that with different groups of students each year or each day, they needed varying approaches because what works for some, does not work for all.

Intuition does not always give a clear indication of what students need to be successful in learning, and experience certainly helps a lot. However, without a good knowledge of learning styles gained through proper assessments, it can take months to work out how students learn best, and then it may not be correct any

longer because the students have grown and their styles have changed over that time. The more that teachers know themselves and their teaching style, the more they can respond to varying learning needs, particularly in adverse situations.

Natural matches between learning and teaching styles

From reflections of teachers on their teaching style preferences, we know that they find it easiest to work with students whose learning styles match their own because there is a natural affinity and understanding between them as both are 'on the same wavelength', a state that is very positive and always enjoyable.

Such natural compatibility is the best that can happen to both teachers and students because it always leads to learning success, satisfaction, excitement, high motivation and energy. For students it creates treasured memories about beloved teachers, and for educators it is the magic working with classes they love and students they get on with so well. The perfect style match is when teachers can say 'This is an easy class'.

How to become more flexible as a teacher

In an ideal world we would always be able to match teachers and students with similar styles but, alas, reality is quite different and it is often only by chance that students meet teachers who are perfect for their learning

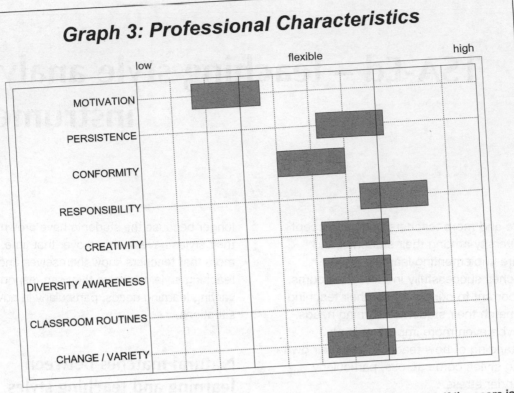

Please note: The graph above shows elements that can be influenced or changed. If the score is in the FLEXIBILE area, it means that attitudes can change according to the situation.

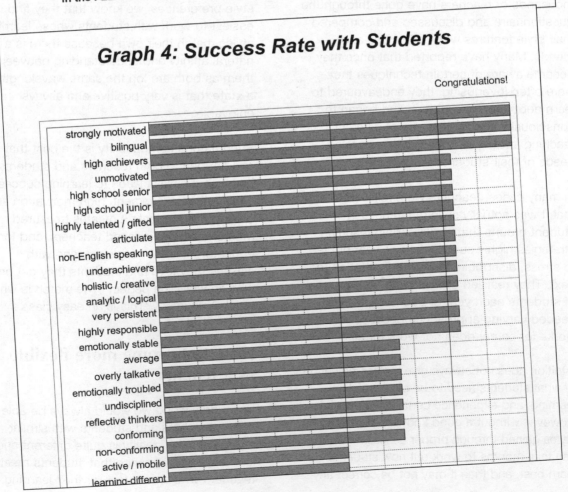

and teachers encounter classes where students learn just the way they are supposed to (in their teachers' minds).

What really happens on a daily basis, often out of necessity rather than by choice, is that teachers have to stretch their teaching skills to the limit to get some learning out of their students, who in return stretch their own abilities sometimes beyond breaking point to accommodate the way a teacher wants them to participate in class. More often than not, neither style needs are met. The result of such a mismatch is that schoolwork becomes more difficult than necessary for everyone concerned.

As teachers cannot change the biological style preferences of their students, only influence their learning attitudes in a positive way, the only solution is for teachers to find out how their students learn best by assessing their learning styles with LSA, and, based on that knowledge, to teach their students with a matching style. This, however, requires flexibility in the way a teacher approaches a class. The saying 'The way you learn is the way you teach' is particularly true for educators who have not had training in diversity and are not aware of different learning styles their students have.

Although becoming more flexible might seem quite scary for teachers who have been teaching the same way, often for decades, it is not as difficult as it looks. When teachers understand their own style features, they become much more aware of how they teach and why they get on with some students really well but find it difficult with others.

So, how DO you become more flexible as a teacher?

First, find out your learning style by using the LSA-Adult assessment instrument. Second, have your teaching style assessed with the TSA-Education instrument and compare both results to see differences and similarities in your teaching and learning styles. You could be surprised how very different (or very similar) both are.

To get the best possible outcome from your TSA-Ed, it is recommended you choose one

(maximum two) particular area(s) in which you want to improve your professional skills, write appropriate steps into an action plan and then execute your plan meticulously. It is most important to choose actions that can be carried out and monitored easily because too much of a change can be overwhelming and often leads to giving up. To prevent that from happening, there is a monitoring system built into the TSA profile through which you can carefully pace the desired changes in your classroom performance.

Remember: less is often more!

In my work with teachers I have seen profound changes in teacher interaction with students once they understand style diversity and true learning needs. I recommend that teachers reassess their teaching style after two years to see what effect the monitored changes have had on their practical approaches. Teachers often report that they are less obsessed with controlling students' learning, but rather support students according to their true learning needs, and find that their increased flexibility leads to less stress in their daily work, even in demanding classroom situations.

With a deeper knowledge and awareness of one's teaching style, educators can draw on their ability to be more flexible, to respond to students' behaviour instead of reacting and stressing out, because self-knowledge is the basis for flexibility and creates the ability to apply different strategies with greater ease. Teachers have told me that by being aware of their students' learning needs and knowing their own teaching styles, they are much more relaxed and confident in their interaction with students, which in turn leads to an improved relationship, better communication and more successful learning outcomes.

Zoe Beasley, the consultant for the LSA pilot project in the Wansbeck area, UK (see pages 51 and 53), found that valuable insights were gained for all teachers involved and reports: *'The TSA provided a lot of information for reflection and staff felt more aware of how they preferred to teach and what they need to do to address the learning styles of all pupils. Many teachers said they did not routinely get time to think because they had*

Suggestions from teachers at a high school in Wellington, NZ after LS training to create an ideal learning environment

Food intake: coping strategies
- You won't starve or dehydrate in 40 minutes
- Drink and nibbles for extended study time is OK
- Eat and drink at lunch and interval
- Regular food/drink breaks in school day
- Water OK
- Consider health and safety issues

Problem: temperature control
- Windows able to be open
- Sun filter
- Heaters that can be regulated in each room
- Re-design staffroom – integrate corridor with room, plus add verandah
- Be more flexible with school uniform
- Good ventilation, especially in corridors
- Adequate fans in each rooms
- Sensible windows

Ventilation
- Fans
- Individual room thermostats
- Grills over big windows so they are able to be opened wide and be safe

Lights
- Priority spending because they are a health and safety issue
- Re-light each classroom (as cost allows) with a less damaging type of light

Stereo/sound
- Every classroom would have speakers installed with following switches:
  1 Tune into centralized school learning music
  2 Plug in your school-provided CD player to play your own music
  3 CD net where you can select music through your PC in your room or via computer network

Classroom: within present constraints
- Display space
- Adequate wall space within reach or with the use of steps
- Free-standing display space
- Means of hanging displays (or students!!!) from rafters or ceiling
- Carpets: to reduce noise and increase warmth
- Furniture: flexible
- Easily moved into different shapes
- Ergonomic
- Heating control:
  - Vents in library covered
  - Adjustable heating in every block
  - Adequate windows on third floor

Fixed classroom layout
- Re-fit the labs, make new space for relaxation
- Group desks differently
- Introduce cushions and smaller more creative desks
- Have separate areas for different activities
- Fixed furniture should be minimized
- Build new and bigger classrooms
- Knock down the school and start again!!!!
- Relocate
- Visit a primary school for inspiration

Class size
- Fewer students
- More teachers
- More classes for senior administrators
- No non-contacts
- Reduce subject options

Fixed timetable
- No timetable
- Students learn where they want, when they want

to move straight on to the next thing. As a nursery teacher said: "Reflecting on your practice is essential if you wish to develop because education is not static" and many members of staff found the information provided by the profile to be extremely accurate: "it's a bit like reading your horoscope, only its true".'

In addition to Zoe's observations, I found that the results were sophisticated and provided insight that staff would not have found in any other way. This was true in the school where I was familiar with staff and also in the schools where I was not. In the school where I was based, the results were detailed, informed and accurate.

In each school, staff commented on the accuracy of the results. Some were sceptical and suggested that data could be input to give a positive report. Although this would obviously be possible, I would question the benefit of this and the instruments have a built-in cross-checking system.

I worked with several members of staff who felt undervalued and said they had found the profile to be enlightening and motivating: 'This has reminded me why I joined this profession. Thank you very much' and 'This has been a personal and professional journey for me. You have given me new confidence and clarity about myself as a teacher and a person' (Year 3 teachers).

It was evident that most teachers teach in their own preference style, which can be very limiting to pupils. Lots of discussion was generated about the traditional education system and how effective it is. Many people rightly identified that it is set up to support more left-brain dominant, analytical thinkers.

One or two staff had experienced negative feedback during lesson observations: 'I understand now why I teach differently from other people. I am a very holistic person.' It was suggested that some changes in the criteria and measures for lesson observations should be introduced. Many staff felt the aspects within the pyramid model should be reflected and valued.

Many teachers said they had learned a lot about themselves and their colleagues. It was felt that this would help them: 'We need to look at the strengths of our staff and build on these. The key is how we communicate with others' (headteacher).

One school requested to spend time looking at the make-up of the staff and how they complement each other. The head and deputy were interested to find out about the composition of the senior management team. They looked at the characteristics of those staff and how they relate to each other as a team: 'That makes perfect sense, we must address people's needs when we communicate with them.'

At this school there was a raised awareness of the needs of the teaching staff. There were staff who needed to know the big picture rather than little details in order to see its relevance: 'This is fascinating and explains why staff can respond so differently to the same information.'

Some staff expressed concerns that the information from the profiles would not induce any change. I would suggest that raised communication is required to ensure all staff feel valued. Through effective communication, individuals are able to share their ideas and actively contribute towards the working ethos and learn from each other. This is possible in schools where the management is willing to take the opinions of others into account.

The TSA report also makes suggestions. Some staff used these to develop performance management targets that would be beneficial to their personal and professional development. Staff are now using different modalities more in their teaching, expanding from VAK to include tactile and the need for mobility.

'I found it quite difficult to teach out of my preferred style at first. I wasn't really even aware that I relied so much on one style until I did my profile. Once I realized I felt I had to do something about it' (Year 4 teacher).

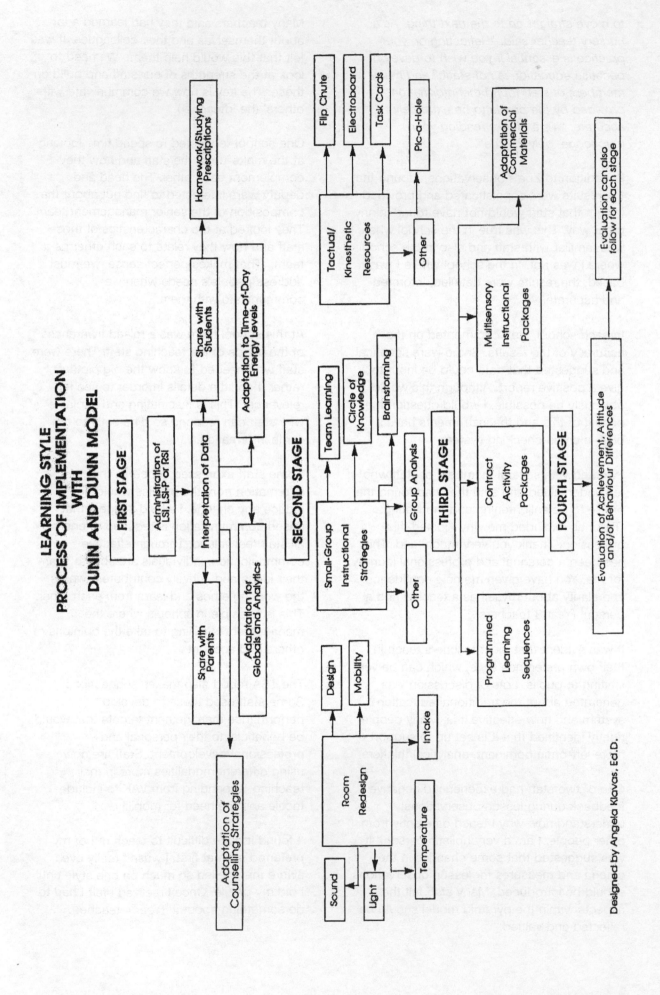

LEARNING STYLE PROCESS OF IMPLEMENTATION WITH DUNN AND DUNN MODEL

FIRST STAGE

Administration of LSI, LS-P or RSI

Interpretation of Data

Share with Parents

Adaptation for Globals and Analytics

Share with Students

Homework/Studying Prescriptions

Adaptation to Time-of-Day Energy Levels

Adaptation of Counselling Strategies

Room Redesign

Sound

Light

Temperature

Design

Mobility

Intake

SECOND STAGE

Small-Group Instructional Strategies

Team Learning

Circle of Knowledge

Brainstorming

Group Analysis

Other

Tactual/Kinesthetic Resources

Flip Chute

Electroboard

Task Cards

Pic-a-Hole

Other

THIRD STAGE

Multisensory Instructional Packages

Contract Activity Packages

Programmed Learning Sequences

Adaptation of Commercial Materials

FOURTH STAGE

Evaluation of Achievement, Attitude and/or Behaviour Differences

Evaluation can also follow for each stage

Designed by Angela Klavas, Ed.D.

Chapter 5

How to start, monitor and evaluate a learning styles programme

Once learning styles are understood and style diversity in the classroom is accepted by teachers, it is necessary to consider how such a programme can be implemented so that it can lead to a change in the learning culture.

To show that learning styles (LS) intervention works – particularly for underachieving students – I suggest the following strategies, which are partly based on my own experiences in schools, some research projects in NZ, the UK and Canada, and on findings based on the original Dunn and Dunn instrument. A prerequisite, however, is that teachers who are carrying out such programmes are well trained in the application of learning styles.

The following strategies have been applied widely and can be used to monitor the success of LS interventions.

1 With a pilot group of 10 to 20 students

Teachers use existing academic records or assess students' academic work (that is, in maths, English, reading and so on) before an LS styles programme is introduced; then students' learning styles are assessed with the LSA instrument; and when all data is collected, teaching is adjusted to the learning needs of the students for at least three months. After that period students are assessed again in the same subject areas for their academic performance, and a continuation with LS applications for another three to six months is highly recommended. After that period a final assessment of students' achievement in the tested subject areas is carried out by comparing academic results from before and after the LS

intervention. Improvements will be noticeable and can be documented statistically.

A variation would be to select one group (or several groups) of underachieving students, collect their past poor results in different academic subjects, assess their learning styles with the LSA as well as their teachers' teaching styles with the TSA instrument and look for natural matches, and then teach all selected students with matched instructions for at least three months (better even for a full school year). After that their academic achievements are assessed as usual at the end of a term or school year, changes are documented and results are compared.

2 Implementation with a whole class

It is most beneficial to establish a trial group and a control group from a parallel class and to ascertain from both groups the students' academic records, attitudes, learning motivation, behaviour, overall discipline, and any other issues important to the class development before the trial; then the learning styles of the trial group only are assessed, after which the LS intervention is used in the trial group but the control group is taught as usual for three months. Changes in the trial group need to be documented carefully, and students' attitudes, learning motivation and so on need to be re-assessed in both groups so that the results can be compared.

After completion of this trial it will become necessary to introduce LS approaches to the control group as well because results in the past have shown that by following this approach, students in this group often feel

Introduction of LS

Quick Guide

Twelve-step implementation plan for a learning styles programme

1 **Start** with a one-day in-service professional development

2 **Assess** students' learning styles with the LSA instrument

3 **Interpret** LSA results with a trained facilitator

4 **Carry out** an observation period of at least seven school days

5 **Share** LSA results with students, organize a parent evening

6 **Introduce** multisensory teaching methods, subgrouping students

7 **Adapt** teaching strategies to suit analytic and holistic students

8 **Begin** with classroom redesign based on group profiles

9 **Introduce** LS tools and let students create their own tools

10 **Monitor and evaluate** the change process carefully, meet with colleagues

11 **Incorporate** new students and teachers into the LS approaches

12 **Become** a model school, demonstrating LS applications

they are missing out. What is even more important, parents also want to see the benefits learning styles can bring to their children.

3 Introduction on a school-wide basis

Once the decision is made to go ahead with an LS programme and all teachers are keen to embark on this change programme, I strongly recommend using this proven implementation strategy by following these 12 steps:

1   **Start with a one-day in-service** (INSET) professional development ('Introduction to Learning Styles') where all teachers should participate, including the principal, so that a uniform knowledge base can be developed.

2   **Assess students' learning styles** with one of the LSA instruments (questionnaires can be completed on screen or on paper); this needs to be done before the next professional development programme.

3   **Interpret LSA results with a trained facilitator** during the second one-day in-service training with the title 'Teaching Styles – Learning Tools – Classroom Management', which also includes understanding teaching styles as well as creating learning tools.

4   **Carry out an observation period** of a minimum of seven school days to gain a deeper understanding about style diversity in the classroom.

5   **Share LSA results with students and parents** to help them understand their own learning styles; organize a parent evening when appropriate; discuss homework and study strategies based on learning preferences with parents and students.

6   **Introduce multisensory teaching methods**, subgroup students according to their preferences and find more and better ways for teaching tactile and kinesthetic learners.

7   **Adapt teaching strategies** to suit analytic and holistic students who have very different information processing styles; learn about and apply 'double tracking' (see Chapter 8).

8   **Begin with classroom re-design** based on the group profiles of each class; involve students – it's their workspace! Invite parents and community members to contribute to setting up LS classrooms; ask for donations if appropriate.

9   **Introduce LS tools**, explain how to use them and let students create their own tools for different subjects and/or teaching units.

10   **Monitor and evaluate** the change process carefully; have regular meetings with colleagues to discuss progress and problems; observe how underachieving students become successful learners by matching their learning needs; and keep the discussion going about how students learn best. Include members of the community if possible.

11   **Incorporate incoming students** into the existing LS approaches; set workable strategies in place to train new teachers for sustaining the change process until learning styles is imbedded as a core component of the school's new and enhanced learning culture.

12   **Become a model school**, demonstrating to other educators that learning styles is the basis for improving styles, academic results, student behaviour and professional skills.

This well-tried approach has been used by schools in various countries with often unexpected positive outcomes as reports throughout the book will explain.

One particular successful application was, and still is, at Forbury Primary School in Dunedin, NZ, as the principal, Ms Janice Tofia describes so impressively in her own words in Chapter 23. It is even more remarkable as this was a failing school, earmarked for closure and only 'radical' intervention could save it. I am pleased to report that LS implementation carried out by extremely committed teachers was at the core of this success.

The Learning Styles Picnic

If you go down to St Vincent's today, you're sure of a big surprise.
If you go down to St Vincent's today, you'll never believe your eyes.
For every style that ever there was,
Is catered for, for certain because
We know the way our children will hit the jackpot.

Every child who is in our school
Is sure to find their own way.
There's lots of wonderful books to read
And wonderful games to play.
We'll meet the needs of those in our care
Who'll get the best as long as we dare
To teach the way our children will hit the jackpot.

We have those who need to talk,
Who need to touch and feel or picture things in their mind to learn.
Some of them like sound around and comfy chairs to help them concentrate.
Some will need to move about,
They'll even sing and dance when trying out something new.
But that's OK 'cause we have the knowledge of how they like to learn,
But now we're tired little teddy bears!

Erica Hewetson 2003

April 1, 2004

Dear Parents,
We have the opportunity to be a part of an action research project that will examine students' learning styles. The title of this project is 'Many Students Struggle in School Because of a Mismatch in Learning and Teaching Styles'. This research is designed to identify each child's learning style and compare with their teachers' teaching style.

Creative Learning from Auckland, New Zealand is supporting this effort. If you would like more information about this process, please see the resources at their website, http://www.creativelearningcentre.com/default.asp?theme=lsat

Your child will be taking a Learning Style Analysis (LSA) at the school and will be bringing the profile home to share the results with you. It would be beneficial to sit down and discuss this profile with your child and try to implement the unique needs that can help your son or daughter to be successful in school. Attached please find a signature line that needs to be signed and returned to me or my mailbox so that I know you have received the profile.

If you have any questions please feel free to contact me via email at:

Thanks for your assistance in this matter,

Regards
Sue Zeeb
Jefferson Academy High School

Implementing LS at St Vincent's

Another primary school, by no means struggling with the severe problems Forbury had, but also in a lower socio-economic area and wanting to improve students' behaviour and academic achievement, is St Vincent's Catholic Primary School, an inner city school in Birmingham, UK, where over 50 per cent of children are entitled to free school meals. Erica Hewetson, the Teaching and Learning Co-ordinator, describes how they got started in her report below and an overview of implementing an LS programme can be seen on page 48.

St Vincent's has an extremely dedicated and skilled staff who constantly strive for the best for their children. As a staff we had been investigating the 'accelerated learning' agenda and found that the methods employed had much to offer our children. I was at this point studying for a Masters in Education, focusing on 'The New Learning' in Birmingham – essentially looking at the learning revolution that was occurring. During this period of training, the headteacher and I were introduced to Barbara Prashnig's work on learning styles and found that it filled many of the gaps that we had highlighted and would provide me with far more material to consider for my dissertation! As she talked about our students' LS profiles, we wondered had she met some of our children as she described their displayed behaviour and style features perfectly! This gave us the confidence that learning styles was something we wanted to investigate further. The problem that now faced us was how to convince the whole staff that this made sense when they had not experienced the training for themselves.

Initial experimentation

I began with some low-level experimentation with a class of particularly challenging pupils to see how it would impact on their behaviour. This group of Year 3 children had an exceptionally large number of pupils with behavioural difficulties in its make-up. Many strategies had been explored to find ways of unlocking the learning potential in the class, such as extensive circle time, inventive rewards and sanctions schemes, child specific initiatives, fastidious keeping of behaviour logs and conferences with the behaviour co-ordinator, and even employing an extra teacher to put the children into two small classes. Each strategy showed some reward, but all were short lived. If LS could help this group of children, then it would be given credence among the rest of the school. I rushed around my house gathering lamps and cushions and set about creating a variety of areas in the room. As our windows are fitted with metal security shutters on the outside of the building, we asked the caretaker to close them on half of the windows in the classroom. We turned the fluorescent lights off and placed the lamps around the room. We moved desks to create a variety of seating arrangements, including desks in pairs, singly and groups, in the bright areas of the room and by the dim lamp light, and set up a large floor area with cushions laid out.

As the children walked into the room the response was instantly different and they sat on the carpet and waited in virtual silence to see what was going on. This was a real rarity for these pupils who would usually come bounding in to the room, full of the wrongs that had been done to them on the way in. My voice was calm and peaceful and so were the children. It was hard to withhold the wry smile that played around my mouth as I heard so many of the elements of the training replaying in my mind!

I explained to the children that they would be allowed a choice of where to work that day, but that it was to be a good learning choice, and any choices that I did not deem to be good for learning would be overruled, unless they could show me otherwise. For the first lesson, the whole class lay sprawled on the carpet. Fortunately I had foreseen this and set work on a piece of paper! At the start of the next session each child evaluated their piece of work and decided if they would be proud to stand up and say that this was their work. If they were not proud, they chose to put it in the bin. All but three children threw this piece of work away. During the next lesson I suggested they considered where was best for them to work given the task they had been set and only three children sat on the floor. They all produced excellent work this time and

Evaluation of learning styles within the classroom programme

Having now completed the Diploma of Holistic Education, I have become more aware of the different learning styles of my children and realized the impact that my personal teaching style can have. By recognizing that children learn in a variety of ways, I am now aware of the importance of providing a variety of learning experiences in the classroom programme.

When looking at the current classroom programme, I realize that many of our learning experiences cater for different learning styles. The Numeracy Programme that is being used throughout the school has many features that help children with different learning styles. At each stage of the programme children use a variety of equipment to gain an understanding of the concept being taught. They have the opportunity to practise their new learning by written recording in their books and through the use of a variety of games and activities that can be used individually or in groups.

Reading is also taught in small group situations with children grouped according to ability. Each group works with the teacher learning concepts particular to their needs. Learning experiences are varied and range from written responses, drama, creating visual aids to puppet shows.

I have realized the importance of acknowledging learning styles when planning and implementing units and assessment tasks. These are both areas that I intend to focus on in the near future.

Some areas of learning styles have been quite difficult for me to implement because they are not my style of learning. During the year, I have had to relax more and accept children who need to move around the room to learn and those who prefer a more informal work environment. I now have cushions that children use when they want and am happy for the children to choose a working space of their own rather than always being seated at a set desk.

NZ primary school teacher

made appropriate choices. We spent time discussing how choices may be different for different activities and these young children rose to the challenge, revelling in the new found freedom and responsibility they had been given.

'The Passionate Room!'

This was enough to tell us that we had to go further, but how to spread the word across the school? During a discussion between the headteacher and our LEA adviser this problem was raised, at which point the adviser made a suggestion that was to prove to be the turning point for LS in our school. Why not establish a 'Prashnig' room (later misquoted by one of the children as 'The Passionate Room'!) where the environment could be set out at the optimum for LS, where resources were appropriate for teaching the LS way and where teachers could go and experiment with this idea in a way that required no investment from them in their own rooms.

This strategy obviously had financial implications, but we were inspired and ready to overcome any hurdle. The room was to be a disused community room that had never really functioned well. It was full of resources that had never found their way back home and was dark and dingy. I wrote to over 50 companies asking for help with this project, promising publicity for this new approach. Almost without exception we were turned down with companies selecting one charity at head office and all branches supporting the designated cause. As a part of an Education Action Zone (EAZ) established to support education in challenging areas, we were made aware of the services of a group of volunteers from industry who took on community projects. This group came and painted the room for us in calming blues. The walls were still painted brick and the room has an uninviting high ceiling, so painting the room in two tones of blue, separated by a dado rail, made it instantly more appealing. A carpet was purchased to replace the worn 1970s off-cut that had adorned the floor, and lighting was supplied by a store that had no ability to sell ex-display models, on the provision that we had them safety tested. Suddenly a new

learning environment was taking shape. We trawled the local shops and found the best deals out there to furnish the room as economically as possible, even buying cushions from pound shops! We carefully arranged the furniture, ensuring a range of combinations available to pupils, and purchased resources to support the independent learning using a grant from the EAZ. These included a large number of self-correcting tools, commercial flip chutes, masks and puppets and, my favourite, a telephone booth with four receivers so that the auditory learners could go and discuss their work with a partner without disturbing the rest of the class. (One teacher used this tool for her auditory learners in a literacy lesson on alphabetical order. Pupils had a name on a piece of paper and they phoned the 'operator' to get the address and phone number, which the operator looked up in the phonebook. The caller then had to locate the street on an A–Z street map using the index!)

With the room intact and functional, it was time to get going. Staff received the first day of LS training and following that they used the room in rotation for a week at a time to experiment with the different environment and put their new found knowledge into action. An extremely valuable activity initiated by one teacher using the room was to ask the children to draw a picture of what they perceived their best learning environment to be, and at the end of the week they produced these pictures again but included the experiences they had had in a variety of scenarios. These second pictures closely matched the LSA-Junior instruments, provided by the online tool, showing that the children had really begun to grasp an understanding of their own learning needs. During the time in the room, I spent one session helping the class teacher observe the children's reactions. We looked at the group profile and in one instance all but one of the children were sitting exactly where their profile suggested they would be most comfortable. When we looked further into this child's profile we discovered that his strong preference for working with peers had overridden his environmental requirements, and in that instance he was placed exactly as

Considerations for implementing a learning styles programme on a school-wide basis

- Begin with an introduction or awareness session on LS to get colleagues excited about the idea.
- Organize LS in-service training for all teachers during which they will receive their LSA and TSA reports to find out how they learn and teach.
- Start an LS steering committee; create a budget for required LSA instruments and LS resources.
- Develop a school-wide management system for implementing the LS programme.
- Help group teachers into learning teams to give them support as they learn more about the concept of LS.
- Schedule morning or after-school meetings to discuss LS approaches.
- Establish an ongoing staff development programme.
- Inform and educate parents, organize parent evenings and working parties.
- Create LS tools and/or purchase commercial resources.
- Recognize teacher accomplishments and establish a feedback and evaluation scheme.
- Help administer the LSA instruments to students.
- Urge teachers to spend time discussing LS with their students.
- Begin with several classes or groups of students.

Tips for implementing a learning styles programme in class

1 Teach all students similarly but make adjustments in the learning environment (classroom set-up).
2 Teach all students similarly but provide a variety of activities to match their LS at one time or another.
3 Use co-operative group learning for about 60–70 per cent of the time as an alternative to traditional instructions.
4 Recognize differences in LS and prescribe LS skills re-training.

E. Hewetson, St Vincent's Primary

described! It was useful to have one member of staff visit each class as they were in the room to ensure that there had been a constancy of experience for the children and that teachers had not simply carried on teaching as before in a different room. This gave teachers the opportunity to ask questions and be reassured that they had understood the message and were transferring theory into practice correctly.

In order to explain this work to our parents, I wrote a song to the tune of 'The Teddy Bears' Picnic' (see page 44) and the school choir performed it at the school's AGM. This was a really simple way of explaining why they had heard about so many changes, giving a whistle-stop tour of the learning styles agenda.

A measurable result

Prior to beginning the LS programme, we carried out a baseline study of pupils' levels of engagement and observed this again for the same children at the end of the first period of intervention.

Where to next?

The visits to 'The Prashnig Room' showed our staff that this approach could work and they are now finding ways of taking this back into their own classroom design. All refurbishment of the school, as has taken place in the Nursery, will be in support of LS classrooms and we are in the process of creating ideas banks for activities to support different learners to aid staff in their planning. In turn, as each policy is reviewed, the question is constantly asked – 'How does this fit with learning styles?'. We are still struggling to find a way of writing a display policy that we can be comfortable with when all our previous training had told us to fill every space, but we're getting there, and the debate is invaluable as it means people are reflecting and considering what they are doing with the children and why.

At times, it feels that we have done very little in moving LS into our school, but when new teachers come to join us, it is apparent just how far we have come as a staff. Things we used to say to pupils, without thinking, stand out so clearly as going against the diversity

agenda and staff are able to instantly draw up new plans for their classrooms as they consider the possible needs of their class. We need to constantly revisit the theory in order to remind ourselves of where we are going in the midst of the heavy constraints of the National Curriculum and statutory testing, but when we do, the team at St Vincent's never cease to amaze me as to how much they now know intrinsically. We still have a long way to go, but we're working on it – and if we could tell all teachers just one tip for success – switch your lights off and get ready to see your children shine!

LS at Pukekohe High School

In one large, semi-rural high school south of Auckland, NZ, Jill Courteaud, the assistant principal, has been instrumental in the introduction of LS for the whole school and I have provided professional development over the past three years. Here is her interim report.

Pukekohe High School's purpose is to be a positive place of learning where individual learning potential is realized. In order to achieve this, we aim to ensure that all approaches to teaching and learning are consistently based on best practice and, in particular, to ensure that teaching takes into account the full range of individual learning styles and that the programmes we deliver are differentiated to meet individual learning needs. We intend to use individual learning style analyses and class profiles of students' learning style analyses to achieve these purposes.

In the first year, 33 teachers elected to undertake day 1 of learning styles training in their own time. Of these, 21 teachers undertook day 2. In the second year another third of our staff attended the second offering of this training and before the end of the school year the final group of teachers (the most resistant ones) also went through the LS training. The day 1 training engendered high levels of enthusiasm and teachers willingly experimented with light (a good number being shocked to learn that many of their students preferred them to keep the lights off

This is Kim's testimonial about her experiences as an adult student at an Australian Technical and Further Education institute. It was sent after her 'thank-you' letter (see page 16) to her former teacher Bob Ayliffe (with permission for publication) and it speaks for itself. Since then, Kim has continued to study successfully at university.

18th March 2004.

Dear Bob,

Inspired by our conversation over lunch today I came home and decided to put pen to paper and write the testimonial again. Bob, you know me: this could go on for pages and pages (or maybe bottles and bottles of wine). Don't be surprised if it takes me days to do this as I try to express everything that you did (and gave) to so many of your students last year. So here it goes. I hope I don't rave on too much. Censor at your discretion.

TESTIMONIAL

This testimonial is dedicated to Bob - my teacher; my mentor; my friend; and my inspiration. Thank you for having such faith, belief and confidence in me as a student. You inspired me to persist with my studies: you dared me to dream my dream; and you encouraged me to pursue it.

Last year you opened my eyes with the LSA and the MI. After being a refugee from the traditional education system, even after some 20 years. I never thought that perhaps the system failed me. I was told that I failed as a student!!!! And was too dumb, stupid, or a hopeless case, many teachers just gave up on me. Most of my school years were spent outside the classroom – in the hallway – for being too talkative, too disruptive, too questioning and for not conforming!!

After doing my LSA, so many light bulbs came on that it was overwhelming. It wasn't me at all; it was my learning style that did not coincide with traditional teaching methods. I was taught in the traditional style, under regimental classroom conditions. You had no individuality!!! You were just another face in the crowd. You were a student and you were there to learn the system's way and that was all there was to it. If you didn't, this was your failure as a student, not the teachers, their methods or the education system. Teachers were never interested in what was happening to you outside of school or on the home front. They never took into account that this may be having an effect on your learning. These two were always kept separate. I remember being told, 'You're here now, this is what you're supposed to be doing, so sit down and concentrate. Everything else gets left at the gate as you enter.' In hindsight I often wonder if they (teachers) had perhaps taken an interest in me as a person, knew the facts of my home life, showed some understanding and compassion, how different schooling would have been for me. How different my life would have been.

Until doing my LSA, I never considered that I have times of the day where I learn better, retain information and actually produce my best work. Of course these hours don't coincide with those of TAFE or school. Early morning is one of my best times to study or learn new concepts; as such; this is when I tackle my maths and science assignments. At home I get up extra early to work on these subjects, I've found by doing this I can accomplish more and I don't find the tasks so complicated or frustrating. If I leave these subjects till later in the day I get bogged down and confused, which makes the tasks stressful and seems to set off a vicious circle and I

continued on page 52

in the classroom), music, Brain Gym®, allowing students to work in groups or pairs where formerly they encouraged more individual learning, informal areas in their rooms, allowing students to work on the floor and so on.

One of the things that was noticeable was that teachers quickly became more flexible – even those who had previously been quite set in their ways. Also, right away, efforts to make small changes were rewarded. Where teachers were fearful of allowing group or pair work, having previously allowed only individual work, they were pleasantly surprised at the levels of engagement of students who opted to work in these ways when the opportunity was provided. A teacher who dreaded the idea of an informal area with sofa and armchairs, fearing that there would be a rush for the area every period, said her fears soon subsided when she realized that the area appealed only to certain students who thrived there, happy to write on their laps, while most students preferred the convenience of their desks. Another teacher was surprised when a previously difficult to 'control', disengaged and underachieving student seized the opportunity to work on the floor when it was offered and completed two periods' work in one!

In the meantime we have made LSAs of all our Year 9 and 10 students available to staff and we provided separate, small group follow-up training on interpreting and using group profiles to maximum effect. Regular time will be provided in our ongoing staff Professional Development Programme for sharing of ideas and experiences and to allow for the writing in to schemes and unit outlines of suggestions for activities for the different learning styles.

A useful resource for activities that cater for kinesthetic learners, such as walk-around surveys or doughnut, the use of two circles of students, one inside the other, with students asking and answering questions then moving around to another partner, is a book entitled *Co-operative Learning in New Zealand Schools* by Don Brown and Charlotte Thomson (2000).

We are looking forward to becoming more skilled in meeting the individual learning needs of students and to providing more flexible, differentiated programmes which enable all students to enjoy learning and achieving their potential.

LS programmes with several schools or district wide

The following is a summary of the LSA pilot project of four schools in the Wansbeck area, UK, which was lead by the Thinking for Learning Consultant, Zoe Beasley.

The LSA is a highly informative educational profiling tool. The information it provides is detailed and precise. There are several generalizations but each profile is unique to the individual and teachers can use the profiles to communicate learning to children and to articulate how learning occurs. This enables the child to have ownership over their experiences and to make informed decisions that will help to support their learning.

Involving pupils in the implementation of the six areas of learning, as shown in the LSA pyramid overleaf, is important. The children can provide suggestions and ideas about how to develop their learning experiences and create their learning environment.

Communicating throughout such a project is vital to ensure the pupils know changes are there to support their learning and the impact these could have. The level of staff development is dependent upon commitment and interest in the project. Most of the staff involved spent a lot of time reviewing and reflecting upon their practice. Many were keen to introduce changes in order to make improvements.

The use of group profiles has been instrumental in meeting the needs of anywhere from 6 to 36 or more pupils. Many teachers have found this extremely beneficial when planning for different groups or classes. It indicates where strong preferences and non-preferences are in their classes and promotes meaningful learning opportunities.

end up getting absolutely nowhere. My LSA also indicated concentration is higher and I'm more alert in the evening. I use this time slot to do my humanity subjects such as English, Australian Studies etc. I've found late evenings are where I produce my best work for these subjects. I'm highly interested and stimulated by topics covered and consequently more motivated to complete my tasks or assignments. This revelation also showed me that my three boys all have their individual times where their concentration is higher.

Well there you have it!!! LSA has become an integral part of, not only my studies and learning, but my children's as well. I started applying these methods in the home, before their school began to introduce some aspects of LSA. However, I feel that they didn't utilize this to its full potential. There are probably heaps I've overlooked or inadvertently left out, but it's so difficult to remember all aspects and how we have used them at home. LSA has become such a natural thing for us we don't often stop to think how or what we use and the above is just a few ways we implement some of it.

Thank you for teaching me holistically Bob, as I use what you taught me with the boys and as such my children have a head start because of you. We remain forever in your debt at showing us this. See the ripple effect you have had, not only did you make a difference to my life, but also to my three boys. Finally finished it, I think!!!!

Forever grateful

Kim

PS: Another bloody book Bob, I wonder how wise you were at asking me to do this. You know me - can never keep things short and sweet. Verbosity is my forte!!

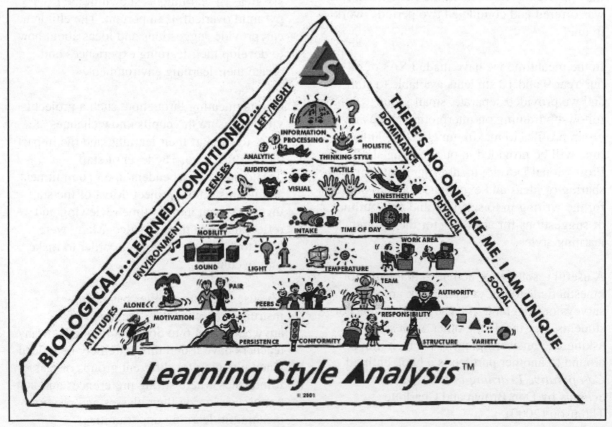

LSA pyramid model showing all elements that influence someone's learning ability

I would advocate that someone who has had relevant training and experience in LSA should lead the project. This means one person has an overview and an understanding of the needs of those involved. It also ensures that the results can be interpreted correctly.

This has been a very exciting project to lead. I have felt privileged to work with hard working and dedicated staff. Lots of changes have been introduced and are being implemented at all levels in the schools I have worked in.

The impact on staff morale has been high. People have told me how motivated and inspired they have felt. It has changed their perspective of teaching and learning and given them the confidence to try something new based on students' learning needs.

I would certainly recommend this model of LSA. It is thorough and confirms the important issues that schools need to address in order to promote enthusiastic and independent lifelong learners. Its principles are the very foundation of an education system that is challenging and wholly appropriate to the needs of both the teacher and the learner.

The work of the LSA pilot project has introduced new enthusiasm and motivation to teachers who strive to develop their practice in innovative ways. When I met Barbara Prashnig to discuss the findings of the project she was keen to hear examples of excellent practice and said the work teachers had been doing in the Wansbeck area was very exciting. After completing this pilot project, we came to the conclusion that these developments are pioneering and revolutionary. Staff and teachers will be inspired by them for a long time.

For a full description of this project see online appendix 7.

Dear Barbara,

Learning styles has changed the way I teach for many reasons. One is the introduction of the idea that you need to cater for different modalities in the educational setting, which I can't imagine not doing now. The freedom you gain as a teacher by understanding the different learning styles of your pupils is immense. We made bracelets so they could fiddle without reserve, once they were allowed to fiddle of course they didn't bother much. We all work on the floor or on low desks when the mood takes us and understand the way we work best which is such an important concept for children to have. They look very relieved when they learn that they work best in groups or by themselves, even when they know already how they work. My classroom set up has never been the same. I spent the other day making flip chutes with my class so they can learn their times tables. They were so excited at what they were doing and so engrossed they worked right through their break and were very proud of their efforts. I only wish I had taken photos. The other reason learning styles has been so important is that it creates an openness to try new ideas with children that I never had before and it means that I have a classroom where the students and the teacher can take risks and survive.

Thank you for the gift of learning styles in my classroom.

Julie McElhinney
St Patrick's School, Invercargill, NZ

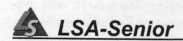

LSA-Senior   15 Seniors - Group Profile

prepared for:	15 Seniors - Group Profile
Network Educational Press	Chris Dickinson
22/02/04	Total number in group = 15

Group Percentages I (preferences)

Graph shows the % of people with preferences in the following areas

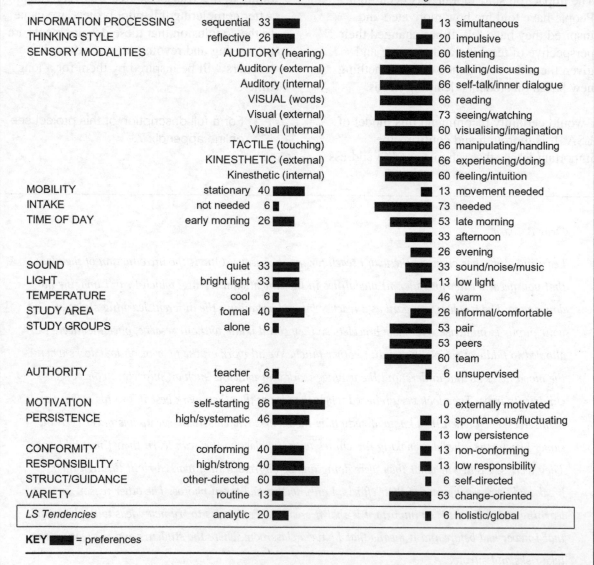

INFORMATION PROCESSING	sequential 33	13 simultaneous
THINKING STYLE	reflective 26	20 impulsive
SENSORY MODALITIES	AUDITORY (hearing)	60 listening
	Auditory (external)	66 talking/discussing
	Auditory (internal)	66 self-talk/inner dialogue
	VISUAL (words)	66 reading
	Visual (external)	73 seeing/watching
	Visual (internal)	60 visualising/imagination
	TACTILE (touching)	66 manipulating/handling
	KINESTHETIC (external)	66 experiencing/doing
	Kinesthetic (internal)	60 feeling/intuition
MOBILITY	stationary 40	13 movement needed
INTAKE	not needed 6	73 needed
TIME OF DAY	early morning 26	53 late morning
		33 afternoon
		26 evening
SOUND	quiet 33	33 sound/noise/music
LIGHT	bright light 33	13 low light
TEMPERATURE	cool 6	46 warm
STUDY AREA	formal 40	26 informal/comfortable
STUDY GROUPS	alone 6	53 pair
		53 peers
		60 team
AUTHORITY	teacher 6	6 unsupervised
	parent 26	
MOTIVATION	self-starting 66	0 externally motivated
PERSISTENCE	high/systematic 46	13 spontaneous/fluctuating
		13 low persistence
CONFORMITY	conforming 40	13 non-conforming
RESPONSIBILITY	high/strong 40	13 low responsibility
STRUCT/GUIDANCE	other-directed 60	6 self-directed
VARIETY	routine 13	53 change-oriented
LS Tendencies	analytic 20	6 holistic/global

KEY ▇ = preferences

How to use LSA group profiles

The key to an easy and successful introduction of LS strategies to a whole class is first to look for extreme results (strong preferences and non-preferences); second, to check how flexible this group is; third, to subgroup students with similar needs; and, last, on a regular basis implement whatever strategies can be used to accommodate different styles. This means teachers do not necessarily need to cater to everyone's individual needs because human beings can be very flexible but any actions they take to match teaching and learning styles will increase motivation and benefit any learning process, particularly when teaching something new and/or difficult.

Subgrouping students according ... to their preferences

Preferences (LSA graph I; page 2)

This graph shows the percentage of students with preferences in their LSA profile.

*Results **ABOVE 60 per cent** are significant and must be considered for devising effective teaching strategies.*

Recommendations for teachers

Look into the areas where you see high results and accommodate these learning needs where you can. For instance, if 85 per cent of your students learn best through feeling/intuition, 75 per cent need authority and 68 per cent need time to visualize what they have heard, seen or read, your teaching strategies must allow for that by making your students feel good the moment they enter your classroom and by presenting learning content in a way that it makes sense to them. It also means that you need to exercise your authority in a positive, non-threatening way to avoid negative feelings that will certainly switch off students with such preferences.

... to their non-preferences

Non-preferences (LSA graph II; page 3)

This graph shows the percentage of students with non-preferences in their LSA profile.

*Results **ABOVE 40 per cent** are significant. These elements should be considered during the introduction of new and difficult learning content.*

Recommendations for teachers

Look into the areas of high scores (above 40 per cent) and try to avoid teaching through these strategies whenever possible. (Except in 'Attitudes' where it can also mean that these are not applicable for some students, such as a non-preference for low persistence means that not following through is not being considered by students who have such a result.)

For example, if 47 per cent of your students do not learn well by listening, 55 per cent find it difficult to concentrate in the morning and 63 per cent cannot sit still, then these must be avoided by reducing your 'chalk-and-talk' approach and allowing students to move around while learning. If it is not possible to avoid teaching through your students' non-preferences, make sure that as many of their other style preferences as possible are matched. This is particularly important when

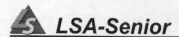 **LSA-Senior**   15 Seniors - Group Profile

prepared for: 15 Seniors - Group Profile
Network Educational Press   Chris Dickinson
22/02/04   Total number in group = 15

Group Percentages II (non-preferences)

Graph shows the % of people with non-preferences in the following areas

INFORMATION PROCESSING	sequential	0		0	simultaneous
THINKING STYLE	reflective	20 ——		— 13	impulsive
SENSORY MODALITIES	AUDITORY (hearing)			— 13	listening
	Auditory (external)			— 6	talking/discussing
	Auditory (internal)			0	self-talk/inner dialogue
	VISUAL (words)			— 6	reading
	Visual (external)			0	seeing/watching
	Visual (internal)			0	visualising/imagination
	TACTILE (touching)			0	manipulating/handling
	KINESTHETIC (external)			— 6	experiencing/doing
	Kinesthetic (internal)			0	feeling/intuition
MOBILITY	stationary	26 ——		— 6	movement needed
INTAKE	not needed	33 ——		— 6	needed

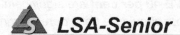 **LSA-Senior**   15 Seniors - Group Profile

prepared for: 15 Seniors - Group Profile
Network Educational Press   Chris Dickinson
22/02/04   Total number in group = 15

Group Percentages III (flexibilities)

Graph shows the % of people with flexibilities in the following areas

INFORMATION PROCESSING	sequential	60		80	simultaneous
THINKING STYLE	reflective	26		40	impulsive
SENSORY MODALITIES	AUDITORY (hearing)			26	listening
	Auditory (external)			26	talking/discussing
	Auditory (internal)			33	self-talk/inner dialogue
	VISUAL (words)			26	reading
	Visual (external)			26	seeing/watching
	Visual (internal)			40	visualising/imagination
	TACTILE (touching)			33	manipulating/handling
	KINESTHETIC (external)			26	experiencing/doing
	Kinesthetic (internal)			40	feeling/intuition
MOBILITY	stationary	20		66	movement needed
INTAKE	not needed	53		13	needed

teaching student groups at a time of day when they are 'brain-dead' and have 'fuzzy' thinking, which is often the case with teenagers.

... to their flexibilities

Flexibilities (LSA graph III; page 4)

This page shows graphically results of all students in a group but the percentage figures show their flexibilities only. To get the most valuable information from this page, add the percentages of preferences and flexibilities from graphs I and III in the same element (e.g. intake or informal study area).

*Where results are **ABOVE 80 per cent**, they MUST be considered for the majority of students in this group.*

Recommendations for teachers

The golden rule is teaching to the majority while catering for the minority. This means incorporating teaching methods for all those who show preferences/flexibilities in certain elements while allowing the few remaining others to learn in a different, often opposite way (e.g. using kinesthetic and tactile techniques with the majority while the minority might use visual and auditory techniques; the use of music in the background for those who concentrate better with sound while those who need quiet can wear disconnected earphones; instead of forcing everyone to sit still, allowing students to move around in class when their concentration and learning improves).

Putting students into learning groups according to their preferences in these areas can be achieved by consulting page 5 of the group profile (see graph opposite).

... to their style combinations

Group Results (LSA group profile; page 5)

This page gives complete LSA profiles of each individual student in a group without revealing names for anonymity.

Recommendations for teachers

These results can be interpreted either

vertically to see, for instance, which students have question marks or a lot of flexibilities, or can be read horizontally to find out how many students have preferences in certain areas or need to avoid certain style elements when learning something difficult. Instead of having to look through individual profiles, teachers can see the results of their students at one glance and can take appropriate action. The names of all the students in a group can be found on page 5 of the Group Profile (under Group Members) correlating with the code numbers in the Group Results (see page 58).

Group Members (LSA group profile; page 6)

This page reveals the names of all the students in this group, their gender, age and when the LSA profile was generated.

Recommendations for teachers

To help you with analytic and/or holistic approaches, square or round symbols can be found in front of the names of those students who show strong overall tendencies in these areas. It is recommended to let students who share the same preferences work together when they are tackling something new and/or difficult. Students without these symbols in front of their names are flexible and can be subgrouped in many different ways.

An important point to note

The more question marks that are visible in a personal LSA profile, the more it is likely that this student:

a) is under stress

b) has had a traumatic experience

c) is currently experiencing confusion

d) is undergoing change in these areas

e) has reading problems, or was confused about the questionnaire (which occurs very rarely).

Question marks can be found in many students' profiles and are generally the result of inconsistencies in answering the questionnaire. However, any of the above scenarios can lead to behaviour problems, loss of motivation, learning difficulties, ill

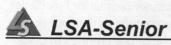 **LSA-Senior**

15 Seniors - Group Profile

Group Results

Chris Dickinson

Group member code number	1	2	3	4	5	6	7	8	9	10	11	12	13	14	15	
INFORMATION PROCESSING sequential																sequential (analytic)
simultaneous																simultaneous (holistic)
THINKING STYLE reflective																reflective
impulsive																impulsive
SENSES AUDITORY (hearing)																listening
Auditory (external)																talking/discussing
Auditory (internal)																self-talk/inner dialogue
VISUAL (words)																reading
Visual (external)																seeing/watching
Visual (internal)																visualising/imagination
TACTILE (touching)																manipulating/handling
KINESTHETIC (external)																experiencing/doing
Kinesthetic (internal)																feeling/intuition
MOBILITY stationary																stationary
movement needed																movement needed
INTAKE not needed																not needed
needed																needed
TIME OF DAY early morning																early morning
late morning																late morning
afternoon																afternoon
evening																evening
SOUND quiet																quiet
sound/noise/music																sound/noise/music
LIGHT bright light																bright light
low light																low light
TEMPERATURE cool																cool
warm																warm
STUDY AREA formal																formal
informal/comfortable																informal/comfortable
STUDY GROUPS alone																alone
pair																pair
peers																peers
team																team
AUTHORITY teacher																teacher
unsupervised																unsupervised
parent																parent
MOTIVATION self-starting																self-starting
externally motivated																externally motivated
PERSISTENCE high/systematic																high/systematic
spontaneous/fluctuating																spontaneous/fluctuating
low persistence																low persistence
CONFORMITY conforming																conforming
non-conforming																non-conforming
RESPONSIBILITY high/strong																high/strong
low responsibility																low responsibility
STRUCT/GUIDANCE other-directed																other-directed
self-directed																self-directed
VARIETY routine																routine
change-oriented																change-oriented

KEY ⬤ strong preference ⬤ preference — non-preference ⬤ flexibility ?? inconsistency

health, underachievement and, ultimately, dropping out of formal education. It is very important that teachers talk to students about these areas in their LSA profile and attempt to find out the reasons for these inconsistencies.

From our work with practitioners we know that group profiles are one of the most valuable sources of information about the learning needs of students, not only in whole classes but also in a whole school or even district. Group results can reveal trends and changes in learning styles and can trace developments in style needs over certain time periods, development phases and student populations.

With LSA group profiles, teachers have for the first time an in-depth analysis of students' true learning needs in large numbers and can keep records about how styles change over time. These results will help educators to adjust their teaching methods accordingly, not only from year to year but also from group to group if necessary.

Learning with the help of an adult

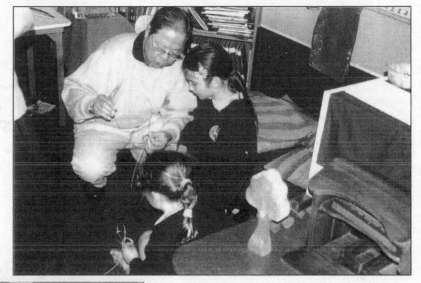

Informal learning at Glendowie Primary School, Auckland, NZ

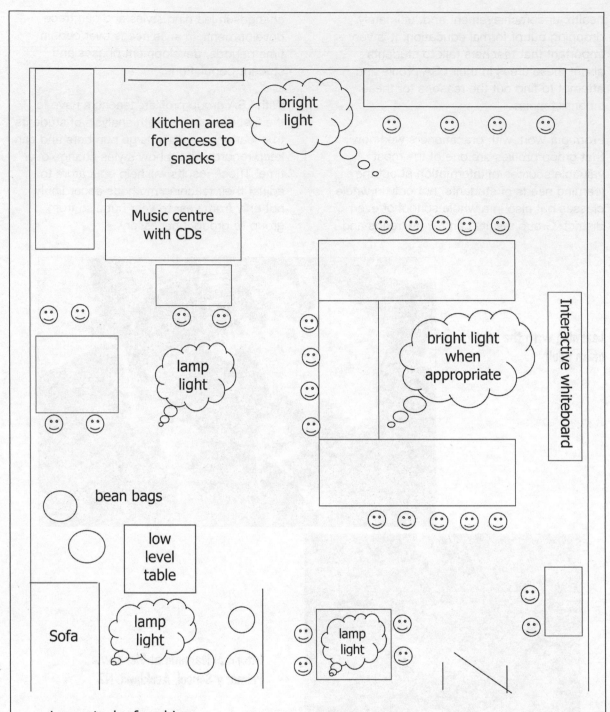

- large stock of cushions
- a range of lighting
- clipboards
- range of music
- access to natural snacks (that is, dried fruit) and water
- headphones for those who do not want music
- koosh balls for tactile learners
- interactive whiteboard aids a variety of learning styles
- display is interactive only – a tool, not an exhibition.

Erica Hewetson, June 2003

Chapter 7

How to create learning styles classrooms

General principles

As many times before, I am deliberately provocative here when discussing this important aspect of education. However, it is not my intention to offend anyone because I know there are many wonderful practitioners out there who struggle on a daily basis to make the best with the little they have got; but there are also, unfortunately, many politicians, administrators, teachers and decision makers in education who do not want to know about style diversity, and do not think it is necessary to have classrooms that suit different learning styles of students or even deny they exist. A strongly held belief is still that with the right support and motivation, successful learning can happen anywhere and too many students are just lazy. If this was true, we would not have increasing numbers of underachievers in virtually all countries, more discipline problems and dropping academic standards, given the numerous attempts to introduce new programmes and support strategies that come and go and cost a lot of money.

Classrooms for frontal teaching with neatly arranged rows of desks facing the 'front' of the classroom have been a familiar sight in schools ever since mass education was introduced. We have all been through schools where such classrooms were the norm and we probably did not think much of it, we just took it for granted that this is the way classrooms are supposed to be because they have always been like that, the furniture just looked a bit more modern and only recently the blackboards changed from green to white. We never questioned WHY classrooms were arranged in this fashion, and teachers, students and parents had no idea how important the physical learning environment can be for succeeding or failing in school. Only since research on learning styles began in the early 1970s do we know that furniture and its arrangement, lighting, sound, colour and temperature can have a profound impact on students' overall well-being, memory, concentration, reading and learning ability.

When faced with such evidence, many teachers reject the idea that these radical changes to their classrooms are possible, practical and workable and cannot imagine that an interactive learning styles classroom is manageable or even useful. The result is that the higher we go in education, the less stimulating learning environments become, so that worldwide in modern mass education we now have lecture theatres and classrooms packed with modern technology but missing the human touch as they are extremely sterile, non-stimulating and uninviting to spend more time in than necessary. These progressive new learning environments (or should I call them provocatively curriculum-delivery factories?) have still not improved learning, discipline, attendance or academic achievements as many reports from different countries are proving each year.

Before going into details, the basic ingredients of a learning styles classroom are: teachers' awareness of the style diversity of their students (no more 'one-size-fits-all' approaches), furniture arrangement and comfort, learning music, light levels, colours, temperature, drinking water and nibbling, social interaction, multisensory instructions,

Evaluation of resources in the Prashnig Room

Please fill in this evaluation as accurately and honestly as you can so as to ensure we move the programme forward in an appropriate manner. Your answers will help to focus priorities for spending and the way in which we interpret Barbara Prashnig's work at St Vincent's Primary.

Please tell me how you found the physical resources in the room. Comments should include how useful you found the resources, were they the right size/type, would something else be of more use to your class. What do you think is the ideal number of the items listed. These things will be different for each class according to their group profile, so please say how you think it works for your group. The empty rows are for you to add anything you feel I have missed! – Please don't miss the behaviour section! If you do not notice any particular changes, please say so.

Item	Too many	Not enough	Just right	Comments
Desks				
Formal chairs				
Bean bags				
Sofas				
Cushions				
Lamps				
Bright lights				
Music – range				
Headphones				
Group seating				
Paired seating				
Koosh balls				
Flip chutes				
Computer stations				
Dried fruit				
Clipboards				
Low tables				
Seat pads				

How was the behaviour of the children while in the room?

Any notable points on levels of engagement during time in the room?

more hands and body involvement, personalized, active learning and movement.

Despite the fact that all these necessary changes might be overwhelming (as it certainly can be in the beginning), creating LS classrooms is a lengthy process, an evolution, starting with small changes, adding further improvements, always involving students and often their parents, even the wider school community, always building on past successes, gaining confidence, monitoring students' improved discipline and academic performance. Many teachers reported that they had to re-arrange their classrooms several times until they found the right setting and the proper work flow for themselves.

The importance of lighting and colour

In over ten years of involvement with style diversity, I have often been asked about the importance of colours and lighting in classrooms. The more I hear and read about the successes educators have with implementing learning styles in their classrooms, the more I have become aware how important light levels are, but equally how important the 'right' colours are for enhancing students' learning. It has been well documented what impact light has on the ability to concentrate and overall well-being, not only in learning situations, but also in daily life. For a closer investigation it is important to distinguish between the different properties of light and colour: the need for light in human beings seems to be very personal, depending on age and preferences for bright or dim light and all levels in between, but the way people react to colours seems to be much more universal, based on the strong emotional qualities of different colours.

Light levels stimulate brain activity in different ways and often generate physical reactions, whereas colours have an impact on human emotions, trigger feelings and undoubtedly have spatial effects in rooms. When light levels and colours are 'wrong' for students, they will switch off, lose concentration,

become discipline problems and often give up on academic learning. For further reading please visit the websites below where much of the information was derived from.

Colours

Regarding colours, there are some basic guidelines and insights, most of which go back to the 1960s when Swiss professor Dr Max Lüscher created his colour test that is still being used as a psychological assessment tool today.
www.colourtest.ue-foundation.org

Here are the basics, applied to classroom environments:

- **Blue**: feels tranquil, cool, serene; certain shades of blue cause the brain to secrete tranquillizing chemicals; can be perceived as 'cold'.
- **Green**: makes people feel secure and 'tended', persistent and self-centred; can be dull.
- **Red**: increases respiratory rates, stimulates eating, can increase blood pressure; feels exciting and invites impulsiveness; over-exposure can result in agitation.
- **Yellow**: is recognized by humans faster than any other colour; evokes spontaneity, is joyful, optimistic; is truly joyous and virtuous in its purest form. It exudes warmth, inspiration and vitality, and is the happiest of all colours, signifying communication, enlightenment, sunlight and spirituality.
- **Orange**: dominant, lively; bright orange is non-relaxing; peachy orange is warm.
- **Terracotta/brown**: evokes 'back-to-earth' feeling; inspires 'groundedness'.
- **Violet**: can be overpowering; pastels are better for background.
- **Black**: avoid it!
www.rockymountainprinting.com

How does colour impact on children (and teachers) in the classroom?

Young children experience space as an emotion, and colour can have a big impact on how a child consciously or unconsciously

Desks near natural light

Working away from
brightly lit areas

Creating dim light area under
umbrella and in tent, Ordrup
Skole, Copenhagen

Table lamps for those
who need more light at
Björken Skola, Sweden

behaves, socializes and learns in space. Colours can encourage introversion or extroversion, cause anger or peacefulness and influence our physiological functioning.

In early childhood settings, there is often an overabundance of colour. Children's clothes provide colour in motion in addition to the bright colours of toys, artwork, furniture and so on. Designers, teachers and parents often use too much colour on the walls and the end result is a kaleidoscope atmosphere that cheers for a short time but wears on the children much of the time. The result is often agitation and then tiredness.

Mood can affect behaviour as well as attitude and the colours in a room can directly affect teachers' and students' moods. Specific colours encourage certain emotions and brightly coloured walls are not appropriate for classrooms.
🖰 www.glidden.com

Practical tips

Deep, 'warm' colours give classrooms an intimate, cosy feeling (red–violet, red, red–orange, orange, terracotta, yellow–orange, yellow).

Light 'cool' colours make a classroom seem more spacious and have a calming effect (green, blue–green, blue–violet; white and off-white also have this effect).

Wall colours can be warm or cool tones, but keep the colours fairly light and not greyed. All colours will have to be chosen carefully and with consideration of the classroom layout, window and sun exposure and so on. A mistake is to go overboard with lots of bright, primary colours, particularly in primary schools. This is just as bad as an all black and white room.

A pale blue or green shade would have to be chosen carefully, just as any other colour considered. Clean, clear, light colours are usually best for a learning atmosphere, but can be varied depending on classroom usage and light. The same colour could be used in all classrooms on the same floor. In future there might be a new role of a colour consultant in schools whose task it will be to create colour harmony conducive to learning and improve visual ergonomics.

Most often classrooms are either too cluttered or walls are stark and monotonous. The best would be a comfortable middle ground. In combination with colour, lighting is of utmost importance and natural light and full-spectrum lighting is the best.

The 'blackboards' ideally should be green and not black, but are mostly white these days, although green is easier to look at over longer periods of time. Walls behind whiteboards should be of the same or slightly lighter reflectance value but do not match the wall colour to the whiteboard. Do not use white or off-white because of too little contrast, which is fatiguing to the eyes.

Keep the children's drawings and crafts away from the blackboard area or the front of the classroom. Otherwise it will be too distracting and busy. Create separate bulletin boards for such items and place them beyond view, such as to the back of the classroom or in the hallways.

Desks and worktables should not be white or very pale. Again, watch out for the glare factor and keep surfaces matt and mid-toned. Wood and wood-like surfaces are excellent as long as they are not glossy.

For special needs children (and adults) stay away from large patterns; especially busy floor coverings, wall graphics and tile patterns. They can be visually ambiguous and confusing. The use of mirrors or glass partitions can also be a problem. Objects reflected in them can be disturbing and even frightening. 'Time-out' rooms should be friendly and home-like.

I saw a very successful colour design in a primary school in Brighton, UK that had transformed an old and ugly brick stone building into a cheerful learning space: each of the three floors had a different yet related colour scheme – brighter colours in the corridors and paler colours in the classrooms, allowing for dim and bright light areas. I heard that it was so beautiful kids would drag their parents in after the first few

Working informally in low light areas

Light diffuser SKY-SCAPES giving the impression of windows in the ceiling

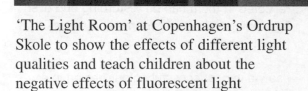

'The Light Room' at Copenhagen's Ordrup Skole to show the effects of different light qualities and teach children about the negative effects of fluorescent light

Diffused lighting in corridor at Ordrup Skole, Copenhagen, Denmark

days of the school year exclaiming, 'Look mum, look how cool my school is!'

Daylight vs. fluorescent light

Current research confirms that we are energized by the full-spectrum light of the Sun. Natural light helps pupils learn better as a new study from Sacramento, California found. It was one of the largest ever done on natural light in schools, and findings suggest that children learn faster and do better on standardized tests in classrooms with more daylight.

As researchers isolate the specific part of the Sun's spectrum that is related to health and well-being, we could eventually create the perfect indoor environment with artificial lighting. Based on extensive research, the cool-white fluorescent tube is legally banned in German hospitals and medical facilities. Yet, most offices, shops, hospitals and schools in NZ, Australia, the USA and the UK still use cool-white fluorescent light!

Full or incomplete spectrum lighting?

In 1980, Dr Fritz Hollwich conducted a study comparing the effects of sitting under strong artificial cool-white (non-full spectrum) illumination with the effects of sitting under strong artificial illumination that simulates sunlight (full-spectrum). Using changes in the endocrine system to evaluate these effects, he found stress-like levels of cortisol (a stress hormone) in individuals when sitting under the cool-white tubes. These changes were totally absent in the individuals sitting under the sunlight-simulating tubes.

Currently the only natural full-spectrum fluorescent light bulbs and tubes that can illuminate details and colour with the same accuracy as natural outdoor daylight are known in Germany as BIO Light – see
🖱 www.narva-bel.de
and is marketed in the USA as Vita-Lite – see
🖱 www.naturallighting.com
Both these manufacturers produce full-spectrum, full-colour, natural-light tubes, portraying true colours that can reduce fatigue, glare and eye strain from VDU screens. This fluorescent lighting is pleasant, natural, bright and stimulating; it can also

reduce SAD (Seasonal Affective Disorder, also known as 'winter blues') and is excellent for ADD (Attention Deficit Disorder).

Practical tips

If you have old, cool-light fluorescent tubes in your class, check out the learning styles of your students first (with the LSA instruments for primary and high school students) and find out how many students need bright light and how many have a preference for dim light. Make sure that there is always a low-light corner or naturally darker area in your classroom and diffuse harsh neon light with loose, transparent fabric. If your budget and the light fixtures allow it, light-diffusing panels can be attached, replacing the white plastic panels that do not diffuse the cold glare. Please visit this interesting website
🖱 www.skyscapes.biz
and look at these very creative products. SKY-SCAPES® are durable, lightweight replacement light diffusers and are easy to install in just minutes per fixture. They have various transparent images such as the blue sky with white clouds (see opposite) or green flowering plants that give the impression that the light segments in the ceiling are actually windows.

The ultimate goal, however, for our schools (and offices) should be to replace all old fluorescent light tubes with full spectrum ones (BIO Light or Vita-Lite) as mentioned before.

There is one little-known phenomenon: fluorescent light distorts colours and the Irlen Syndrome (described below) is another problem many students encounter. In one New Zealand primary school we found 85 per cent of students suffered from this visual distortion. In this situation coloured eye glasses or transparent, coloured plastic overlays for reading are a great remedy when diagnosed early enough.

Irlen Syndrome

Scotopic Sensitivity Syndrome (SSS) is a type of visual perceptual problem. Bright lights, fluorescent lights or glossy paper will often make the problems worse, as the extreme contrast will increase the problem of persistent images. The Irlen Syndrome

Classrooms equipped with learning styles aids at Glendowie Primary School, Auckland, NZ

Cushions, couches, formal/informal seating, low tables, whiteboards, teacher learning centres, bean bags, and classrooms have been set up to allow for formal and informal seating.

Tape decks in each room.

OHPs in all Junior rooms, and between rooms in the Middle and Senior School.

All classrooms have koosh balls or tactile feeling tools.

Computer/printer in each room.

Access to earphones/ear muffs.

Learning Centres to provide a range of visual and tactile resources especially in mathematics and topic work.

Classroom layout has changed to cater for a variety of furniture and varying light conditions.

Multiple changes of music have meant teachers adapt the music to the learning taking place, thereby reflecting music at 40 beats to 120 beats from slow absorbing information to energizing music.

Koosh ball circles and speaking tools have greatly aided oral language, sharing and discussion of viewpoints.

Teachers are finding the noise level in classrooms is diminishing, while background music is playing, or by using a variety of speaking tools to alert the children to focus on the teacher.

One of our special needs teachers has trained on the Irlen Syndrome and is becoming a school resource person for identifying children with visual/perceptual problems, and is now able to offer solutions/alternatives for student with this problem.

Learning Style Budget and Support Budget programmes have been set up to allow for individual teachers to purchase or have made learning style tools for their classroom. Teacher-aides are being paid for the extra work this entails.

A set of books, tapes, videos and a master file of learning style modules has been assembled to support this programme.

The special needs budget has an emphasis on purchasing self-correcting tools, tactile literacy equipment, audio-visual equipment (e.g. Rainbow reading programme).

manifests itself most strongly when reading words or music, because of the repetitive patterns on the page. The patterns of words on the page and persistent images when the eyes scan across the page will jumble in a manner that is difficult for the brain to interpret properly. The Irlen Method screens the individual with a wide array of colour filters to find the most suitable colour. This stops the confusing light signals from being sent to the brain, and the person will see the page more normally and easily. The treatment also usually helps individuals experiencing other problems, such as depth perception or night vision difficulties. For more information see

www.irlen.com

and

www.readingandwriting.ab.ca

LS classrooms in primary/ elementary schools

There is no doubt that creating LS classrooms during the early years of education is easier the younger the pupils are and most junior classrooms already show many elements of learning styles. However, the older the students get, the less emphasis is put on comfort and a child-friendly atmosphere, individuality and learning needs. When children start school everything is there: bright, warm but not agitating colours, soft toys, lots of learning tools, hands-on activities and manipulatives, cushions, room to move, child-friendly chairs and desks in a stimulating environment. There is even the danger of over-stimulation through clutter, but at least children are still allowed to use their hands, move their bodies and even learn on the floor!

Although I have visited many such classrooms around the world, I have hardly ever seen a conscious use of all these wonderful tools and techniques based on learning style needs. What is still missing in most classrooms is the awareness for different light levels, and sadly most classrooms have far too much light and teachers have a tendency to always switch on the fluorescent lights without being aware of the damage it can do to young learners. Teachers MUST accept that most young students and many teenagers need much

less light than they do because human beings seem to need more light when they grow older. This creates a serious discrepancy between teachers' needs and students' needs, which has to be overcome by creating low and bright light areas in every classroom and more flexibility from teachers who need to adjust to their students' needs and not vice versa, as is often the case in traditional classrooms.

It is most important that these necessary components of a well-functioning LS classroom are not reduced and left out completely when students grow older. When primary school classrooms begin looking like impersonal high school classrooms, it is no surprise that learning becomes more difficult and discipline deteriorates. Many students still have the same needs for low light, comfortable seating and hands-on learning because for many these preferences do not change, just because they are a few years older. There is anecdotal and research evidence from many schools that a change of classroom environment to accommodate learning styles has brought about an instant change in behaviour, together with interactive strategies and better academic performance, particularly for problem students.

LS classrooms at high school level

When pupils move from primary school to high school, they bring with them not only their expectations, and often fear and trepidation, but also their personal learning styles that are still evolving during puberty. This means that traditional classroom settings are totally unsuited for many students (particularly underachieving boys) who have informal style needs and find it extremely difficult to function well in formal classroom settings. There is plenty of proof that a prolonged exposure to mismatched learning environments leads to underachievement, frustration and, ultimately, to school failure. However, teachers fear that if students are allowed to learn in a more relaxed and comfortable environment with activities suited to their styles and classmates who have similar needs, then the result will be mayhem.

Breakout area in the Learning-to-Learn Centre at Cramlington
High, painted in soothing blue-tone colours

In nearly every Scandinavian primary school classroom there
is a kitchen area

Quite the opposite is true: our own experience and past research shows that discipline and academic achievement improves when learning needs are understood by teachers and matched in their daily classroom work. I remember the comment made by one headteacher in Hartlepool, UK, who said that these boys who in the past were causing serious problems would no longer be at school if it was not for learning styles, and I have seen it time and again that even a partial LS classroom keeps them at school and engaged in learning! It cannot be emphasized enough that the learning environment has a huge effect on students' (and teachers') concentration, memory, behaviour and well-being. Therefore, high school classrooms also need to cater for different styles and despite fractured timetables and students moving from classroom to classroom, the most important elements need to be available, which are: cushions and soft furniture, switching off fluorescent lights, dimming the lights or creating permanent low light areas, table lamps, background music at a very low level, a quiet area, possibilities for group, pair and individual work, learning tools that students love to make themselves once they know how, and some room to move. Temperature regulation in classrooms is often difficult but very important and many classrooms are over-heated during the cold weather months or in hot climates, which can make concentration very difficult for those students who need it cool. School uniforms often enhance an uncomfortable feeling, which can also impact on learning ability. Teachers need to be creative in re-organizing desks and chairs if they are movable and discuss with the students how they would like to re-arrange the classrooms to accommodate style diversity based on the group profiles of their LSAs.

Although many teachers might not believe it, students know how they want to set up their classroom; they love to be involved in this creative process and have often much better ideas than their teachers because it is THEIR work area and they will look after such classrooms much better. We have reports from teachers that graffiti, destruction and neglect is non-existent in LS classrooms and research has shown the same results. This is not hard to understand, because generally people do not damage or destroy what they like – they protect it, defend and improve it. When LS results are revealed and understood, it is amazing to observe how teenagers who could not care less about their classrooms before, suddenly become engaged and get protective of their new, more inspiring learning environment.

The best situation for students is when ALL teachers of a school are LS trained and accept and understand style diversity because then it is possible to re-arrange all classrooms to different degrees for learning styles and even if students have to move around a lot, they still find learning environments that enhance their learning. The secret is that when different groups of students use different classrooms, they occupy similar areas according to their style. It is important that there is continuity between departments, because it can be very unsettling for students to be in LS classrooms for English, geography and history but to be in classrooms where NO learning style features are accommodated for maths, history and science. If teachers collaborate to create the best possible learning environment for their students, as I have seen in many high schools, the atmosphere changes for the better not only between teachers and students but also between colleagues.

LS classrooms in adult education settings

When adults go back to study, they often find themselves in classrooms they know well from their schooldays and many still resent the traditional set-up because their learning style is less formal. Here it is important that individual and group LSA results are discussed in class so that students can create a more suitable learning environment for the whole group, respecting different learning needs. Like younger students, many adults learn better with reduced light, background music, hands-on exercises, body involvement, and need the option of either studying alone or with others, based on their LS preferences, which their lecturers or tutors

If we could only have one thing from this room in our room it would be...

If we can't have all these things in our room, then these are the ones to leave behind...

What we think of the new classroom
by class
Date we left the room

What we enjoyed about our time in the room...

What we didn't enjoy about our time in the room...

Learning on soft furniture during professional development

Learning on the floor with task cards

should know. For this age group it is also most important to create the right learning environment at home to be able to take full responsibility for self-study.

What to do in very small classrooms

Think outside the box, re-arrange furniture together with students, be creative with the use of space, remove some desks, utilize corners, windows and walls differently, even areas outside the classroom as breakout spaces. The rule in these situations is when the physical environment cannot be changed much, teachers MUST COMPENSATE with in-depth knowledge of their students' true learning needs and more appropriate teaching strategies for each group. If there is not much room to move, then more hands-on techniques and stretching exercises will help students learn better; if the small space is crammed with desks, be daring and re-arrange them in unusual ways, creating more space, and cushions can be used any time, any where to help those who need more comfortable sitting. In my visits to schools in many countries I have seen horrific classrooms with appalling environmental conditions, students stuffed into matchbox-like compounds where nobody would voluntarily spend more than one hour unless they were prisoners. And that is exactly what teachers and students are and it is no wonder that learning and teaching is very hard and everyone wants to escape – at least mentally! But even under such extreme conditions I have seen what is possible: desks arranged for individual and group work, dim and bright light areas, cushions and bean bags, background music, sensory stimulation and different work stations.

What to do in lecture theatres

COMPENSATE! Discuss students' different learning styles; let them subgroup themselves according to their social learning needs; teach with multisensory instructions based on group preferences, which might be different from group to group; use good visuals with big print and colours; switch your techniques from holistic to analytic presentation and always 'double track' (see Chapter 8) in your delivery; change light

levels if possible, initiate short movement breaks, have buzz groups after lecturing for no longer than 15–20 minutes; allow water bottles (no soft drinks!); be interactive; involve students; and, finally, encourage them to arrange their study environment at home according to their personal style preferences to make their preparation time more effective.

What to do in labs or fixed-furniture classrooms

Again, know your students and COMPENSATE! If furniture cannot be re-arranged, have stretch breaks, alter light levels, use background music and more hands-on techniques, allow students who need quiet to wear disconnected headsets or ear plugs for their work periods, and use similar techniques as described above for lecture theatres. Involve students actively in the decision-making process for re-utilizing their learning environment. You might be surprised how well students know what works best for them in learning.

If a full implementation of the LS concept is not possible in a classroom, even some minor changes can have a hugely positive effect and here a little is better than nothing. I have reports from teachers where one cushion on the floor made all the difference to a student who was never able to sit still and concentrate. Never forget: this is the MICRO LEVEL of teaching and learning where small things can and do make a huge difference together with the knowledge of WHY you are doing this.

> # IF YOU CAN'T JUSTIFY
> # WHY YOU DO
> # WHAT YOU ARE DOING
> # IN CLASS –
> # DON'T DO IT!

Left–right brain strategies for double tracking

Pre-school: Lesson on rhyming words
- **Teacher**: brainstorm for one minute rhyming words students know
- **Analytic students**: listen for words that rhyme as you read *Cat in the Hat*; recall and repeat them
- **Holistic students**: pantomime rhyming words that they know or hear in the story

First grade: lesson on the kinds of objects magnets pull
- **Teacher**: pretend to be a magnet and attract objects held by the children
- **Analytic students**: examine available objects and list them on a chart in two categories
- **Holistic students**: fish for objects with magnets on a string

Second grade: lesson on sums of money to 99c
- **Teacher**: review coin values with large visual chart
- **Analytic students**: complete the workbook page on adding money
- **Holistic students**: play 'shop' in small groups using examples from workbook page

Third grade: lesson on the order of the planets in the solar system
- **Teacher**: show a video to the class; search the internet
- **Analytic students**: write a silly sentence to remember the order of the planets
- **Holistic students**: draw the solar system in order; a small group may create a model

Fourth grade: lesson on the important mountain ranges in the USA and the states that they include
- **Teacher**: introduce the lesson to the class with a chalk–talk
- **Analytic students**: make a chart listing the states in each range
- **Holistic students**: create an advertisement to lure tourists to each mountain range

Fifth grade: lesson on the important events in Columbus' life
- **Teacher**: create a time-line on the whiteboard or overhead projector while tracing the events
- **Analytic students**: make a set of puzzle cards matching dates and events
- **Holistic students**: form small groups and dramatize an event from his life

Sixth grade: lesson on a country's geography
- **Teacher**: present lecture with available maps, pictures and photos
- **Analytic students**: create a dictionary that lists the important features of the country
- **Holistic students**: create a relief map of the country or tourist brochures

Seventh grade: lesson on cell division
- **Teacher**: use video to introduce the topic
- **Analytic students**: read the chapter and answer the questions
- **Holistic students**: create a skit on cell division and perform it in class

Eighth grade: lesson on drug abuse
- **Teacher**: invite a youth counsellor to introduce the topic
- **Analytic students**: in small groups, write poems on the dangers of drugs
- **Holistic students**: pretend to be a drug and dramatize its effect on the body

Once your students become familiar with a variety of alternatives, hold a 'wild card' session where they design their own follow-up activity. Their left and right brain creative forces may surprise you!

Based on an article by Freeley and Perrin, in *Teaching K-8*, Aug/Sep 1987

Chapter 8

How to 'double track' when teaching analytic and holistic students

Classroom teachers are well aware that in each student group there are different types of thinkers, not only as far as the speed of their thinking is concerned but also whether they are logical, focused and well organized with their thoughts or 'all over the place' with little ability to focus on details. Given that teachers also have diverse thinking styles, often not matched to their students' way of thinking, it is no wonder that communication frequently breaks down and teaching strategies do not always show the desired outcome.

Since working with the concept of human diversity and learning styles, it has become very obvious to me that the biggest divide between human beings is how they process information based on their overall natural brain dominance: either analytically, rational and 'left-brain dominant', or holistically, feeling based and 'right-brain dominant'. These two very different style combinations are responsible for virtually all communication problems, misunderstandings and ultimate breakdown of interactions between parents and their children, teachers and their students, bosses and their workers, as well as between people in private relationships. The differences show up in every learning, life and work situation and need to be understood to be managed successfully.

For educators it is therefore very important to recognize and accept these often profound natural (biologically based) style differences, to accommodate and utilize them in their everyday classroom work. When teaching new and/or difficult content, it is advisable to subgroup students with these respective

preferences into an analytic and a holistic group according to their LSA results, and assign flexible students to one group or the other.

Apart from knowledge about the different style combination of LSA elements in analytic and holistic students (as described in detail in my previous book *The Power of Diversity* in Chapters 5 and 7), teachers need to develop skills in delivering their lessons in 'double track' mode. This means switching from one style to the other consciously and at regular intervals so that no students are left behind or need to suffer from teaching methods and explanations that do not make sense to them and switch them off.

In other words: analytic, step-by-step teaching is *confusing for holistic students* who need the big picture and tend to learn well when they can be emotionally and physically involved in a fear-free learning environment.

But holistic, unstructured, self-directed lessons can be very *unsettling for analytic students* who need routine, order and guidance in a predictable, more traditional learning environment.

Many students have the flexibility in their style to adjust to different teaching styles and somehow make it; unfortunately underachieving and at-risk students do not have this flexibility and cannot learn successfully in traditional classroom set-ups with analytic teaching methods and therefore cause endemic discipline problems and school failure, often compounded by social

Brain Gym® exercises for integration

Brain balloon game to determine left- or right-brain dominance – learning by doing

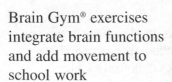

Brain Gym® exercises integrate brain functions and add movement to school work

problems in the home, poor health, and emotional and nutritional deficiencies.

The younger the students are, the more holistic they are, and in the early years in primary schools their way of thinking and learning is usually accommodated through more playful teaching methods. However, when students get older, they are increasingly being taught in analytic, logical and sequential ways, no matter whether this is the way they can learn best or not. Serious problems arise when holistic students constitute the majority in a class (sometimes even without flexible students counted in) and teachers do not accept or do not know that these students cannot learn analytically. Such teachers find it particularly hard to deliver curriculum content in a non-sequential fashion because they most often teach academic, scientific subjects and have been trained to teach this way. This is the reason why so many students find subjects like mathematics, chemistry, physics, and often music, so difficult, begin to dislike them and ultimately drop out if they can, or hang in, just get by and scrape through at exams or study very hard under a huge amount of pressure. In any case, when they have some school success, it is often success without satisfaction because the price for participating was too high and they are usually lost to further formal education.

To avoid the frustration of losing holistic students' participation because they easily get off track and cannot concentrate for longer periods of time, high school teachers in particular need to put extra effort into developing instructional methods that cater for holistic learners while not neglecting analytic students.

Tips for 'double tracking' in class

➤ Always introduce lessons holistically, giving the big picture so that students know where they are going; after that explain the rules and what is expected from them at the end of the unit.

➤ Put holistic students in groups where they can do experiential learning, have fun and participate in learning games; supply or let them bring resources for discovery learning; for analytic students hand out specific directions, learning objectives and let them work through those individually or in pairs, usually in a more quiet part of the classroom or in a breakout area.

➤ Be aware that details are very important for analytic students but overwhelm more holistic students; give test dates and instructions for analytics at the beginning and for holistic students after they have become familiar with the new content.

➤ While students with holistic style preferences and their flexible classmates can work in small groups with hands-on learning tools and resource materials other than just books or handouts and little supervision, students with analytic preferences need step-by-step guidance and direct instructional methods with closer teacher supervision.

➤ Once holistic students have used interactive learning materials, they can then switch to worksheets and writing tasks to reinforce what they have learned in a multisensory way at the beginning; analytic students will then use the learning tools and activities as their reinforcement of the learned content – this way all teaching resources are being utilized by everyone, just at different times and in different sequences according to their preferences.

➤ Be aware that holistic students need more learning tools, they are the practical, hands-on learners, whereas analytic students learn well with traditional methods, reading, writing and worksheets, and are generally more academically inclined.

➤ When giving feedback for holistic students, always be positive, personal and encourage even small achievements – many need it desperately because their self-esteem in learning has suffered over the years and they easily give up; analytic students need regular feedback on details and on how they are progressing; they love written comments and often do not learn for praise or emotional acknowledgement but because they are hungry for knowledge and often learn to

Guidelines
for teaching ANALYTIC and HOLISTIC students simultaneously
(after subgrouping them into learning groups with similar preferences)

To be successful with both types of students do the following:

1 **Introduce to the whole class to new and/or difficult curriculum content holistically with a funny or personal story, or a joke, and always give an overview.**

2 **Then let students do the following activities at the same time:**

ANALYTIC Students (left-brain dominant)	HOLISTIC Students (right-brain dominant)
a **begin with direct instructions, giving facts and data first (worksheets)**	a **set up a team-learning exercise with open instructions**
b **then arrange a team-learning exercise with closed questions**	b **give facts with different multisensory learning tools**
c **followed by creative applications including different learning stations**	c **followed by creative applications including different learning stations**
d **for revision and reinforcement, multisensory learning tools should be used, role play and learning games**	d **for revision and reinforcement, worksheets and writing exercises can be used, role play and games**

Mini lectures with multisensory, analytic–holistic presentation for all students can be inserted and then the double tracking continues.

Let holistic students learn in a team with open questions and then follow up with facts, while analytic students hear and read the facts first and then answer closed questions.

Summaries need also to be done in double tracking mode:
Analytic students present what they have learned in sequential order, giving the final overview at the end to wrap up their learning.

Holistic students begin with a grand reflection of what they have learned, then deducting facts and details from the overall content.

Both groups present to each other in their preferred style.

please parents – be mindful of these emotional differences!

Tips for 'double tracking' in lesson planning

➤ Make sure you plan according to the results in the group profile of your class(es) with particular emphasis on frequently switching between holistic overview and analytic, step-by-step instructions.

➤ Analyse every exercise and activity in your lesson plan according to its analytic or holistic qualities and add more fun, multisensory experiential activities if you realize that there is too much 'chalk and talk'. Your students will be very grateful.

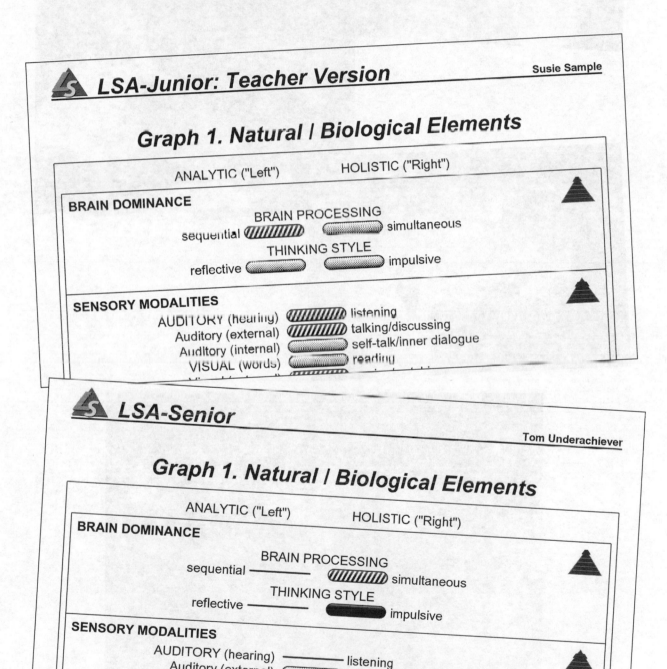

LSA-Junior: Teacher Version   Susie Sample

Graph 1. Natural / Biological Elements

ANALYTIC ("Left")   HOLISTIC ("Right")

BRAIN DOMINANCE

BRAIN PROCESSING
sequential ▰▰▰   ▰▰ simultaneous
THINKING STYLE
reflective ▰▰   ▰▰ impulsive

SENSORY MODALITIES
AUDITORY (hearing) ▰▰▰ listening
Auditory (external) ▰▰▰ talking/discussing
Auditory (internal) ▰▰ self-talk/inner dialogue
VISUAL (words) ▰▰ reading

LSA-Senior

Tom Underachiever

Graph 1. Natural / Biological Elements

ANALYTIC ("Left")   HOLISTIC ("Right")

BRAIN DOMINANCE

BRAIN PROCESSING
sequential —— ▰▰▰ simultaneous
THINKING STYLE
reflective —— ▰▰ impulsive

SENSORY MODALITIES
AUDITORY (hearing) —— listening
Auditory (external) ▰▰ talking/discussing
Auditory (internal) ▰▰ self-talk/inner dialogue
VISUAL (words) —— reading

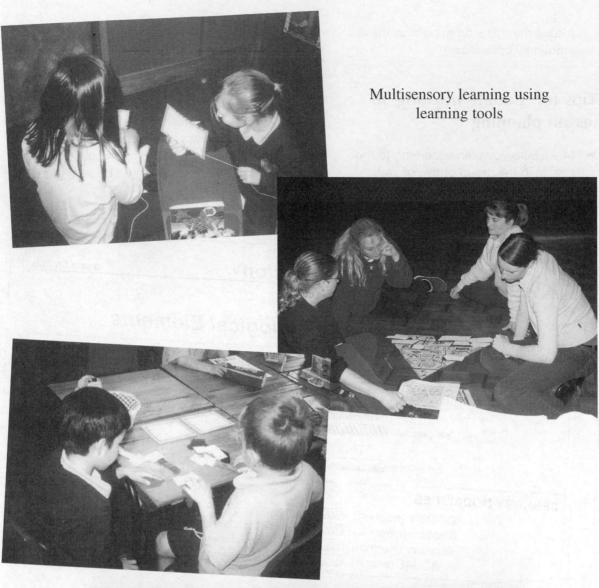

Multisensory learning using
learning tools

Informal learning with tactile discussion during LS training at
Rivergum Primary, Melbourne, Australia

Chapter 9

Multisensory teaching and learning

LSA instruments measure much more than VAK and even in the modalities they make the very important distinction between tactile (hands-on) and kinesthetic (experiential/doing) learning; in addition to these there are sub-modalities that are equally important but not fully covered in the VAK approach. (See also Chapters 10 and 11.)

VATK

Using multisensory teaching techniques in regular classroom settings is being described throughout this book, and every LSA report has detailed explanations of how students need to use and combine their senses when they learn something new and/or difficult. For many teachers who are familiar with VAK, it will not be too difficult to make a distinction between tactile and kinesthetic methods and add more tactile activities, allowing students to do more hands-on learning.

The letter below is representative of the experiences of many classroom teachers when they embrace LS and enhance their teaching with multisensory methods.

VATK CONSIDERATIONS FOR WRITING WORKSHOP

SENSORY MODALITIES
Visual: Reading and writing tasks, imagination, observation, posters, worksheets.
Auditory: Verbal instructions, role plays, discussions.
Tactile: Synonyms card game, koosh balls, alphabetical order task cards.
Kinesthetic: Role plays about Greek myths.

PHYSICAL NEEDS catered for
Mobility: Movement activities, brain breaks.
Intake: Children allowed to eat snacks while working.

ENVIRONMENT
The environment was sometimes quiet, with music playing softly in the background. At other times it was quite noisy as children prepared their role plays and when they were working in teams for the Language Olympic Games Tasks.

Light and temperature were hard to control as we were in an air-conditioned room with artificial light. Children could choose where they wanted to sit. They all chose to sit at desks but some children were allowed to move around when they needed to.

Rachel Mitrovits, Sydney

THE FOUR SENSES DRILL
for Wayne's golf practice

The Four Senses   by **waynethomas**   Date_____

Student name   _____

Internal		External

Kinesthetic

Tactile

Visual

Auditory

K	(External) Experience, doing
	(Internal) Feeling, intuition

T	(External) Touching, handling, manipulating

V	(External) Reading, seeing, watching
	(Internal) Visualization, Imagination

A	(External) Listening, talking
	(Internal) Self-talk, inner dialogue

Shot routine
1. Notice any don't do's / do instruction
2. Visualize what I want
3. Notice how I sense it
4. Do it
5. Observe the outcome
6. Match senses to outcome
7. When everything matches what emotion is present?

Matching senses to the outcome
1 Low...High
2 Low...High
3 Low...High

_____

© Wayne Thomas 2002

In reviewing the results with students at the end of the session, every person who has done this exercise with me reports a slowing down of time and a clear mind free from all distractions, internal and external; some have described it as being in a trance-like state or 'in the zone', having a full understanding of both their mental and their physical patterns without even trying and producing results far beyond what they thought themselves capable of.

Wayne Thomas

On my many visits to classrooms in various countries I have seen wonderful examples of multisensory teaching, and many practitioners have sent me their reports, describing how they practise VATK. But it was not until I became familiar with the golf coaching work of Wayne Thomas in Melbourne, Australia, that I learned how well multisensory instructions can be applied to golf coaching. As I was lucky enough to experience them myself, I know his technique works – it has enhanced my play and given me a new confidence as a learner.

Although this approach is used for playing golf, it is obvious that it can be transferred to many other learning situations, even to more theoretical ones. By describing this technique in detail I hope to help educators to make this transfer into their own subject area. Here is an extract from Wayne's report that explains about VATK.

I have found catering for learning styles in golf coaching an interesting challenge. The majority of my clients are between the ages of 27 and 65 and conditioned to learning a particular way with many inflexible to opening their minds and learning in new ways. For the most part they tend to be conditioned to over analyse and find it difficult to let go and integrate both left and right brain. One of the biggest challenges of playing golf is to switch from the analysis of a given situation to gaining an understanding of what is required, sensing the swing motion that produces a desired outcome and then letting go trusting oneself and having it occur.

There is no question in my mind that we all intake, process and apply information differently; believing this to be so I set out to develop a standard systematic approach to every shot a golfer played that catered for the diverse learning styles of each individual.

The result was what I call 'The Four Senses Drill' (see opposite). This drill trains the individual to clearly identify through the four senses – kinesthetic, tactile, visual and auditory – how they process information before every shot they play. This session or lesson takes approximately one hour to complete and has the student in touch with how they visualize and sense the shot before it is played, letting go and trusting their senses, and observing the outcomes for future reference.

Before we begin, students receive their LSA or working style analysis (WSA) profile and I give them a brief on the sensory modalities and sub-modalities (internal visual, auditory and kinesthetic), explaining this will be like taking a snapshot of their thought processes so as to self-train to maximize their performance. I explain to the student: the end result will have you able to clearly identify your own unique thought patterns, how these thought patterns influence human movement and performance and have you hitting great shots free of conscious instruction. You will have developed a new thought process or pattern that produces results far beyond what you know yourself capable of. A bold statement and usually received with mirth.

Opposite is the practice sheet used by students at the beginning of the session and at the end to record their results for future reference. Throughout the entire session I take great care not to prompt or put forward suggestions that may influence how the student responds; I just wait until the person communicates to me what they are sensing.

 For a full report see online appendix 13.

Using LS tools in schools

Elizabeth Good, an Attitudes to Learning co-ordinator in one of 15 schools in Brighton, UK that form an Excellence in Cities (EiC) cluster, describes how she has introduced LS tools in her school.

When the EiC began, Attitudes to Learning co-ordinators were given the task of proposing projects that would improve children's attitudes to learning. Among other things, one of the projects that I was involved in was to put together a toolbox. The aim was to produce a times tables toolbox for each school in the EiC cluster. The box included examples of visual, auditory, tactile and

An example of VATK activities for storywriting

Visual	Auditory	Tactile/Kinesthetic
1. Have objects to use as prompts	1. Listen to a tape of a story as a stimulus	1. Act out their story as a plan **K**
2. Use pictures to add labels as planning	2. Listen to a recording of a character talking	2. Dress up as a character **K**
3. Draw pictures of parts of the story then progress to writing it **V/T**	3. Think, pair, share for formulating ideas	3. Be the character in the hot seat
4. Cut up parts of a story and sequence them **V/T**	4. Record their ideas on tape	4. Sequence pictures before writing a story **V/T**
5. Watch dramatizations	5. Watch a video as a stimulus **V**	5. Build words with magnetic letters before writing them **V/T**
6. Watch a video as a stimulus	6. Question characters in hot seat	6. Provide objects to stimulate senses – e.g. eat fruit from *Handa's Surprise*, make models of the three pigs' houses **K**
7. Prompt writing through questions such as 'What would it look like?' **A/V/T**	7. Use variety of voices for characters	7. Use sign language for keywords when introducing stimulus **V/T/K**
8. Give the children scrap paper to jot possible spellings on **V/T**	8. Involve in group discussions to focus on key elements	
	9. Signing spellings/story keywords **A/V**	

Erica Hewetson, St Vincent's Catholic Primary, Birmingham

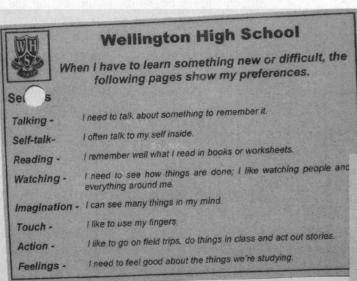

Official LS cards for students at Wellington High, NSW, Australia

kinesthetic learning tools with the specific intention of enhancing recall in tables. I was very inspired by some of the tools I had seen on a recent course with Barbara Prashnig and was keen to introduce them to other teachers.

Such a toolbox included flip chutes made from orange juice cartons, wrap-arounds, learning circles with clothes pegs, Electroboards, bingo cards, website links, Pelmanism games, ideas for physical movement and for classroom tables games.

All the tools were intended to be easy and cheap to reproduce – the common cry among primary schools is that there is never enough money!

A toolbox was given out to all EiC cluster schools and the feedback has been very positive. The LEA Numeracy team has asked for a box to show to other schools in the area. Other schools outside the LEA have seen the box and are very interested. There is a thought now to do something similar with Literacy – maybe making a 'punctuation' toolbox. At this stage it is not definite.

I spent time with our teaching assistants reproducing some of the tools for each class in our school – by popular demand from the teachers. That had the added advantage of having people trained in the making of these tools for future use.

I tested my class on their tables three times over this term, and found there was an average of 30 per cent improvement in tables recall, with one child improving by 68 per cent. Verbal feedback from children has been very positive:

'I like the way we can do it at our own speed. We don't have a teacher asking us to answer too quickly.'

'When the answer comes out and I get it right I go "aah!".'

Although koosh balls are not self-correcting LS tools as all the other ones described here, this learning tool must be considered as very important, particularly for highly tactile students. Elizabeth gives a very enlightening

description about using these useful learning tools:

Koosh balls have been a major success in our class. I began by ensuring I had one for each child in the beginning, so there would be no argument over who had one. We had to be quite strict at first about their use – anyone using them to distract others would have to put them back. We call them 'fidget toys'. I have been experimenting and recently bought two soapstone eggs that are quite heavy and beautifully smooth. Some children prefer to stroke these while they are sitting listening on the carpet.

One child said, *'I like having something to fidget with. It makes a change from teachers saying, Stop fidgeting!'* Another said, *'I much prefer it. I used to pick up bits off the carpet to play with. Now I don't have to.'*

How to create self-correcting learning tools

Creating and using self-correcting LS tools is the ultimate level of LS teaching. Any teacher not using these tools cannot rightfully claim to have introduced the full LS concept because without these tools no LS approach is complete. As only a limited number of such LS tools is commercially available, teachers, parents and students need to make their own to have new resources available, particularly to enhance the learning of visual/tactile students.

Some US companies such as Hamlyn sell such tools, mainly wrap-arounds, and one NZ company exports a wide range of self-correcting tools to various countries. They are very durable and can be found under:
🖱 www.smartkids.co.nz or
   www.smartkids.co.uk

If schools cannot afford to buy such resources, they can be created from recycled materials and in primary schools parents often help to make these tools whereas in high schools students make their own, and tactile students particularly love creating them, already learning curriculum content during the production. They are also very effective for hands-on adult students who are struggling with theoretical content.

LS tool making at Forbury
School, Dunedin, NZ

Pic-a-hole

Wrap-around

Learning circle

Electroboard

Flip chute

How to use multisensory tools

Flip chute

Take the question from the side pocket; read the question on the card. Think of an answer, then put the card with the question facing you into the top slot. Watch for the card to come out the bottom slot with an answer on it. Do this with each of the cards and you will see that it is an interesting tactile way to learn. When you finish all the questions, please put the cards back into the side pocket and put the flip chute back into the box.

1 Be certain all the cards in the envelopes belonging to this topic are facing you so that the missing corner is on the upper right side.

2 Read the question on the first card and try to think of an answer.

3 Insert the card face up into the top slot of the flip chute.

4 The card will come out of the bottom slot with the answer showing. Is it what you thought it would be?

Learning circle directions

1 Take out the large coloured circle with the clothes pegs attached to it and remove all the clothes pegs.

2 Match each of the eight words/phrases on the circle with the word or phrase on each clothes peg by clipping the clothes pegs in place on the circle.

3 When you have finished doing this, turn the circle over. On the back of the circle, you will see eight different designs/letters.

4 If the designs/letters match the designs/letters on the clothes pegs, you will know that you have matched the items correctly.

Pic-a-hole

Take out the rectangular-shaped material with the three holes at the bottom. Read each card and choose an answer by placing the attached golf tee into the hole. If you are correct, the card will come out; if you are incorrect, the card will remain in place. So, try again! After you complete the pic-a-hole, please put it back into the box where you found it.

1 Take the golf tee that is attached to the pic-a-hole out of its pocket.

2 Read the question in the top window.

3 In the smaller, bottom window are three choices to answer the question. Only one of them is correct.

4 Take the golf tee. Put it into the hole under the correct answer.

5 Gently try to pull the card out of the pocket. If your answer is correct, the card will slide freely from the pocket. If you choose an incorrect answer, however, the card will not slide out.

6 Continue until you have answered all the questions.

Electroboard

Take out the Electroboard. In order for this to work, you need to use a continuity tester, which is available in the box. Put one end of the continuity tester onto the question being asked on the left-hand side. Put the other end of the continuity tester onto the answer you think is correct on the right-hand side. The continuity tester will light up if you chose the correct answer. No light will show if your answer is incorrect, so try again! After you have worked with the Electroboard, please put it back into the box.

1 Take the continuity tester and lay it out in front of you.

2 Put one end of the tester near the question, or left side of the board.

3 Put the other end of the tester near the right, or answer side of the board.

4 Read the word or phrase on the left side.

5 Place one end of the continuity tester on the silver/gold circle next to that question.

6 Read the answers on the right side.

7 When you find a match, put the other end of the continuity tester onto the silver/gold circle next to it.

8 If you choose the correct match, the continuity tester will light up.

9 If it doesn't light up, try again.

10 Continue until you have matched all the items on both sides of the Electroboard. Try to remember the answers to each question. Write them down and compare with others.

LS tools in action
in Oslo

Flip chute

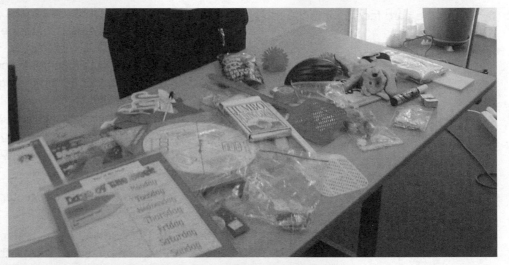

LS tools for
language learning

Flower trays for
tactile spelling at
Rivergum Primary
School, Melbourne,
Australia

Chapter 10

How to help tactile students learn better

Every teacher has seen students in class who fiddle most of the time, play with their pens, tap their fingers and can never keep their hands still. If it is not their whole body, there are always hands and fingers in motion. Such behaviour shows that these are highly tactile (tactual) students and the younger they are, the more they need to involve their hands. This strong need disappears in many when they grow up but in a large number of people these strong tactile needs remain with them for life, more so in males than in females.

Tactile learning in primary/elementary schools

During the early years in education there is usually plenty of opportunity for children to involve their hands and they are allowed, actually encouraged, to touch and manipulate objects while learning and playing. That is very fortunate for these young learners, but when they grow a little older they are often told 'Hands off', 'Don't touch' and many learning tasks in academic subjects get reduced to listening, reading and writing. Teachers' justification behind reducing hands-on activities is that they need to prepare students for the 'real' learning later in high school, forgetting that tactile students will always learn best by using their hands combined with other sensory stimulation.

Recommendations for teachers

Acknowledge your students' need to fiddle, have their fingers/hands engaged.

Be aware that tactile students will often have their hands on other students and often on things that are not theirs; if they also have strong kinesthetic style features, they can get very physical with other students and often become a bully.

Discuss their tactile needs in class and assure them that there is nothing 'wrong' with them, they just need more hand or finger stimulation than others.

Allow them to fiddle and play with things as long as they stay on task, do not disturb others and show better discipline and learning outcomes.

Set clear guidelines for using tactile support tools (such as koosh balls or other manipulatives including LS tools).

Be firm when students abuse their privilege to use LS tools and reduce their activities to just listening, reading and writing; very soon they will discover that working properly with tactile stimulation feels much better and their behaviour will improve.

Prepare learning tasks that need hands-on involvement – instead of just reading and writing, let them cut and paste information, build and manipulate learning resources, let them take apart and re-build concrete learning content.

Create self-correcting learning tools (see Chapter 9).

Teach them how to make and use these tools for their future learning tasks – they will love these hands-on activities, will feel better and learn a lot.

Let them use their own LS tools when they are learning something new and/or difficult before they move on to writing and other learning tasks.

Tactile LS tools
for learning
science concepts

Auditory/tactile
learning at
Wellington High,
NSW, Australia

Use these LS tools even for testing because tactile students will have better results that way.

Modify and **Use** board games with curriculum content.

Inform parents about new tactile LS tools and why you allow certain students to fiddle in class and how fiddling enhances the learning ability of tactile students.

Encourage parents to allow the same at home when their children are doing homework, it will help resolve many a conflict.

Tactile learning at high school level

Although younger students are generally more tactile, there are huge numbers of students in high school who remain highly tactile, particularly boys (and especially when they are also kinesthetic, physical learners). As soon as they enter high school, their tactile stimulation during classes is drastically reduced to handwriting (which they do not like) and to computer work (which most of them love). Any other activity with their hands – such as doodling or playing with pens – is forbidden and often punished. Despite all the warnings and reprimands, these highly tactile students will not stop fiddling, particularly when they are bored, have to listen and/or concentrate hard.

In addition to these restrictions, students are forced to sit still, listen, read, write and discuss when the teacher demands it. It is no surprise that many cannot learn as requested and will fall behind, become discipline problems, underachievers and at risk of dropping out. Many such negative developments could be prevented if teachers and parents would just know how to support these tactile students in their learning.

Recommendations for teachers

(In many aspects similar to the tips for primary school teachers.)

Acknowledge your students' need to fiddle, have their fingers/hands engaged.

Accept that students with a tactile/visual preference will often doodle to enhance their listening and even more so when they are bored; you will often discover how talented they are – utilize that talent to enhance their learning.

Be aware that tactile students will often have their hands on other students' possessions and other students' bodies, which can lead to inappropriate behaviour.

Discuss their tactile needs in class together with their other LS results from the LSA and assure them that there is nothing 'wrong' with them, they just need more hand or finger stimulation than others.

Allow them to fiddle and play with things as long as they stay on task, do not disturb others and show better discipline and learning outcomes.

Show them how to manage their strong tactile needs in a positive and learning-supporting manner to control excessive fiddling (often combined with body movements and sound generation, more often in boys than in girls).

Set clear guidelines for using tactile support tools (such as koosh balls or other manipulatives including LS tools).

Be firm when students abuse their privilege to use LS tools and reduce their activities to just listening, reading and writing; very soon they will discover that working properly with tactile stimulation feels much better and their behaviour will improve.

Prepare learning tasks which need hands-on involvement – Instead of just reading and writing, let them cut and paste information, build and manipulate learning resources, take apart and re-build concrete learning content, even convert abstract content into something tangible, touchable (that is, build mathematical models, equations in algebra, geometric rules with brick stones and other materials) to help students understand and remember through touch.

Create self-correcting learning tools (see Chapter 9).

Teach them how to make and use these tools in different subject areas – they will love these hands-on activities, will feel better and learn a lot.

Let them use their own LS tools when they are learning something new and/or difficult before they move on to writing and discussing.

Hands-on learning tools at Cramlington High and Wansbeck Primary, UK

Use these LS tools even for testing because tactile students will have better results that way.

Modify and **Use** board games with curriculum content; invite students to create their own learning games for different subject contents.

Inform parents about new tactile LS tools and why you allow certain students to fiddle in class and how fiddling often enhances the learning ability of tactile students.

Encourage parents to allow the same at home when their teenagers are doing homework, it will help resolve conflicts around homework, give parents more peace of mind and avoid their constantly trying to make their daughters and, particularly, their sons study 'the right way'.

Tactile learning in adult education

In higher education and particularly in vocational institutions, there are many students who want to study but find it quite difficult to concentrate and use traditional study techniques because their personal learning style does not match such approaches. Generally they did not do too well at school, still carry a stigma and know they are not 'academic' learners. Most often they are very practically oriented, hands-on people and get very frustrated when they have to learn theoretical content through reading, writing and discussing only. Although in practical subjects of their training courses they do very well, they often fail in theory and therefore tend to drop out and leave qualifications incomplete. Instructors need to understand that tactile students learn differently, even more so when they also have a strong need for movement and do not have preferences for listening and reading. In these situations tactile stimulation and some movement during study sessions can make all the difference (see Chapters 11 and 12).

Recommendations for tutors/ lecturers

Acknowledge your students' need to fiddle, have their fingers/hands engaged when studying.

Accept that adults with a tactile/visual preferences will often doodle to enhance their listening and even more so when they are bored.

Discuss their tactile needs as shown in the LSA results and assure them that there is nothing 'wrong' with them if they cannot learn well by listening and reading only, they just need more hand or finger stimulation than others.

Show them how to manage their strong tactile needs in a positive and learning-supporting manner to control excessive fiddling (often combined with body movements and sound generation, more often in males than in females).

Introduce tactile support tools (such as koosh balls or other manipulatives including LS tools) for studying difficult, theoretical content if they struggle.

Create self-correcting learning tools if appropriate in your course, lectures or tutorials (see Chapter 9).

Teach them how to make and use these tools for different content – tactile students will love these hands on activities, will gladly make them, feel better, have fun and learn a lot.

Let them use their own LS tools when they are learning something new and/or difficult before they move on to writing and discussing.

Encourage students to use tactile study techniques at home and tactile tools (such as koosh balls) when reading and preparing for exams.

Learning by doing at the Diploma in Holistic Education course, Auckland, NZ

Chapter 11

How to accommodate kinesthetic learners

Among all the senses, teachers of so-called 'academic' subjects find it most difficult to use kinesthetic methods in their subjects because experiential learning, full-body involvement and learning by doing is generally not their own way to learn. Such methods, often considered as 'childish', 'gimmicky' or 'belonging to playtime in kindergarten' and not 'serious learning' are the only way underachievers and non-academic learners can make sense of difficult academic content. Whether teachers like it or not, or actually believe it or not, the introduction of active learning into theoretical, academic subjects makes all the difference between success or failure for many students.

It is important to point out that kinesthetic exercises always have multisensory components, involving visual, auditory and tactile activities, which in combination are always the best way to learn, particularly for students who have learning problems. A widely held misconception is that when a bit of movement is added to learning tasks, they become kinesthetic. Unfortunately that is not the case. Allowing students to move around while they learn is certainly helpful for those students who need mobility (and only for those who need it – for others it can be quite distracting), but it is still not kinesthetic, as often claimed by advocates of 'accelerated learning', because it is not learning THROUGH the body to create understanding and long-term memory.

The distinction between kinesthetic and tactile learning and the need for mobility is most important and generally not well understood. The explanation given here should help to eliminate this confusion and assist teachers to create or select learning activities that include all of those, but applied to different students in different ways according to their style needs.

There is one more aspect worth mentioning: the importance of the kinesthetic internal modality in feeling-based learners. This means that students with such a preference will always have a strong feeling about the learning task, the content, the learning conditions and especially about the teacher. If they like what they have to do, they will do it well, often surprising themselves and others, but if they do not like what they have to do, when they do not feel good about HOW they have to learn, they will not do it, despite their ability to do so. This is very unsettling for teachers who know these students could accomplish certain tasks but do not want to or cannot be bothered; an attitude frequently found in underachievers who often do well with one teacher or in a certain subject but underachieve in other subjects, mainly academic ones.

Parents get equally frustrated because their children who have a strong internal kinesthetic aspect to their learning style will struggle with homework and studying, doing it well and with alacrity when they like it, but can't bring themselves to complete tasks or even start them when they do not like what they have to do. Such children are often described as 'lazy' and 'could-do-better' because nobody seems to understand how important it is for them to FEEL GOOD about a learning situation.

Learning by doing: using the whole body and feeling good

Kinesthetic maths exercise

In our field studies around the world we have found many underachievers, more often boys than girls whose LSAs show the combination of strong preferences for kinesthetic internal and external, for tactile and the need for mobility. These are learning needs generally not accepted and catered for in traditional classroom settings, particularly not in high schools.

If parents and teachers could understand how important and overriding kinesthetic internal (also called intuition, gut feeling) can be in some students, they would be able to support their learning in practical, often unusual ways, but the outcome will always be worth it. For many kinesthetic learners who often have a highly developed 'practical' intelligence, such support might even be a 'quick fix' and sometimes the only prevention from school failure.

'Body learning' in primary schools

During the early primary school years children mainly learn with all their senses, they are encouraged to learn by doing and experiential learning ranks very high even in classroom activities. But unfortunately for many highly kinesthetic learners, the older they get, the less full body involvement is provided in formal classrooms; experiential learning is greatly reduced in favour of more 'academic' learning mainly consisting of listening, reading, writing and discussing subject topics. However, most teachers working with younger pupils provide plenty of physical activities to teach curriculum content, involving all their students' senses.

A very kinesthetic child in Finland

Raija Leskinen from Helsinki, who works with all age groups in education, is sharing her experience through several short contributions.

A teacher told me that there was this very kinesthetic boy in the first grade. When he had done his schoolwork in class he got restless, started to talk with others and thus disturbed them. The teacher understood the situation, asked this boy to fetch a glass of water or to empty the paper basket or to sharpen the pencils and so on, when the others were still working. This way this first grader got some activity going and afterwards could again concentrate on the schoolwork for a while.

In another case I came across, there was an older teacher, close to retirement, who could not understand a kinesthetic boy. His teaching style was very authoritative and mainly auditive. The boy was active and disturbing others in the classroom. The teacher removed the child from the classroom to the corridor time after time. Under the circumstances the learning results of the boy were quite poor. There were several meetings with the parents, teacher and headmaster of the school and the result was that the child was taken out from that class and put into another. Fortunately, there was a younger teacher who understood the LS of the boy and could adjust her approach accordingly. She used more interactive methods and the boy was allowed to get more physically involved and use his hands and body in learning. There were no more behavioural problems and the learning results were greatly improved.

'Body learning' at high school level

Emma Burns, a registered psychologist in Australia describes how she works with mainly kinesthetic students, utilizing their LS to bring about behavioural change.

I work as an educational psychologist in the compulsory school sector, with those children who are considered to be in the top one per cent of severely behaviourally disturbed.

Having attended Barbara's two-day course on learning styles in May 2003 and having been considering the pitfalls of the 'one-size-fits-all' models in existence, I began investigating how LS might be used to individualize therapeutic programmes.

Since that time I have worked with a large number of young people, mainly assisting them to reduce aggressive and other antisocial behaviours. Part of my initial assessment now involves administering the LSA instrument, in order to discern how the student learns best, and then this knowledge is applied to the development of the therapeutic intervention.

Kinesthetic learning outdoors at
Rivergum Primary, Australia

Kinesthetic presentation of
learned content and learning by
doing under time pressure during
the Diploma in Holistic
Education course, Auckland, NZ

For example, when the student has a predominantly auditory learning style, I will focus on more of the 'talk-based' therapy for anger management. However, for the more kinesthetic learner (which seems to be the majority of students struggling in the high school setting), I use more of a physical approach. For example, one adaptation of the cognitive approach might be to lay down paper stepping stones, symbolizing the sequence that leads from an incident to an angry outburst, then have the students walk over them; in doing so they learn that there are steps in the path to anger, and that they have the choice of which ones to step on, and hence the choice of the outcome. Overall I have found LS a very valuable tool in meeting the needs of our young people.

'Body learning' in adult education

Again, Raija Leskinen describes how this kind of learning is of great benefit to kinesthetic learners in that age group.

I have followed in my professional life complementary training for adults who have a lower education level. It seems that these people are more kinesthetic/tactile or more often kinesthetic learners than adults with a higher education. In the training they need more action and activating tools/exercises because they cannot sit still for a long time and they cannot learn easily by listening, reading and writing. I have also noticed that very often during the lesson kinesthetic adults need something to drink, that many (actually most of them) smoke cigarettes, that they want to speak with each other and that they can hardly concentrate for longer than half an hour.

Typically as a child they have had low grades from the school and did not want to continue their studies. Later on as grown-ups they notice that they are not less intelligent than people with more education, they just need to learn in a different way. Nowadays, in the adult training system in Finland there are more activating exercises and practical workshops, which make studying easier for a kinesthetic adult. As children, most of them had learning problems, because the traditional teaching methods were, and still are, more

adapted to auditive learning styles. These kinesthetic adult students are often very creative and have a strongly holistic thinking style.

'Body learning' from a parents' viewpoint

Raija continues with a parent's view of diverse learning styles.

I have not been very good at school because of my kinesthetic and visual preferences and I also have an integrated thinking style. When I was at school the teaching style was very authoritative and auditive. The teachers spoke in front of the classroom and by the table. Students had to listen. If there was an opportunity to disturb the schoolwork, I was always ready to participate.

Because of my kinesthetic/tactile style I have always done a lot of hand work during lectures, such as knitting pullovers. I remember that once when I had to study geography, which I consider very boring, I found that it was easier to study if I knitted at the same time and I made a pullover in one week while studying for my exams.

My son is more analytic but has a specially integrated thinking style; he is very good in mathematics, he is also very good at organizing activities and his handwriting is perfect. He likes to play on computers or other games. He loves football and basketball but he does not like to read books at all.

I have also two daughters. Both of them have a holistic thinking style; they do their schoolwork on the floor or on the bed. They are not very good in mathematics but they are very creative. The younger daughter is very visual and also highly kinesthetic. She likes to read but not so much. My son and my younger daughter also had dyslexia. When learning to read they mixed the order of the letters in the words and they were a bit slow to learn to read. Luckily, this has had no impact later on. I feel that there might be a connection between their early learning problems and their kinesthetic learning style, especially since they are not auditive.

LEARNING STYLE IMPLEMENTATION

to standardize the improvement at Tumbarumba High, Australia

by Sheila Ayliffe, principal

Having discussed the types of teaching strategies that are appropriate for each group we are also comparing notes on which types of activity better engage students. Two of the collegial group teach English to the profiled students and one teaches both English and history so we are also comparing strategies which work better in each subject. We have developed the following lesson plan proforma and are looking at ways to further improve this so that teachers can have an electronic proforma which can easily be adapted for different class groups.

Lesson Planning using Learning Styles

Unit Title: Media   Unit 1: Newspapers   Class: Year 7/8 Date: _____

Learning Style Preference	Learning Activity *I learn new and difficult things best when I can:*
AUDITORY (external)	• Read out my letter to the editor • Debate a current issue • Participate in an academic controversy • Use an inside-outside circle to discuss newspaper features
AUDITORY (internal)	• Think – Pair – Share • Use the 'comfort zone' to read • Have background music during reading quiet time
VISUAL (words)	• Write a letter to the editor • Copy notes from the board or overhead • Work independently using a pre-prepared information booklet
VISUAL (external)	• Use a Venn diagram to compare broadsheet and tabloid newspapers • Study survey data
VISUAL (internal)	• Use visual stimuli as a scaffold for my writing tasks • Design the front page of a newspaper
TACTILE (touching)	• Enter survey data into a spreadsheet • Cut and paste definitions and search for examples of identified characteristics in newspapers
KINESTHETIC (external)	• Conduct a survey on people's newspaper preferences • Role-play a newsroom • Choose a costume to inspire a newspaper feature story
KINESTHETIC (internal)	• Describe my emotional reaction to a current newspaper report • Debate a current issue from both points of view

As a mother, I consider it very important that I can support the different learning styles of my children. I know that it is not easy to support them in big classrooms of 30 students and more. Nevertheless, it would be very helpful if schools could support the different learning styles.

LS at Katikati Primary School

On the other side of the globe there is a primary school in Katikati, New Zealand, where Jeannette McCallum was the deputy principal under whom the LS concept was introduced with emphasis on holistic education and kinesthetic learning for these young students. Here is part of her report about the development at Katikati Primary School.

Kinesthetic learners may learn to spell by 'air punching' or 'taking the long walk' (a long walk is a dance with a letter for each step) or throwing a koosh ball while their partner checks the spelling is correct.

Tactile learners may use playdough or sand to form words or build words with magnetic letters. Visual learners may use lots of different colours when writing out words and auditory learners may test their partner or sing or rap the words.

New concepts are taught through all the senses (auditory, visual, tactile and kinesthetic). An example of multisensory learning at Katikati Primary School is Letterland for Year 0 to 2 children. Each alphabet letter is a character who lives in Letterland and there are songs, rhymes, dress ups, stories, games and puzzles to learn from. Last year a research project found those children learned sounds and letter names better than the children in a control group who did not participate in Letterland activities. The teachers notice a huge shift in reading and writing skills since Letterland has been introduced. Another programme introduced at Katikati is the PMP (Perceptual Motor Programme) that the three youngest classes participate in. This programme teaches children perceptions and understandings of themselves and their world through movement.

If you visit classes you will see a variety of workspaces. Children choose where to learn. It may be on bean bags, kneeling at a low table, sitting on cushions or sitting at desks. Some prefer to work on their own with headphones and others prefer to work with a buddy or in a team.

To keep brain-fit, children enjoy snacking on healthy food and sipping water when they wish to. You will probably hear Mozart or baroque music playing in classrooms as children learn. Teachers report that snacking on healthy food not only means learning is improved, but children are also learning to bring more fruit and vegetables based foods and bread to school instead of junk food.

After breaks, relaxation gives children a chance to get back into learning mode. Peaceful baroque music plays while they relax. Baroque music also plays before school when the teacher greets the children in classrooms. A relaxed body and alert mind is the state children need to be in for effective learning.

From the age of five, children are guided towards thinking about how they learn best. A learning styles poster is in every classroom and teachers encourage each child to reflect on their learning, using the poster as a graphic guide. In Year 4 every child has their LS analysed and the results are shared between child, caregivers and teacher. Parents report that the LSA is useful for them to understand how their child learns best when doing homework.

High expectations and consistency combined with the LS approach means we are noticing an improvement in behaviour and achievement, especially in literacy and numeracy.

For full report see online appendix 6.

Arabian Society for Human Resource Management Conference 1997, Bahrain
Transformational Leadership for the Next Millennium

Energizing exercises during Barbara's conference presentation

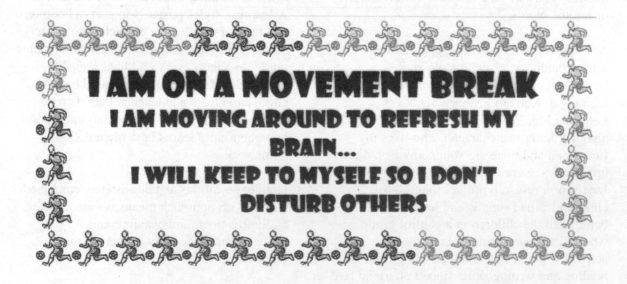

Cards used by children who need to move while learning and thinking and are allowed to wander around outside their classroom without being told off

Learning Styles in Action

Chapter 12
What to do with students who cannot sit still

Before giving answers and practical advice to this complex problem, I want to ask a few questions :

➤ Why is it that up to 30 years ago no one had ever heard of ADHD (attention deficit hyperactivity disorder), even though famous people throughout history have displayed restless behaviour (for example, Benjamin Franklin, Winston Churchill, Albert Einstein)?

➤ Why is ADHD the most common behavioural disorder in many schoolchildren today, particularly in the USA?

➤ Why is it increasingly diagnosed in NZ, Australia and the UK?

➤ Why is it three times more likely to be diagnosed in boys than in girls?

➤ Why can ADHD be found as a common feature in adults who either seek help for their relationship problems, violent behaviour and/or drug abuse, or, more interestingly, in adults who have criminal convictions from an early age?

➤ Could LS be the missing connection between ADHD and mismatched parental and educational treatment of children whose behaviour problems are mostly a result of 'unfortunate' style combinations?

➤ Has this nothing to do with a lack of intelligence but is actually based on their physical needs, and their behaviour is a desperate cry for help?

The list on page 114 compares the commonly observed symptoms of ADHD (and LD – Learning Disability) with the style features of strongly holistic students who struggle in formal education. It also explains in detail how holistic students work best, although they are rarely allowed to do so, which results in problems for all concerned. It is common knowledge that ADHD is always connected to learning problems and underachievement; an understanding of LS can turn such struggling students around in 6–8 weeks and often shows instant results in improving behaviour. Once this is achieved, real learning can take place.

The most important and usually not generally accepted approach with children who cannot sit still and display other undesirable behaviours is to focus on even minute positive aspects in a student's overall style and behaviour, noting what works and building on it.

What can be done when students find it impossible to sit still?

First: accept this need and stop attempts to control or suppress it. Such a physical need will only get stronger when suppressed and if this happens long enough, it cannot be suppressed any longer and the behaviour gets out of control.

Second: know their learning styles and discuss their learning needs, assuring them you understand and are willing to help when they are willing to learn. Teachers and parents will be surprised HOW willing such children are when they are allowed to learn THEIR WAY, which might look unusual for so-called 'normal learners' who can sit still.

Moving: The younger the children are, the more mobility they need

Sitting still: Girls can sit still for longer periods than boys

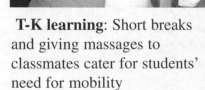

T-K learning: Short breaks and giving massages to classmates cater for students' need for mobility

Mobility: Formal and informal classroom set-up allows children to move around while learning

Third: allow them to learn through their preferences, to move around, use their hands and body for learning, work on the floor and so on, but doing all that without disturbing others during the learning process or breaking rules. Make these students understand that these are privileges that they are entitled to when their behaviour as well as their academic achievements improve. They will be withdrawn when behaviour lapses because LS needs are not a free ticket to selfish and unacceptable behaviour.

Fourth: draw on their flexibilities because once students know their strengths, their somewhat unusual learning needs and understand that they cannot always have it their way and cannot always be in motion, they practise sitting still for a while and then are allowed to move around again. Whether you believe it or not, this works! The reason is that students feel better (these are highly feeling-based learners) when they know they can learn in their own way most of the time, they will do it willingly and also do it in other ways (for example, sitting still) when required and when it does not last for too long.

It also has to be noted that boys generally need more mobility and find sitting still more difficult than girls and the younger the students are, the more mobility they need. This does not mean they are all kinesthetic learners, as so often claimed with VAK in the accelerated learning approaches (see also Chapter 11).

Teachers and parents will never succeed in keeping their children's bodies still, particularly while reading, writing or listening because movements actually enhance their learning ability; sitting still makes them feel very uneasy, leading to behavioural problems that then can easily get out of control. Many adults need to move their bodies when thinking or talking of solving problems. Why do we accept it here but not in our children?

Erica Hewetson from St Vincent's Primary reports that one of the children who had initially come to mind during the author's training has shown real benefits from being allowed a different way of working. The child found it extremely hard to control her physical need to move and constantly bounded around rooms disturbing anyone she got a chance to. During one lesson she was to be seen highlighting her literacy poetry text while pedalling on an exercise bike (given to the school free as it had been left over at a parish bazaar!). It has been difficult for staff to retrain themselves to consider fiddling, doodling and moving as acceptable conduct in the classroom, but when they manage it, the impact on behaviour is enormous.

The above situation is a paradox of LS, observed worldwide: the more teachers and parents accept and acknowledge this style need, the more the need goes down! This is particularly true for fiddling, for being in motion, for moving arms or legs. This paradox also applies to more adult students than we like to admit, because many who have a strong need for mobility during learning, never continue to go to school or never complete their courses. Theory and academic studies are just not for them and they would rather give up. If they had lecturers and tutors who understood their learning style, many students would find they are not 'dumb', would regain their self-esteem and would understand that learning in their own way by using hands and body more has a profound impact on their lives. (See 'Dear Bob Letter', page 16.)

So, next time when you as a teacher are inclined to say to parents their child cannot sit still, reconsider your judgement and see how you can utilize the need for movement in a positive way to enhance your students' learning.

Practical tips

➤ Students are allowed to go on 'movement breaks' (I have even seen in two schools children carrying cards which say: 'I am on a movement break', see page 102).

➤ Cushions and soft furniture in classrooms reduce fidgeting and the need to change body posture frequently because of uncomfortable, hard chairs.

➤ Ask students how they could build their need to move around in a meaningful way into their learning activities.

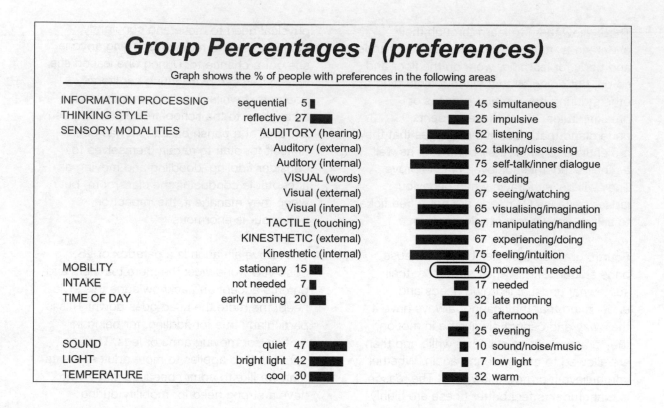

Group Percentages I (preferences)

Graph shows the % of people with preferences in the following areas

INFORMATION PROCESSING	sequential 5	45 simultaneous
THINKING STYLE	reflective 27	25 impulsive
SENSORY MODALITIES	AUDITORY (hearing)	52 listening
	Auditory (external)	62 talking/discussing
	Auditory (internal)	75 self-talk/inner dialogue
	VISUAL (words)	42 reading
	Visual (external)	67 seeing/watching
	Visual (internal)	65 visualising/imagination
	TACTILE (touching)	67 manipulating/handling
	KINESTHETIC (external)	67 experiencing/doing
	Kinesthetic (internal)	75 feeling/intuition
MOBILITY	stationary 15	40 movement needed
INTAKE	not needed 7	17 needed
TIME OF DAY	early morning 20	32 late morning
		10 afternoon
		25 evening
SOUND	quiet 47	10 sound/noise/music
LIGHT	bright light 42	7 low light
TEMPERATURE	cool 30	32 warm

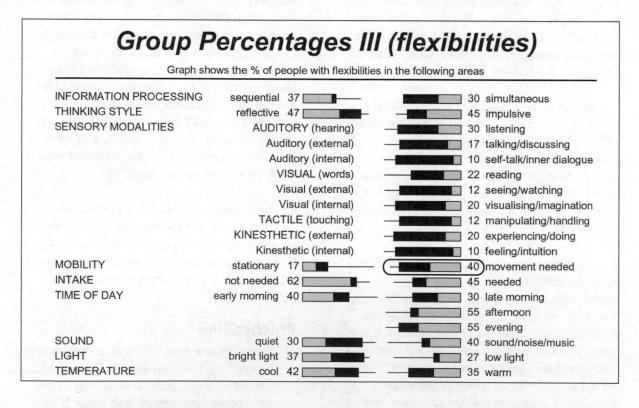

Group Percentages III (flexibilities)

Graph shows the % of people with flexibilities in the following areas

INFORMATION PROCESSING	sequential 37	30 simultaneous
THINKING STYLE	reflective 47	45 impulsive
SENSORY MODALITIES	AUDITORY (hearing)	30 listening
	Auditory (external)	17 talking/discussing
	Auditory (internal)	10 self-talk/inner dialogue
	VISUAL (words)	22 reading
	Visual (external)	12 seeing/watching
	Visual (internal)	20 visualising/imagination
	TACTILE (touching)	12 manipulating/handling
	KINESTHETIC (external)	20 experiencing/doing
	Kinesthetic (internal)	10 feeling/intuition
MOBILITY	stationary 17	40 movement needed
INTAKE	not needed 62	45 needed
TIME OF DAY	early morning 40	30 late morning
		55 afternoon
		55 evening
SOUND	quiet 30	40 sound/noise/music
LIGHT	bright light 37	27 low light
TEMPERATURE	cool 42	35 warm

Nearly 100 per cent of students in this group need movement to learn best (this result is gained from adding up preferences and flexibilities in the area of mobility and that adds up to 80 per cent). Students will NOT sit still for long, particularly when they are bored or not interested in a learning task and discipline can deteriorate very fast.

➤ The whole class should be involved in discussions about their different needs for mobility; those who need to move a lot can describe to their classmates what it is like having to sit still and why they find it so hard. Those who can sit still have a chance of explaining how they can be distracted by the constant movements of others.

➤ Through such discussions based on LSA needs, students learn to become more tolerant of each other and practise more self-discipline.

➤ RELAX! Stop telling them off for fidgeting! Restrain yourself from controlling them in their every movement. Acknowledge that some need to be in motion and you will see that their strong need will be reduced.

Use of learning styles in the learning to learn course at Cramlington High School, UK

The following report was supplied by Wendy Heslop.

In September 2003 my class undertook the learning styles analysis. The results were staggering – 65 per cent of the group were kinesthetic learners and needed mobility, 60 per cent of the group liked to study in teams or pairs and most preferred an informal/comfortable study area with low light and music. (I imagine most of these young people had been taught in a formal classroom situation all of their lives.)

What did I do? Well, I only really had one choice: in order to maximize the learning potential of my whole group I had to adapt and change not only the way I taught but also the way they could interact with the learning space.

The students were invited to remove shoes, sweatshirts and ties – whatever made them feel constrained or formal. In addition, I bought bean bags for my room and stopped insisting that they sit on a chair. RESULT: most students removed shoes and ties and nearly all students wanted to sit on a bean bag so they simply brought cushions from home which they sat on. When doing whole-class inputs the students were 'all over the place', some on formal chairs, some on tables but most lay out in front of me. Were they fully engaged? Yes! And their ability to listen, remember and concentrate improved.

➤ *The power of the koosh*
In my lessons I made a big thing about concentration, resilience and managing distractions. To focus the mind when processing difficult information we simply used koosh balls and the tactile students loved them and used them responsibly.

➤ *Getting up and moving around*
Brain Gym® became integral to our lessons. When we were learning for two hours or more, actually doing Brain Gym® became refreshing and allowed us to quickly refocus. In addition, we used breakout areas where students could work; they were allowed to walk around the room and for a while, at the start, this was a novelty but later, because of the different use of space, they rarely did it!

➤ *Bring personal possessions to the classroom*
Part of my policy when we were learning for extended periods of time was to allow them to bring personal possessions into the classroom – they often brought soft toys and placed them close by. It helped students to feel secure in the classroom and to engender a feeling of belonging.

➤ *Feed the body/feed the brain*
It was clear from my group LSA profile that most of my students required intake while learning. We discussed this as a group and they were allowed to drink water and eat fruit.

Overall, doing the LSA profile for my group revolutionized my classroom in a way that I could not have foreseen. As I start a new year with a new class, I am beginning again to change the mindset of my pupils – they are on a journey of ownership and empowerment. And for me? I know what to expect this time: freedom, security and confidence in myself and, more importantly, in my students as capable learners.

For Jack and Jenny - the kids who didn't fit the system

It was early summer. Outside our inner city classroom the world beckoned; ships made their way up and down the Clyde, fruit market tradesmen called to their customers in florid Glaswegian cadences and I could hear the factory workers across the road busy at their whirring machines.

We were inside, trapped. The teacher was, as usual, berating Jack because his work was not up to standard. I knew she would start on Jenny next. She always did. I didn't understand why our teacher couldn't see what we all saw – that Jack and Jenny were different. They needed different ways of learning.

I knew I would be next, in trouble again for dreaming out the window. It was the only way to escape the gut wrenching boredom of the school room. 'Frances marches to the beat of her own drum,' our teacher said. I wasn't sure what it meant but I knew it wasn't good. Our teacher never said anything nice.

It is memories like these which have stayed with me throughout my teaching career: from the hair-raising experiences of teaching in 'no go' areas of inner city Glasgow to the rarefied atmosphere of Oxford, teaching the children of university dons, my focus has always been the same – reaching those hard-to-reach students, who by reason of disability, social dysfunction or giftedness do not fit into the system.

Frances Hill

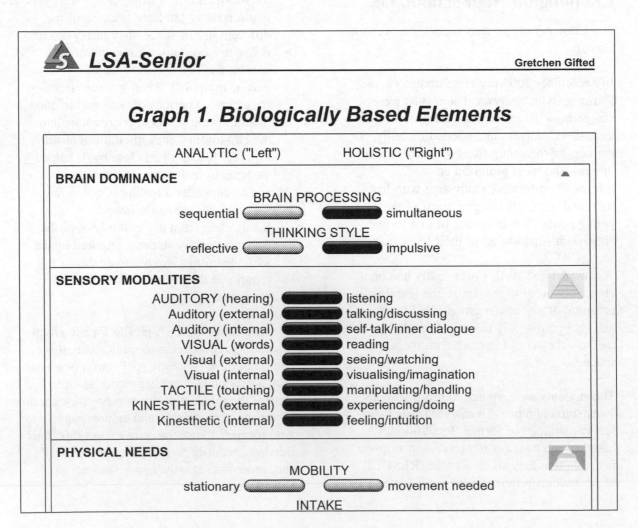

Chapter 13

How to work with 'problem' students

Underachievers

Greg Riceman, principal at Malfroy School, Rotorua, NZ, describes how LS are helping problem students to improve their learning and behaviour at school.

I left the LS course very enthusiastic and went back to school and implemented the use of learning styles in Whakamaru School, with the help of all staff, in the next six years, which was extremely beneficial.

We unfortunately could not afford to use your company training though as it was too expensive for us at that time.

At Whakamaru we were picking children up from other schools who were not achieving (a lot had been suspended from school), who were upset with everyone and school was a real pain for them. During this time our school roll doubled; we started at the school with a roll of 98, we left after six years with the roll hitting 204 and all of this was in an area where there was a population decrease.

After introducing the LS approach we cut down on truancy, behaviour problems (stand-downs cut from 10–12 a year before we started with LS to one in six years!).

The children left the school heading off to different secondary schools and were doing extremely well – head boy or girl getting scholarships and so on. I have just heard from two ex-students both who went directly from sixth form to university and have got their degrees. One of these told me that he had the best ever year at school that year. (He was in Year 8 when we first implemented LS.)

My wife and I also used the LS approach in Arorangi School (a private school in Tokoroa which has since closed). The approach was really good as it improved the children's perception of themselves and what they could achieve. They really believed in themselves and what they could do. It was great.

I know that the use of LS is absolutely essential in the overall academic achievement of students, and in building up a sense of self-worth. They become proud of who they are and realize that they can do well in school.

Gifted learners

Despite high intelligence and above average learning ability, gifted learners can also cause problems in class because they are often bored, frustrated, misunderstood and very lonely. Frequently they do not fit into the mainstream and not all 'gifted programmes' might suit their special learning abilities.

Again, a knowledge of their LS can profoundly change how teachers and parents interact with such students. The LSA sample profile opposite shows a combination of style features often found in these students and should help all concerned in coming to terms with the fact that they think, function and study differently from their classmates. They need a very different support than underachievers, and without it there is a danger that they will become isolated, lonely, desperate and, in extreme cases, suicidal.

IDENTIFYING GLD STUDENTS
by Frances Hill former principal, Te Moana School, South Canterbury, NZ

The usual methods of identifying gifted students, namely high progressive achievement tests (PAT) scores and an IQ test, do not readily identify GLD students because of the blocking effect of the learning difficulty which those students experience. A holistic method of identification is required. These procedures outlined do include the above. In addition they use careful teacher observation and an accurate history of the students' early development and current interests and attitudes.

Step 1: PARENT INPUT
It is my experience that parents are aware of, and are puzzled by, their child's unusual behaviours and characteristics long before the child attends school. GLD pre-schoolers may display precocious thinking patterns and mature oral skills while appearing to be socially immature and delayed, often in the key area of motor skills development. Information gleaned from parents regarding their child's early development is invaluable as it highlights key characteristics of students' early development such as those listed below.

CHARACTERISTICS AND TRAITS OF A GIFTED PRE-SCHOOLER
Compiled by Dave Lawrie and Ann Bonifant covers the following:
- Early linguistic development (talks, reads early – lots of questions)
- Psychomotor development (early motor milestones, active and independent)
- Personal characteristics (adult oriented, sensitive)

SAWLOR'S PARENT REFERRAL
This checklist gives an accurate picture of the student's present characteristics.
Areas noted include interests/resourcefulness/social ease/imaginative qualities.

GLD students' home behaviours often vary greatly from their school persona. They may reveal their giftedness when relaxed at home or they may take out their frustrations on their parents by displaying anger and destructiveness. The two checklists above are easy to use and are an invaluable way of providing an accurate picture of the student's home behaviours.

TEACHER INPUT
Busy classroom teachers are often puzzled and a little frustrated by the variable performance of GLD students who alternate between displaying characteristics of giftedness and of learning disability. Using the tools below helps teachers to clarify their thinking regarding a GLD student.

TEACHER OBSERVATION SCALES
I use the NCER Teacher Observation Scales which cover:
- Learning characteristics
- Social leadership characteristics
- Creative thinking characteristics
- Self-determination characteristics
- Motivational characteristics

Assessment instruments to diagnose GLD:
Learning Style Analysis (LSA)
developed by Creative Learning Systems (see chapter 3)
WHITMORE CHECKLIST for underachievers
provides a holistic picture of the students' abilities and learning characteristics and is particularly useful when identifying GLD students.
PAT and other test results
Any academic records which highlights both the strengths and the perceived academic weakness of the students are useful. These are used to provide baseline data which will form the basis of comparison between the GLD student's academic performance before and after the intervention programme.
THE WECHSLER PRE-SCHOOL and PRIMARY SCALE OF INTELLIGENCE
is the final tool in the identification process. Unlike other IQ tests which do not meet the needs of GLD students because they only give an overall score, I prefer the Wechsler test which reveals the classic subset scatter which is indicative of GLD students' performance. Study of the Performance Scale and Verbal Scale subset contained in the report will reveal areas of strength and areas of deficiency. A difference of more than 11 points between the Verbal and Performance Scale is indicative of a GLD student profile.

Step 2: ANALYSIS OF NEEDS
The next step in the process of meeting the needs of GLD students is to gain an accurate picture of the strengths and disabilities of each student. For this purpose I use the tools outlined below.

LEARNING STYLES ANALYSIS (LSA-Junior)
In order to create a targeted learning programme I need detailed knowledge of the student's learning profile. For this I use an LSA Profile which provides an accurate picture of BIOLOGICALLY BASED ELEMENTS (Brain Dominance, Sensory Modalities, Physical Needs, Preferred Environment) and CONDITIONED/LEARNED ELEMENTS (Social Preferences and Attitudes) as well as LEARNING STYLES TENDENCIES (Analytic/Holistic thought patterns).

A SPECIFIC LEARNING DISABILITY REPORT (SLD)
An SLD report, as it is commonly referred to, provides an in-depth assessment of motor development, spatial concepts, visual and auditory perception, sensory integration, oral development and academic achievement levels. The SLD report, together with the Wechsler IQ test with its revealing subset scatters, provides an accurate picture of the GLD student's strengths and difficulties.

GLD students (gifted learning disabled)

The following is an interview with Frances Hill, the former principal of Te Moana School in South Canterbury, NZ. She was chosen to be an adviser for LS and GLD in the Forbury Project in Dunedin (see Chapter 23) and is an experienced LS practitioner who has, for the past ten years, implemented a successful programme for students who experience difficulty in fitting into the education system. Prior to teaching in NZ, she has worked extensively in the UK, teaching pre-schoolers to high school students. Frances is a trained primary and secondary teacher who also has an interest in pre-school education. She is the creator of the Building Blocks Pre-School programme, which provides an innovative approach to the education of young children. Frances also works with the George Parkyn National Centre for Gifted Students which has run one-day schools for gifted students since 1996.

B.P.: GLD students – who are they?
F.H.: In the course of my teaching, I have become aware of a significant sector of the school population who fit into the above category. These are students who are gifted but suffer a specific learning disability. They are usually labelled as underachievers or who puzzle their teachers by displaying an excellent verbal ability which sadly does not transfer to productive outcomes. Characteristically there is no overt learning difficulty that could account for the reluctance because the above average intelligence of these students masks the severest effects of a learning disability. The students tend to perform in the average range with the exception of their advanced verbal facility and their highly developed thinking skills. A strong creative streak is usually present as well.

B.P.: Aren't such students often seen as 'unmotivated', 'not interested in learning' and often described by their teachers as 'Could do much better'?
F.H.: Yes, there is a tendency for the misinformed to label these students as disengaged or lazy. There is rarely a pattern of acting out in school; rather these students tend, initially, to withdraw into themselves, causing little disruption at school but displaying patterns of negative behaviour at home or of illness that worries their parents. As the students progress through school, they become increasingly anxious as the discrepancy between their strengths and weaknesses becomes wider. They may become moody or withdrawn, behaviours that result in social dysfunction and alienation from their peers. The keen sensitivity displayed by these students arises from a self-critical function which tends to be perfectionist and that damages self-esteem. The combination of high intelligence and a learning block produces a great deal of frustration and suffering for these students and their families.

B.P.: Can you give us an example of how a GLD student can be helped and how the changes occur?
F.H.: With pleasure. Here is a case history based on my own experience:

Anthony displayed the classic early characteristics of a gifted learner. He was a sleepless baby who seemed to be interested in everything. His mother reported that she had, from an early age, to carry him around in a sling so that he could view the world. He spoke complex sentences at 12 months, learned to read by two years of age and asked endless 'Why?' and 'What if?' questions. He did not play with other toddlers but loved the company of adults. Anthony's idea of play was to dismantle the clock to see how it works or, on one occasion, to attempt to take the toilet system apart. He was late in walking and seemed to lack both gross and fine motor skills. He often fell over and was fearful of playground equipment. He did not play in the expected way and avoided other children.

By the age of three his parents were convinced that something was wrong with their son and so consulted an educational psychologist. Anthony loved the sessions with the psychologist, who provided lots of interesting conversation. The psychologist's conclusion was that Anthony was a bright child and the parents were worrying over nothing. He entered school on his fifth

Depending on the results of the above assessment I may consult the following agencies to identify the disabilities which underpin the GLD student's learning difficulties. Each of them will provide detailed reports and advice on the best way to remedy the problems. The most often consulted ones are:

OCCUPATIONAL THERAPISTS
to assess fine and gross motor skills development and to highlight possible problems such as dyspraxia or lack of sensory integration.
DEVELOPMENTAL OPTOMETRISTS
to detect visual perceptual problems such as eye tracking difficulties or Irlen Syndrome
AUDIOMETRICIANS
to detect hearing difficulties such as central processing disorder

Step 3: CREATING THE PROGRAMME
Following identification and analysis of needs, an individually tailored programme is created for the student and monitored. The purpose of the programme is to remedy the learning difficulty and to celebrate the gift. Targeted programmes are highly effective in eliminating the learning disability and in freeing GLD students to access the higher order thinking skills which characterize their performance.

Elements of the Programme are:
1. **Training in Metacognition**
    GLD students suffer greatly from a sense of frustration and hopelessness. They need to come to terms with the learning difficulty which has affected them and to learn how to use their giftedness to overcome the effects of the learning difficulty. They literally need to learn how to learn. Above all they need to believe in themselves as successful learners who, against the odds, have overcome a major learning difficulty and are able to go forward.
2. **Regular Conferencing Sessions**
    It is vital that students overcome the sense of learned helplessness which afflicts them. They must be partners in their own recovery. Together with teacher, teacher aide and parents, the student plans the programme, sets achievable goals and reviews progress. A signed contract and daily timetable provides details of the elements of the programme.
3. **Slaying the Dragon**
    Provision of a daily programme to address the problem which underpins the learning difficulty. This may take the form of a perceptual motor programme, eye tracking exercises or auditory processing training depending on the need of each student. The agencies previously mentioned provide strong support for the class teacher by providing exercises and success indicators.
4. **Direct Daily Intervention**
    This programme is written by the teacher and is supported by a teacher's aide. The programme targets the specific learning difficulty which is experienced by the student. Careful study of the LSA and SLD reports and of the Wechsler IQ report will assist teachers in devising a programme. The programme is revised weekly and adjusted in the light of the rapid progress which GLD students invariably make.
5. **Curriculum Compacting**
    I use curriculum compacting to find the correct learning level for each student and then use a judicious mixture of acceleration and enrichment to provide the optimum learning programme which will allow the student to excel in those areas of giftedness which have been identified. The programme includes accessing those higher order thinking skills which gifted students display.
6. **Celebrating 'The Gift' (at every opportunity!)**
    GLD students rapidly lose their sense of helplessness by using their gifts to help others in buddy and mentor programmes, by being the class spokesperson in whatever interests them.
    Give GLD students responsibility – they will thrive.
7. **Mentor programmes**
    Find someone who shares the student's passion – perhaps a local artist or science teacher, inventor or enthusiast, anyone who can spend some time with the student. I find that local community members are willing to come to school to spend some time with a student who shares their interest. It may only be a matter of a few weeks' contact, just long enough to validate the student's belief in themselves and to make them feel that they are not as strange and different as they had feared.
8. **Counselling Sessions**
    In addition to the above programme, support should be offered in the form of counselling for both students and families to enable individuals to come to terms with the unusual needs of GLD students.
    It may simply take the form of contact with other families in a similar position or it may need the assistance of an outside agency.

Even without additional funding available from the Ministry of Education, creating such a programme is well within the reach of all primary schools as it requires little additional cost. The key to success is the collaborative support which is offered to the student. Freed from the fear of being 'different' or 'strange', freed from the deep-seated loneliness, students experience renewed hope and energy. The fact that they are agents in their own renaissance is also vitally important. They are able to use their giftedness, their insights and their thinking skills to overcome the worst effects of their learning difficulty. The most rewarding aspect of working with GLD students is the speed with which they overcome and/or accommodate their learning difficulty and are able to access the regular gifted students' programme.

birthday. An astute teacher noted his intelligence but also remarked upon his lack of social and play skills and on his inability to dress himself properly despite instruction in how to do so. By the third week of school Anthony was unhappy. He asked his parents 'Why do the children not accept me?' Anthony, who was always full of energy and enthusiasm, became reticent. The light faded from his eyes. He became withdrawn. As he moved from class to class the pattern was always the same. Initially his new teacher would enthuse over this delightful new child in the class. Invariably, by about the third week, the teacher would telephone to express concerns about Anthony's lack of play skills, lack of co-ordination and generally disorganized behaviour.

His reading age was four years above his chronological age and his oral language skills were highly developed. The children called him 'The little professor' because of his sophisticated speech patterns. On two more occasions concerned teachers referred Anthony to an educational psychologist for assessment. On each occasion the response was the same. There is nothing wrong with this child. He must have pushy parents!

Anthony's handwriting was large and poorly formed. He could not complete simple physical tasks such as using scissors. Teachers reported that he was becoming increasingly withdrawn and tended to 'space out'. Although highly imaginative, he could not produce a legible, ordered piece of writing. Learning tables was a nightmare and number work presented a challenge because he could not grasp sequences. A specific learning disability (SLD) assessment noted Anthony's verbal ability but pinpointed delays in gross and fine motor skills. The Wechsler Intelligence test showed the classic GLD wide subset scatter of abilities with exceptional ability in the area of verbal performance and deficits showing in the areas of visual perception.

At the age of nine Anthony finally found help. He visited a motor skills specialist who diagnosed dyspraxia, a condition which affects motor planning. This specialist also expressed concern about Anthony's ability to see, which she suspected was more severe than the short-sightedness that caused him to wear glasses.

Anthony was referred to a developmental optometrist who found that Anthony had no binocular vision. He was able to read because he unconsciously shut off the vision from one eye but for other activities he saw double. He had poor stereoscopic vision so he had no appreciation of depth and he had limited peripheral vision so he could not see much beyond that which was directly in front of his eyes.

He also had slow motor speed, which accounted for the difficulty he had in finishing a piece of written work. Despite these severe problems Anthony's school performance was average or slightly below average in certain areas with flashes of high verbal ability and problem-solving skills. His intelligence had masked the worst effects of severe physical impairment.

I began to teach Anthony using the programme that I devised and that is outlined opposite. Within weeks he changed, becoming once again the lively child he had been before entering school. He used an alpha word processing machine to write. Freed from the stress of having to form letters that he could not see clearly, he became a prolific writer. In the first writing competition he entered he won a book. The next competition he entered was the Ursula Moray Competition for Creative Writing. Anthony was competing against children several years older than himself but he won the cup. That was a wonderful day and was a validation of all the people who had helped him and for Anthony himself who struggled against severe learning impediments but never gave up.

Anthony continued to go from strength to strength. He is now a senior school student. His ambition? To become a teacher of special needs students. The anguish that his family experienced is typical of the pain that the families of GLD students suffer. In my work with GLD students I have often seen a similar pattern repeated. The good news is that GLD students respond rapidly to provision of an

Comparison of students with

LD & ADHD symptoms   vs   Holistic Learning Styles

LD & ADHD symptoms	Holistic Learning Styles
1. often fidgets or squirms in seat	1. needs mobility, highly kinesthetic
2. has difficulty remaining seated	2. strong need for mobility, kinesthetic
3. is easily distracted	3. short attention span, 'scatterbrain', fluctuating persistence
4. has difficulty awaiting turn in group	4. impulsive thinking, impulsive behaviour
5. often blurts out answers to questions	5. typical holistic, impulsive, right-brain thought processing
6. has difficulties following instructions processing	6. non-sequential, random brain low auditory preferences in information intake
7. has difficulties sustaining attention to tasks	7. fluctuating persistence, works in bursts, externally motivated
8. often shifts form one uncompleted activity to another	8. multi-task oriented, non-analytical, needs variety, is easily bored with just one activity at a time
9. has difficulty playing quietly	9. needs/prefers noise/sound in combination with movement and physical activities during play time
10. often talks excessively	10. needs social interaction, has preference for talking, is peer/group oriented
11. often interrupts or intrudes on others	11. impulsive information processing style combined with high non-conformity and low responsibility
12. often does not seem to listen	12. low auditory preferences in information intake situations, always needs overview, hands-on instructions, experimental learning
13. forgetful, often loses things necessary for carrying out tasks	13. 'scatterbrain', multiple interests, strong right-brain processing with little attention to details
14. often engages in physically dangerous activities without considering consequences	14. high kinesthetic/tactile preferences combined with high need for mobility, low responsibility, high non-conformity, and creative, right-brain processing, resulting in high risk-taking behaviour

appropriate programme of intervention and enrichment. Anthony was the first GLD child I taught and would like to close this interview with a quote from John, a recent GLD student in my class whose family were moving away for employment reasons. His parents were concerned that the rapid improvement he had made while on the intervention programme might not be sustained when he moved to another school. John, however, settled our fears with a few words: 'Wherever I go, I'll be fine. I now know who I am.'

ADHD students

Attention deficit hyperactivity disorder is being diagnosed in ever-increasing numbers among students in many countries and most teachers find it extremely difficult to deal with their disruptive behaviour. Although there are some students who have neurological disorders causing ADHD and benefit from taking certain medication, many students are misdiagnosed. Their behaviour problems are only partly because of deprived family situations – they are largely based on poorly understood LS needs and style combinations that do not fit traditional norms. The comparison shown opposite gives a comprehensive overview of LD and ADHD symptoms in contrast to holistic LS needs.

A very interesting website dealing with ADHD is ⌨ www.drhuggiebear.com where Dr Frank Barnhill describes how many diseases can masquerade as ADHD. He calls these 'zebras' because they are hiding like zebras in tall grass and cannot be seen well. The following is an extract from the website.

1 Thyroid disease. I've seen many girls, who were diagnosed as ADHD without hyperactivity, because they daydreamed in class, were very shy and seemed too sleepy to pay attention. Fortunately, we found the hypothyroidism (low thyroid hormone) before it affected their growth and puberty. Within weeks, parents and teachers could see a big difference in energy levels, attention spans and, of course, grades. Likewise, I have seen boys who were so hyperactive they disrupted the classroom and home-life so much that everyone wanted to get away from them. Some were hyperthyroid (high thyroid hormone levels) and responded within one month of treatment. These kids usually became very good students and rarely continued to cause problems at school and home.

2 Seizure disorders. This is a new topic in behavioural science. Some children labelled ADHD with or without hyperactivity actually suffer from mild seizures. Petit mal seizures (called absence seizures or staring episodes) can appear to be inattentive or spacey when they occur many times an hour. If the child becomes confused or scared, then periods of hyperactivity may follow. If you or any other member of your family has seizures, then you should have your ADHD tested.

3 Post concussion syndrome. Mild cases of trauma to the brain that leave no physical evidence of having occurred can lead to symptoms of ADHD. It is felt that brain cell pathways may have been damaged leaving the child poorly able to utilize higher brain cognitive and executive level thought processing abilities. When a child can't interpret his or her sensory input properly, confusion and frustration may lead to hyperactive states. PET (positive emissions tomography) scans of the brain are used to identify these 'damaged' areas.

4 Effects of certain foods. Everyone knows how 'hyper' kids get when fed a lot of sugar. But, have you ever thought about too much caffeine causing hyperactive states? Each and every child has a different metabolism. So some tolerate large amounts of sugar and caffeine without becoming hyper, while others consume little of these stimulants and start bouncing off the walls.

5 Malnutrition including multiple vitamin deficiencies. No child can adequately focus and concentrate when hungry. With prolonged periods of forced fasting, kids become tired, irritable and unable to process visual-auditory-tactile sensory input correctly. In addition, vitamin B12 deficiency can cause fatigue, wasting and depression.

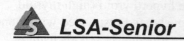 **LSA-Senior**

Tom Underachiever

Profile Summary

Tom, your preferences are your strengths when you can use them in difficult learning situations, and your non-preferences become your weaknesses when you have to use them over longer periods of time. This can lead to frustration, concentration problems, low motivation, and learning difficulties. When you are allowed to learn YOUR way, you will enjoy studying more and your academic performance will improve.

Key elements of my learning style
when I have to learn something NEW and/or DIFFICULT:

My Preferences: (how I learn best)

BRAIN DOMINANCE: simultaneous, impulsive

SENSORY MODALITIES: visual (external), visual (internal), tactile (touching), kinesthetic (external), kinesthetic (internal)

PHYSICAL NEEDS: movement needed, intake, evening

ENVIRONMENT: sound/noise/music, low light, informal/comfortable study area

SOCIAL: team

ATTITUDES: externally motivated, non-conforming, low responsibility, self-directed, change-oriented

My Non-Preferences: (what I need to avoid when learning something difficult)

BRAIN DOMINANCE: sequential, reflective

SENSORY MODALITIES: auditory (hearing), visual (words)

PHYSICAL NEEDS: stationary, no intake, early morning, afternoon

ENVIRONMENT: quiet, formal study area

SOCIAL: alone, peers, teacher authority

ATTITUDES: high/systematic persistence, conforming, high/strong responsibility, routine

6   Vision and hearing problems. It is obvious that children who can't see or hear well will have problems integrating sensory input from their environment. It's always surprised me how often parents and doctors fail to have these important aspects of learning assessed.

7   Visual-tactile-auditory integration problems. These are very specialized problems that affect a child's or adult's ability to interact with one or more aspects of their sensory environment. Some children learn best when they hear and see what they are supposed to learn simultaneously. That's why we advocate use of tape recorders for recording classroom lectures so the child can listen while reading later. Sometimes, students must touch and listen at the same time. This is the way most surgeons learn to operate.

At-risk and dropout candidates

Under Ruth Chalkley and Dawn Gilderoy, the Feel the Dream project in Hartlepool, UK developed innovative learning experiences for students with strong kinesthetic learning tendencies who might be at risk of dropping out once they move to high school.

Out-of-hours sessions beginning at primary through to secondary school have helped pupils to develop effective tools for learning and an understanding of their own learning style. Pupils attending these activities were of mixed ability, and through the variety of visual, auditory, tactile and kinesthetic learning activities each pupil experienced success in developing their own skills, knowledge and learning tools. The achievements of all pupils were celebrated in a ceremony at the end of each project in primary and secondary where pupils shared their successful learning experiences with parents and members of staff in schools.

Conclusions from the Feel the Dream project

What has been achieved?

●   Training of members of the learning team to audit their own learning styles/ intelligences in order to match their own learning with that of students.

●   The successful creation of a 'Matched Transition Curriculum' for both out of hours activities at both Y6 and into Y7 along with the summer school curriculum.

●   Development of the logical use of University of the First Age principles to link with aspects of the Key Stage 3 strategy and the foundation subjects strand.

●   Development of monitoring, observation and evaluation systems that take account of learners' needs.

●   Establishment of successful LS identification procedures for students.

One finding was that students who have the poorest attendance records were those with very strong kinesthetic learning preferences. Due to the small sample number these findings cannot as yet be concluded as statistically significant but are still an interesting trend to consider.

Recommendations from the Feel the Dream project:

1   'Schools need to consider the possibility of providing flexible teaching which takes account of differences in pupils' preferred learning styles (paying particular attention to gender differences); in this way fewer pupils become disengaged.'

2   'It will be important for schools to provide a record of "successful practices" which schools can use and build upon.'

For full report see online appendices 2 and 3.

A continent away, Holly Corman, a passionate teacher of troubled students in Ontario, Canada, has also found that Learning Styles have been a salvation for those who cannot learn in traditional ways.

I work with learners who have been expelled from mainstream schools as a result of weapons or drug use, assault or truancy. For these young people, school had been a battle ground, a torture chamber or a commercial enterprise to make money – certainly not

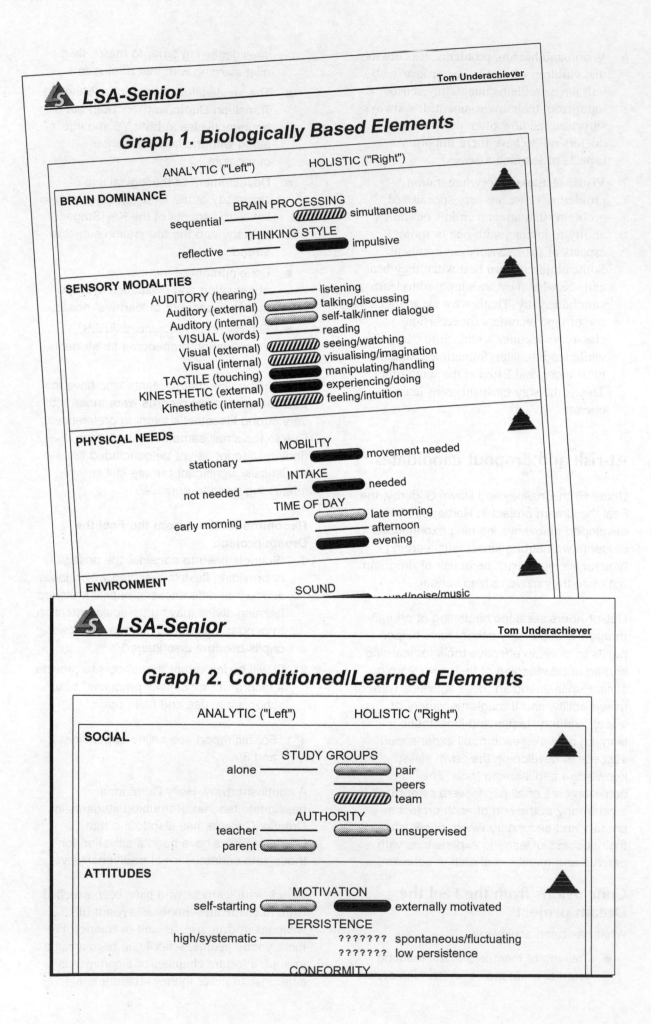

LSA-Senior
Tom Underachiever

Graph 1. Biologically Based Elements

	ANALYTIC ("Left")	HOLISTIC ("Right")

BRAIN DOMINANCE

BRAIN PROCESSING
sequential ——— simultaneous

THINKING STYLE
reflective ——— impulsive

SENSORY MODALITIES

AUDITORY (hearing) ——— listening
Auditory (external) ——— talking/discussing
Auditory (internal) ——— self-talk/inner dialogue
VISUAL (words) ——— reading
Visual (external) ——— seeing/watching
Visual (internal) ——— visualising/imagination
TACTILE (touching) ——— manipulating/handling
KINESTHETIC (external) ——— experiencing/doing
Kinesthetic (internal) ——— feeling/intuition

PHYSICAL NEEDS

MOBILITY
stationary ——— movement needed

INTAKE
not needed ——— needed

TIME OF DAY
early morning ——— late morning
——— afternoon
——— evening

ENVIRONMENT

SOUND
sound/noise/music

LSA-Senior
Tom Underachiever

Graph 2. Conditioned/Learned Elements

	ANALYTIC ("Left")	HOLISTIC ("Right")

SOCIAL

STUDY GROUPS
alone ——— pair
——— peers
——— team

AUTHORITY
teacher ——— unsupervised
parent

ATTITUDES

MOTIVATION
self-starting ——— externally motivated

PERSISTENCE
high/systematic ——— ??????? spontaneous/fluctuating
??????? low persistence

CONFORMITY

Learning Styles in Action

hallowed or welcoming. By a happy coincidence, when I accepted this position, I was reading *The Power of Diversity*, and Barbara's ideas corroborated my own experience of teaching. I thought the online analysis might be the kind of hook my new students needed to begin a process of self-discovery.

I decided to use the LSA profiles as the basis for an entire learning strategies course, geared to guiding each learner to a greater awareness of how they learned in different contexts. I hoped this understanding would enable them to take charge of their own learning, while gaining a greater tolerance for others. I also planned to use the group profile for my own action research projects. I was curious if the learners in our group would have similar profiles and if there were strategies schools could use to engage these students before they were expelled.

Four years later, I am still working and learning with expelled students. Each student who has moved through our programme completed an LSA profile. Overwhelmingly these students have demonstrated preferences for an impulsive thinking style with strong preferences for self-talk, feeling/intuition, manipulating/handling and experiencing/doing closely followed by preferences for visualization and discussion.

It hardly seems surprising then that these students were expelled from a system demanding quiet, reflective, listening, reading and watching. Indeed, the fact they subsisted for nine or ten years in a system that so perfectly mismatched their learning needs is really quite remarkable. Their resilience and coping mechanisms became the basis of our weekly counselling sessions along with a close examination of how their LSA profile is often reflected in other aspects of their lives, especially communication and conflict resolution. Learners often expressed relief after the initial debriefing of their LSA profile. Many harboured the nagging suspicion that something was wrong with them because they didn't understand what the teacher was saying or they didn't see the world the way other people seemed to. The LSA profile validated

what they were afraid to put into words and has been a wonderful tool for externalizing the process of self-examination. Having a hard copy of the profile also helps learners begin to see similarities and differences in their peers and in their teachers. Recognizing a difference is often the first step to understanding and tolerance.

When our students are reintegrated back to mainstream, the LSA profile becomes an integral part of their portfolio. To gain re-entry, students must 'sell' their future success by presenting the contents of their portfolio to a panel including school board officials, administration, teachers and parents. Panel members are often amazed by our students' willingness to reveal who they are and their ability to accept responsibility for poor choices in the past. LSA has been a big, first step in that journey to self-understanding and change.

Slowly, our school system is becoming aware of subtle shifts in teaching that can generate enormous changes in how both students and teachers feel and perform. As a result of our successful reintegration of expelled students, school administrators have been requesting professional development. I use the LSA group profile to illustrate the kinds of shifts that need to take place to match teaching and learning styles. For example, allowing water bottles, turning off the lights or providing background music are simple, inexpensive changes that can dramatically improve student performance.

Some teachers and administrators are beginning to examine why they do things the way they do and are now looking for another way. Completing a TSA can also be an eye-opening experience. One principal confided in me, 'The TSA was the most important PD we've had all year. Teachers began to see that there are other ways of perceiving the world, even among themselves – and teachers tend to be a pretty homogeneous group. This revelation made them more open to the possibility that maybe kids could see things differently too.' Certainly dialogue about learning between teachers, administrators and students is positive. While shifting from teaching as the transmission of information to a transaction between learners

Key Activities Developed for Secondary 'K Club'

All activities developed to match KS3 Y7 science framework at Hartlepool for highly KINESTHETIC students struggling with academic learning

■ Brain Quiz using kinesthetic sticky boards

Each student was given a copy of Brain Quiz laminated with velcro strips attached under each question. Answers provided on separate velcro strips. Students were given the task to complete the quiz and after this had been completed a group discussion was held.

■ Brain in Action

This activity was used to build upon the knowledge pupils had gained through University of the First Age 'Building a brain' activity. Statements outlining activities that would use a particular part of the brain were given to students who had to use their prior knowledge to decide whether the activity would involve using the left side, right side, corpus callosum or reptilian part of the brain. Four areas (left, right, corpus callosum, reptilian) were set up around the room that students had to gather at when their decision was made. Activity was followed up by a short discussion of why each student had chosen which area of the brain.

Examples of 'brain in action' statements

Right Side
I'm playing three blind mice on my recorder, which part of the brain am I using?

Left Side
I'm in class working through a maths problem with one of my classmates. Which part of the brain am I using?

Reptilian
We are having a class discussion about my favourite books, suddenly the teacher asks me a question in front of all my classmates and my mind goes blank. I can't think of the answer. Which part of the brain am I using?

Corpus Callosum
I'm training for the Great North Run by going jogging every night. Which part of the brain am I using when I am jogging?

■ Pin the organs on the body

Working in groups, students were given an outline of the human body with cards of organs to place on the body.

Stage one: Students were given the task without any supporting materials.

Stage two: Students were provided with instruction cards outlining descriptions of the organs.

Stage three: Students were provided with instruction cards outlining the name and function of the organ.

Throughout the stages of the activity one of the co-ordinators was available in the role of 'ask the expert' where students could receive guidance on how many organs they had placed correctly so far.

■ Kinesthetic Mind Maps

Students were provided with pictures and information on 'MRS GREN' processes of life and had to put together their own kinesthetic mind map matching organs of the body to the processes of life.

continued on page 122

and subject is still too giant a leap for many, I hope tools such as LSA will encourage others to build bridges spanning the gap.

A road to follow

At River City Training Academy in Hamilton, NZ, Damon Whitten has used a creative learning approach and LS with his students in a 'Road Code Course' and was pleased about the positive outcomes:

'Power Up' is a course designed for adults with little or no literacy skills. Most of my students are the classic school dropouts. The learning simply moved too fast or they were bored or they just could not remember the information when the time came to prove it, leaving them frustrated and disillusioned with learning. The need for obtaining a driver's licence is paramount to most people in this class.

However, sitting down and reading through the Road Code is not an option for these students and would accomplish little anyway except to further frustrate them and their motivation to learn. After a few lessons motivation has been and still is very high. In fact, they are learning so fast that I could add a lot more information into the following lesson plans. This has been extremely encouraging for me as a tutor and I have now begun to use these techniques with other subjects as well with great success.

Application of LSA to dyslexic adult students

Michael Buckle, the director of the Danish training institute Ordkløveriet (translated as 'The Quibbler'), has for ten years worked with adult students who endure more or less severe cases of dyslexia and reports how the training of these students is largely based on the principles of LSA.

Ordkløveriet in Holstebro doesn't only offer basic skills training, but also recognizes a big need for personal development; in the following text, however, I am primarily focusing on the use of LSA at Ordkløveriet. The average student in our institute has initially a sense of being below his/her peers, being less intelligent, and to have completely failed in traditional learning situations the public school system has offered.

The prospect of having to learn how to read and write at an adult age, often provokes fear of failure in other areas and leads the dyslexic student to avoid training situations at any cost. This happens because training at an adult age is still connected to the memories of earlier tutorial fiascos. In order to have these students commit to a training situation, it is imperative that the methods applied are different from the earlier negative educational experiences they had.

The training conducted at Ordkløveriet is based on the following didactic ideas: learning has to happen at a multisensory level, to enable the brain to remember through practical application and usage of educational material in non-traditional situations. LSA is used to determine what senses need to be stimulated in relation to the student's personal preferences for best results.

We call that educational principle 'enzyme learning'. The amount of energy needed to absorb and process training material can be reduced through the actions of the teacher and the learning environment in which the student is placed. A process of normal digestion is enabled by having the body use an amount of energy. By introducing enzymes into this process the demand for energy is reduced even though the digestive result is the same. In a learning situation the teacher and the environment can be the enzyme that reduces the level of energy needed for efficient training with successful outcomes. In knowing what LSA preferences the individual student has, the teacher is able to reduce the amount of 'energy' needed and can therefore facilitate a smoother, more appropriate learning process.

The connection between the holistic and the analytic part of the brain must equally be made stronger in order to enable dyslexic students to remember and apply the rules of spelling, grammar and reading. This is achieved, for example, through the use of computer programs that strengthen the link of

Making kinesthetic mind maps

■ MRS GREN goes to the doctor

Project co-ordinator acted the part of MRS GREN and role-played with the students who had to move to a picture of the organ that they thought was the cause of various complaints by 'Mrs Gren'. Organs were placed on different areas around the room to encourage movement.

Note: MRS GREN=

Movement	Growth
Respiration	Reproduction
Sensitivity	Excretion
	Nutrition

Factors that make memorizing mind maps memorable...
you will help your memorizing if you can make what you learn...

Colourful

Outrageous

ALLITERATIVE

Rhyming

Sexy!

Emotional

Sequenced

Associated

Numbered

Dynamic

Empowering Lifelong Learners through Knowledge of Individual Learning Processes:

A Case Study at Iowa Lakes Community College

Ellengray G. Kennedy, Iowa State University

This study was motivated by the concern that learning often eludes students due to ineffective study strategies, poor understanding of teacher expectations, and limited knowledge of individual learning processes. The purpose of this study was to determine if students, and specifically students from a small, rural midwest community college, can learn strategies that enhance their ability to learn, reduce intimidation, and thus manage stress during the learning process in order to maximize learning potential. Thus, the study examined learning strategies and styles from the perspective of the learners. It examined how learners can benefit from an understanding of how they learn best, and how the individual learner can use this understanding of learning strategies and styles to take responsibility for creating an environment that maximizes learning potential.

Tools, such as the LSA instrument and training, were available to assist individuals in assessing their preferred learning styles. According to Prashnig (1998), the learning style model developed by Dunn & Dunn is a research instrument containing scientifically researched style elements which are biological and remain fairly stable over a lifetime.

Research Questions:

Two overarching research questions and four exploratory questions were developed for this study:
Overarching Research Question I: What are the changes in learning when individual learners gain knowledge of their preferred learning styles?
Exploratory Questions:

1. As a result of the LSA tool and training, how, if at all, do learners feel empowered and responsible for their learning, thus creating an environment conducive to successful and satisfactory learning?

the left and the right side of the brain, by physical learning activities, or holistic/analytical focused training.

In the process of enhancing the students' reading abilities we use the LSA first to determine the brain dominance of the students. Recent research on reading abilities shows a link between reading difficulties and brain dominance.

Students with reading difficulties can now roughly be divided into two categories: analytical/sequentially weak readers and holistic/simultaneously weak readers. With the LSA profile we can detect the brain dominance and hence focus on training either the analytical or holistic skills of the student.

Personal growth follows an increased skill level as the student experiences learning success. The application of LSA into the training has a very important secondary benefit apart from facilitating an optimal learning environment. Through understanding a student's personal LSA the assumption of being lesser reduces. Students come to the conclusion that they are alright. It isn't the student, but the earlier undifferentiated learning processes that have produced frustration and a poor outcome of skill. Through this clarification our students experience typically a renewed energy towards learning and a strengthening in reading and spelling skills.

Ordkløveriet has over the past years recognized some preferences common to dyslexic students that have been taught at the institute. In general they are holistic, tactile and kinesthetic, and prefer to work in a non-traditional learning environment. It is essential for any training session that this group of students feels confident with the methods and the materials introduced in the process. The institute has through the application of individual LSA profiles and group profiles been able to construct the educational course in such a manner that students experience that their learning needs are largely met.

The institute's physical settings have been carefully established as a learning lab in order to accommodate the different learning styles the students need to have matched.

Examples:

➤ small and large rooms, where seclusion and silence is possible;

➤ traditional classrooms where the position of chairs and desks is determined by the students;

➤ a 'holistic' room with gym balls, couches and bean bag chairs;

➤ computers in the traditional and holistic room organized in order to facilitate learning;

➤ daylight as the main light source through the day;

➤ headphones are being distributed so that music is possible all over the institute without disturbing the students who need silence.

The result is that all our dyslexic students with the deep anxiety towards learning situations experience a major change of mind, within a fairly short period of time. Through a training scheme designed to match personal learning profiles, the students absorb knowledge and acquire reading and writing skills in a manner that doesn't produce the usual stress, reduces the amount of energy needed and eradicates fear of failure.

Our students feels empowered through the knowledge that they have the right to assert and apply their personal learning style. Through this empowerment rises a personal motivation to continue the positive learning experience towards new academic goals that previously would have been unthinkable.

Conclusion

From all the reports I received about working with problem students one aspect stood out very clearly:

Education systems fail them because they are NOT academic learners and function quite differently during the learning process, whether their teachers like it or not. The lists below give educators a quick overview of the main differences between high and low achievers in our school systems.

2. How, if at all, has the LSA learning experience changed student grades?

Overarching Research Question II: What do students perceive as the outcome of the LSA tool and training on their educational and personal lives?

Exploratory Questions:

3. How has the LSA learning experience affected students' satisfaction with their educational experiences?
4. Do students feel more or less stress with their academic experiences?

Conclusions and Implications:

The community college in this study should continue to use the LSA tool and training, increase faculty involvement and add additional follow-up tools for the students. In addition, the two-hour Discovery Session has been attended on a voluntary basis and should be available to all faculty, especially newly hired faculty. Based on the results of this study, more extensive use of these resources would ensure that faculty involvement in the LSA initiative is college-wide.

There is potential for continued development of new tools and applications. The LSA tool and training includes a Junior Version for middle school, a Senior Version for high school and an Adult Version for the college student or lifelong learner. The college should continue to reach out externally, giving presentations at conferences, elementary and secondary schools, other community colleges, and four-year colleges and universities.

Data from the student focus groups and faculty peer debriefing interviews support the need to develop formalized follow-up sessions to ensure that the students review the LSA tool and training periodically. Further application and understanding of the implications of the tool would be evident for each learner. To maximize the benefits of the LSA tool and training for all students, follow-up and reinforcement should be discussed, planned, implemented and assessed on a continuous basis by students and faculty to ensure further understanding and effective application.

This study has implications for students, as well as faculty, who are interested in maximizing learning potential through learning strategies that reduce intimidation and manage stress during the learning process. With regard to improved communication between students and faculty, I believe this research indicated that the use of assessment tools, the LSA tool and training in particular, ensures effective communication that builds skills to improve lifelong learning. Without changing the expectations of the curriculum or the desired outcomes, individuals can gain increased learning and knowledge within an environment that is less stressful because of increased confidence.

This study revealed that changes took place in the learning of the students when the individual learners gained knowledge of their preferred learning styles. In addition, the majority of the students in this study perceived the outcome of the LSA tool and training on their educational experience as positive. The reduced frustration (stress) and the increased confidence with their educational experiences would most likely benefit their personal lives.

Generalizations from this study should be made carefully. Whereas the findings of this study were significant for those involved, the study is not without its limitations. This study involved research participants from only one institution, a small, midwest community college located in a rural area. The results and conclusions cannot be presumed to be representative of, or transferable to, other similarly sized community colleges. In addition, regional differences could affect the transferability of the conclusions to other areas of the country.

This study provided evidence for additional research on the effect of increased awareness of individual learning styles. While this study revealed that the perceived outcome of the LSA tool and training on participants' educational lives was positive, this study did not determine the statistical significance of these effects

Continued research should be done on the validity of the LSA tool and training that was used in the study. In addition, the complementary roles of usage of the LSA, Myers Briggs Type Indicator, and the theory of multiple intelligences should be further investigated. Studying the significance to learners if the three tools were used in tandem and/or parallel to each other would be beneficial. In order for students to fully benefit from learning styles, higher education should utilize every opportunity to integrate the information into the learning-centred methodology.

For a report on the full case study, the bibliography, methods used and results gained, see online appendix 1.

High achievers

are analytic – like formal, quiet classrooms with bright light – don't need intake while learning – have high persistence.

Low achievers

are holistic – like informal classrooms with low light levels and sound – need intake and have low persistence.

High achievers also

are highly motivated to learn, show high responsibility, are conforming, need structure and guidance, work better alone, accept authority, prefer routine tasks, like the morning hours, need little mobility, are reflective thinkers and auditory/visual.

Low achievers in contrast

are not motivated to learn, show low responsibility, are non-conforming rebels but need structure and guidance, something they don't like, work better with peers, reject, often despise authority, prefer variety, are evening creatures, need a lot of mobility, are impulsive thinkers, not auditory, but tactile/kinesthetic.

LSA-Senior

Gretchen Gifted

PERSONAL REPORT AND STUDY GUIDELINES

The following Report contains a detailed interpretation of your results shown in the graphs on Pages 3 & 4. If you act on the recommendations in your Personal Report, you will not only enhance your learning abilities and problem solving skills, but also improve your academic achievement.

BRAIN DOMINANCE

BRAIN PROCESSING:
You are a more simultaneous, right-brain processor who tends to engage the creative right hemisphere in problem solving. In learning you need the big picture first and then the reasons for a task before you are ready to start. You prefer working with people who have a sense of humour; and your overall comprehension improves when you have concrete examples or hands-on techniques during the learning process. You are probably a multi-task learner who likes to do things simultaneously and most of the time you can't be bothered with details. You probably thrive on "creative chaos" and might be quite random in your thought processing. Usually you seem somewhat disorganised and it is most likely that you also have a time management problem. To improve your school performance, set priorities, practise time management, or learn to follow certain routines, but make sure you feel good about it, and that you enjoy the learning process.

THINKING STYLE:
You have an impulsive thinking style. When you are pondering on things you tend to go off on tangents because your mind is quick and constantly creating new ideas. You may find it hard to follow one train of thought, only because you have a multi-track thinking style which allows you to mentally work on several issues at the same time. With this ability, however, you might find that your mind is easily distracted and that you may have difficulty with really focusing and concentrating on just one thing for longer periods of time. You may need to remind yourself to stay on task and organise your school and homework so that you can accommodate your quick mental processes. Fast-paced, multi-task assignments and creative learning environments would suit your thinking style very well. It is important that your parents and teachers understand your style and help you stay on track.

SENSORY MODALITIES

Drinking water is necessary for good concentration and enhanced brain functions

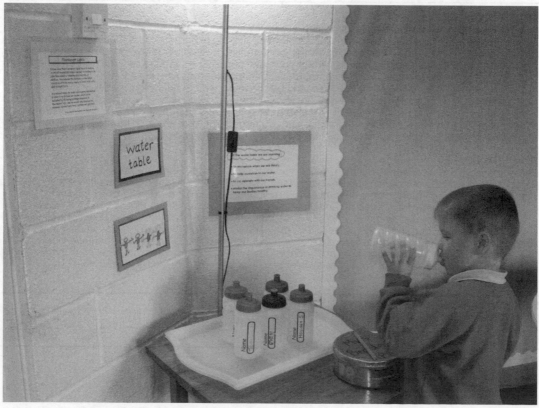

Chapter 14

How important are time preferences and the need for intake?

Once style diversity in the classroom is accepted by teachers, they need to consider that different learning needs or personal preferences have very different influences on students' behaviour and learning success. Time of day and intake are often overlooked or considered not so important because they are generally interpreted as laziness or students' fancy. This is not the case and these two elements can play an important role in a student's learning success or failure.

When strong time-of-day needs are mismatched over long periods of time, they lead to reduced concentration, fatigue and, often, an unwillingness to participate in learning or even going to school. This is particularly true for students who have a non-preference for early morning and find it very hard to concentrate at a time when their brain is not fully alert and they suffer from 'fuzzy' thinking. Many timetables favour academic subjects during the morning hours (when students are fresh and alert – so the argument goes) and teachers cannot understand that many students are 'brain dead' at this time when they themselves function best.

When students have to concentrate on new and/or difficult content at a time of day that is not their best, they will find it very hard, lose concentration easily and suffer from exhaustion. For morning learners that is no issue, but for evening people it makes all the difference for the worse: once they have spent all their energy in the morning, often to just stay awake, they have no more energy to concentrate on difficult content in the afternoon and all they do is just survive. This

leads to the false believe among teachers that for these reasons it is much better to have academic subjects in the morning because in the afternoon it is even worse. As many teenagers are evening learners, they are suffering this mismatch for years during their high school time, until it is too much and they give up or drop out.

I am fully aware that a time-of-day matching to students' biological learning needs is, as far as organizations go, a very difficult one, but awareness, multisensory teaching and some accommodation of time needs can help tremendously, even with discipline problems and truancy.

Students who have to take exams at a time of day that is not their best, are certainly disadvantaged but as this is obviously no human rights issue, these mismatches will go on, more so in high schools than in primary schools. It can only be hoped that with better understanding of style diversity, teachers learn to apply more and more strategies for reaching all students and compensate in situations that cannot be changed.

The need for intake does not seem a very important component of someone's learning style and yet, if not matched, it can cause frustration, disruption and loss of concentration. This need manifests itself not only in the need to eat, nibble and drink while learning, but more often in the need for mouth stimulation, and students who have a preference for intake will chew anything they can get hold of. Be it pens, pencils, hair, clothes, fingernails or paper, they will chew it, particularly when they are bored, frustrated or

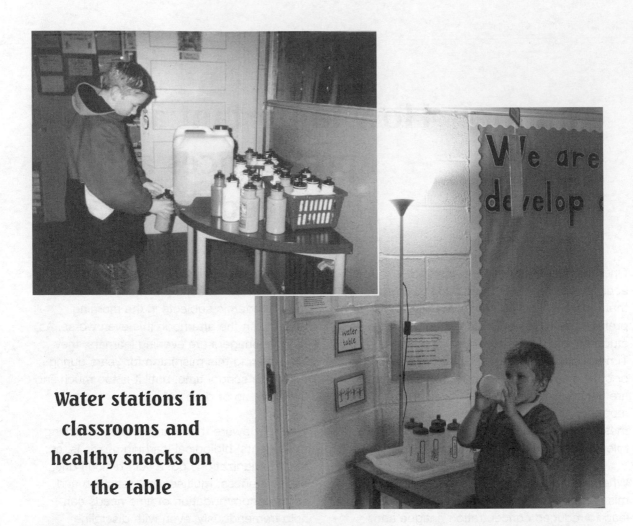

Water stations in classrooms and healthy snacks on the table

have to concentrate hard. Our observations, original research and LSA results have shown that particularly holistic, right-brain dominant students need mouth stimulation to enhance their concentration, whereas analytic, more left-brain dominant students find eating, nibbling and drinking quite distracting and do not need mouth stimulation while they learn.

Although many teachers also have a preference for intake, they do not allow their students to chew or drink during lessons and chewing gum is not permitted in most schools. If students understand their need for intake, when they accept that it is a privilege to have a water bottle or nibbles to chew on, even allowing chewing gum in classrooms will be managed differently and used responsibly without making a mess. Even if teachers do not allow any form of intake during their lessons, students who have a strong need in this area will always find something to chew and pens or fingernails are always available, whether teachers like it or not.

There is one more aspect teachers and parents need to know when it comes to the need for intake. If students also have a strong need for tactile stimulation, there is the danger that they will become smokers. To satisfy these two biological needs, cigarettes are an ideal medium and socially desirable, despite their danger to health. Once students are hooked on nicotine it is very difficult to give up this habit because the addiction is threefold: strong biological needs of intake, tactile stimulation as well as the chemical addiction in the brain and body. Under pressure, smoking increases because satisfying these needs has a calming effect, but to beat that habit, the smoker has to replace the pleasure that comes with smoking, which is most difficult and not easily achieved. As the need for intake does not go away, ex-smokers tend to eat more and often do not know what to do with their hands. It is relatively easy to satisfy the need for tactile stimulation through the use of a koosh ball or something else that can be used to fiddle with, but beating the chemical addiction is extremely difficult and sometimes impossible.

As students these days begin to smoke at an ever younger age, parents and teachers need to make them aware of this particular style combination and the dangers it can harbour. Although some people might not agree, we have seen the results in hundreds of LSA profiles: it is not peer pressure that gets young people into smoking, it is the combination of two biological style features – the need for intake/mouth stimulation and the need for tactile stimulation and finger involvement.

56	simultaneous
30	spontaneous
36	listening
60	talking/discussing
56	self-talk/inner dialogue
40	reading
36	seeing/watching
73	visualizing/imagination
53	manipulating/handling
46	experiencing/doing
66	feeling/intuition
33	movement needed
53	intake needed
30	late morning
26	afternoon
33	evening
23	sound/noise/music
33	low light
46	warm
36	informal/comfortable
20	pair
33	peers
26	team
3	unsupervised
3	externally motivated
3	spontaneous/fluctuating
0	low persistence
33	non-conforming

Extract from group profile percentages for preferences: over half the students in this class need tactile stimulation and intake (53 per cent)

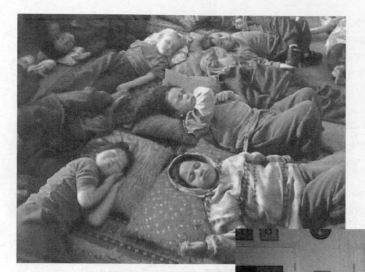

Children relax to Pachelbel's 'Canon' every day after lunch (Malfroy Primary School, Rotorua, New Zealand)

Learning about Mozart by listening to his music, while the teacher tells the story of his life and students give each other a massage (Björken Skola, Gävle, Sweden)

Auditory learners at the listening centre while other students do different activities (Rivergum Primary School, Melbourne, Australia)

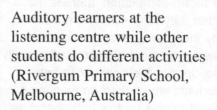

Energizing exercise with music (courtesy of Moulsecoomb Primary, Brighton, UK)

Chapter 15

What to do when students cannot work quietly and need sound

For many teachers one of the most uneasy aspects of style diversity in the classroom is the need for sound in many students. Traditionally, most academic classroom work is carried out in silence and most teachers whose LSA we have assessed internationally show a preference for quiet learning. This is in stark contrast to the needs of many students, particularly male teenagers who can concentrate much better with sound. It seems that the need for sound increases exponentially during teenage years, combined with the need for intake, especially in young males. We are not quite sure why that is so, but it is assumed it has to do with hormonal changes happening in the bodies of these young adults. Teenage girls do not seem to need that much sound and naturally prefer to learn when it is quiet. This may be linked to higher auditory preferences in females, which means they have less need for sound and often perceive background music as distracting over-stimulation.

If you are a practising classroom teacher, it will be easy to find out if your students naturally need a quiet environment or if they work better with sound or music in the background. If students' LSA profiles show a non-preference for sound, do not just accept that happily, observe what they do when they are bored or frustrated or how they learn when content is new and/or difficult for them. Do they make noises, click their pens, hum or whistle, drum with their fingers or pens, chat a lot but do not concentrate well when they have to listen or work quietly? How often do you have to say 'Quiet please!' during a regular lesson? Are they noisy before or after class? A 'yes' to any of these questions indicates that your students actually DO need sound but have been conditioned into learning in quiet environments.

Many students say they learn best in quiet classes because that is all they have ever been exposed to. They often do not even know that they could learn better with the right learning music and are not aware that they make noises because a quiet class is nearly unbearable for them.

If, however, your students work well when it is quiet, none of the previously described, often disruptive, behaviour will occur.

But what do you do when your students need sound for better academic performance?

First, ACCEPT the need for sound in many students, especially when they are more holistic, right-brain dominant. By nature, it seems, they need sound stimulation when they concentrate, and learning when it is quiet is very difficult for them. Although we often see in LSA results that students who have a right-brain dominance in their overall LS say they prefer quiet or are flexible in sound, we have discovered that a preference for quiet classrooms can also be learned and acquired over the years. The reason is simple: if students are made to learn in quiet classrooms, they will do so but with effort and are often not aware that they would function better with background music. However, those students who have a strong preference for sound stimulation will NOT be able to suppress this need and adjust to it. They will make their own sounds and noises when forced to learn in silence and will often

On a recent visit to this school in Sweden, the children gave me pictures they had drawn about their preferred LS and, interestingly enough, most of them needed sound while they were concentrating, symbolized by their earphones.

disrupt quiet work periods because anything for them is better than being quiet.

Remember: noisy students need SOUND. No matter how hard you try to keep them quiet, they will ALWAYS find something with which they can make a sound. Chatting and making noises therefore is often the simplest (but certainly not best) way to have sound stimulation.

Second, learn more about the use of music as a learning enhancement tool and how music influences the brain; find out which music is best for which learning activities; start a collection of suitable pieces for your music library; and encourage your students to also collect suitable music and use it at home during homework time. Background 'learning music' must always be INSTRUMENTAL because the lyrics of songs interfere with the words of the learning content. Please do NOT succumb to your students' pleas to be allowed to use 'their' music, which does not have the right beat and rhythm to stimulate the brain for better learning. This modern music belongs to breaks, if acceptable, and/or outside the classroom. To introduce baroque and classical music to enhance teaching for young students does not pose any problems as children accept it willingly and enjoy it, but with teenagers there can be resistance as they are more used to loud, beating music. For such situations 'bridging' music, as I call it, is very useful. For more information about suitable learning music, see my previous book *The Power of Diversity* (2004: 161–169).

Third, begin to include learning music in your classroom management according to the learning needs of your students as seen in the LSA group profile. Background music should never be loud; it has to be low in volume because it is the sound stimulation that enhances learning, not the volume of the sound.

Therefore the rule of thumb is:

the use of music for some students must never disrupt the learning of those who need it quiet.

And finally, for subgrouping students do the following:

1 If the majority in your class needs sound (all those students who have a preference and those who are flexible put together), they should be allowed to learn with background music, close to the source of sound (usually a CD player at low volume) while they are doing 'quiet' activities such as reading, writing, calculating, brainstorming, mind mapping and so on.

2 Those who need it really quiet should be seated as far away from the source of sound as possible; these students could also wear ear plugs or disconnected headsets during these activities.

3 While the teacher speaks, the music stops, the ear plugs come out and students listen to announcements or a mini lecture.

4 If there are only a few students in your class who need sound, separate them from the rest who need quiet and only under these conditions I would recommend that the few who need background music are allowed to have a Walkman, MP3 player or iPod but are only allowed to listen to the accepted learning music, approved by the teacher.

A word of caution: as soon as the use of individual, personal gadgets is allowed in a classroom, it will be very difficult for the teacher to control the music students are listening to and can be easily interpreted as a special privilege. This has to be avoided at any cost and I always recommend to use only ONE source of sound, to keep the volume low (barely audible but noticeable when the music is not there). Feedback from teachers from around the world proves that the proper use of music does enhance students' behaviour and their academic performance considerably.

Music in class has to be enjoyable and is not there for entertainment but solely to enhance students' learning.

ICT Meets VAK & T

by John Davitt

One key message for teachers will be that it's time to trust themselves. Within a curriculum framework there should be space for teachers to take the kitbag of curriculum content, learning styles, formative assessment and the tools of ICT and deploy them as they see fit to make the best difference for the children they teach. This year perhaps the theme might be fewer set ideas and more flexibility for teachers. There is a growing sense of the need to give teachers the confidence to do things differently with the new tools available. For in learning we know that one size never fits all.

The tectonic plates of curriculum fixity are once more on the move and as a result some landmass will disappear. ICT the subject may be an early casualty – for to unleash the true catalytic qualities of ICT as an agent of deep and wide learning opportunities we may need to signal its demise as a curriculum subject. Come to think of it the Victorians had few lessons on slate use or classrooms dedicated to its use. Other subject barriers will also blur, as Margaret Doran from Stirling Council asked in her statement last June to the parliamentary education committee's inquiry on the school curriculum. 'Are we to continue to teach compartmental subjects or do we develop the capacity of every teacher to teach the whole child?'

If we trust teachers to get it right in their own contexts the cross-curricular objectives of many past curriculum designers may no longer be an aspiration but an inevitability. ICT is poised as the enabling tool to make this happen. To balance rigour with flexibility is the next challenge. The model of learning which, alongside guidance from the centre, each school must develop and adjust for themselves should include range and diversity along with precision and perseverance. Some guidance in this area will come from the pragmatic use of learning styles theory.

Learning styles audits and instruments have provided us with useful tools for examining difference and preferences in learners. In addition to thinking skills and emotional intelligence work, many schools now log the learning preferences of their students and use the information gathered to inform developments in teaching and learning. A central precept to these approaches is that we all learn in slightly different ways but that patterns emerge regarding individual preferences for learning by hearing, doing, seeing and touching.

These style preferences are then given the slicker titles of auditory, kinesthetic, visual and tactile (the touchers). As if by magic, just as our knowledge and understanding of the brain and learning theory is developing, we now have new classroom tools to help us support many of its key principles. Carefully used, data projectors linked to computers can fill a classroom wall with a still or moving image and provide new opportunities for showing the big picture at the start of a lesson. Interactive whiteboards at times provide teachers and students with a visual, kinesthetic and tactile learning opportunity. Animation and sound recording allows students to bring the hands-on and the auditory alongside the textual – telling their story in a medium over which they have considerable mastery. Another challenge now is to get beyond the 'office mentality' in terms of physical environments and software used in schools.

continued on page 136

Chapter 16

How to combine LS with information communication technology (ICT)

A recent independent research report in the UK (ImpaCT2) showed that information communication technology (ICT) can help raise standards. It looked at the relationship between pupils' use of ICT and their performance in exams and the finding was that high ICT users performed better than low ICT users. The difference in performance was the equivalent of a whole term or a grade at GCSE.

Can ICT change or influence the development of LS features in students? Researchers also noted that high ICT use leads to a change in learners' learning style. The research study reports that students were able to study better by themselves and were more independent and not so reliant on a teacher to give them all the answers. One might say that is OK, but what does it really mean in the context of daily classroom practice, particularly when it comes to discipline problems and low learning motivation? To me it seems dangerous making such statements and drawing conclusions without having a good knowledge base of what LS actually are.

But it gets better. The British Council website states: 'ICT is changing the learning styles of many UK classrooms. Teachers are doing less of the talking, students are doing more work in pairs or groups and students are finding out more information by themselves, guided by a teacher.'

This is a typical case of mixing up teaching practices and learning strategies. Even IF teachers do less talking, does this actually mean they are 'changing' their students'

learning styles? Does it not mean that teachers are actually using more matched instructions and does that mean ALL students then benefit from such strategies all the time?

Analytic vs holistic thinking

When it comes to internal information processing, learners will always use either sequential/analytic or impulsive/holistic brain processing and will either need to reflect or think simultaneously about the learning content. Therefore ICT learning situations and course organization need to take these style differences into account and digital resources must be used with an understanding of students' LS differences. Understanding and application of learning styles in a digital world can support students' learning activities and personalized learning should be offered, particularly in distance learning.

Sensory modalities and ICT

How we perceive and how we process information constitutes the uniqueness of our learning style, our most comfortable way to learn new and difficult information. Even if we agree that learning is more than an information transmission process, we need to look at how students can optimize their learning capacity in ICT through using their personal LS in learning situations they perceive as difficult.

Here is what we could call the core elements of the LSA model:

- the area of perception (Sensory Modalities)

Perhaps if Microsoft were really serious about education they would develop some software called 'School'. For much of what we have at present from most software providers are specific suites of software developed for the business world given a retread and sold to schools as state of the art. This would be OK if schools and offices were similar but of course schools are far more challenging and complex places. Perhaps the homonym ossification meaning 'hardened conventionality' gives us a clue as to the software cycle we need to break out of. 'Officacation' is the enemy of flexibility.

We have hardware aplenty but our software toolset is still poor in terms of providing cognitive challenge. What we need now are software tools which make it easy to integrate media, show up connections and share. Software that allows students and teachers to mark up existing resources such as web pages and images and add value through annotation and linking. A resource that allows you to tell and share your story in the tools for your time from Stornaway to Soweto. Ideally these new tools should be open source (free to all and non-proprietary) and built around open file formats like the JPEG for pictures and MP3 file format for sound. There is a historical precedent.

Way back in 1700s ships could navigate but not accurately because longitude, that second fix on position, was still 60 years from discovery. Without it no captain knew with certainty the position of his craft and many ships foundered. In one sense we live in similar times – technology allows learners to cover great distance at a single mouse click – we can copy and paste with ease and send messages to flit the globe – but often genuine challenge is missing and we are not sure where we are or what to do with what we have found. The longitude prize was a prize offered by the British government in 1714 for the precise determination of a ship's longitude. Here's an idea … why not get government and commercial sponsorship for a prize for the development of software to help us find our digital longitude. Free to the world, open source … unsponsored … allowing learners to turn resources into unique and shareable learning maps. That might help diversity at the heart of the curriculum.

> *'Compromise does not satisfy, but dissatisfies everybody; it does not lead to any general fulfilment, but to general frustration; those who try to become everything to all people end up by not being anything to anyone.'*
>
> *Ayn Rand*

- the area of processing (Brain Dominance).

Both of these are crucial for the organization of e-learning itself and the choice of ICT tools.

If we consider the senses in this context (visual/auditory/tactile/kinesthetic) as a 'filter' through which information is taken in, then they must be used in designing computer and web-based learning materials. The only modality that cannot be accommodated yet through a computer is K – kinesthetic (learning with and through the whole body). Although one could say virtual reality programs with holographic displays come close, they are still not REALITY, no matter how 'real' they might seem.

Blended learning

This is where 'blended learning' is so important for many students. As teachers involved in ICT are well aware, this is learning that combines online and face-to-face approaches, and, as I see it, this is the only way to accommodate learning needs of highly kinesthetic learners.

They need to get away from the computer, move their body and DO something with the information they have just received via the screen. Learning sessions for these students will be successful only (and hopefully lead to understanding, skills, competencies and knowledge) when they have physically experienced and/or done something.

Generally, blended learning gives greater choice in delivery methods and leads to greater complexity, but learning situations will vary. As John Helmer in an article in the Think Tank Series in 2003 states: blended learning offers a multiplicity of paths towards a common goal – supporting individual learning styles – some blends will necessarily be strictly sequential. For full report see
www.epic.co.uk

Male and female differences

Are there differences between males and females in learning or working with ICT? Microsoft research (2002 and 2003) has revealed the following: there are gender differences in navigating through 3D environments – women are 20 per cent faster in navigating 3D environments on computers when they have large screens and optical flow cues or continuous visual cues for navigation. This is particularly important for graphic design, architectural walk-throughs, games and various e-learning programs. The general conclusion is that both males and females can navigate through desktops more efficiently when using large screen displays that offer a wider field of view.

Apart from these gender differences it is also interesting to find out how boys and girls learn to use computers – if they do it in the same way and how they assess their own computer skills. This overview has been conducted on the basis of data from the PISA 2003 survey, focusing on young 15 year olds in 18 countries in the Eurydice Network.

The general findings were: almost all young people in that age group have already used a computer. Boys have done so for longer and more frequently than girls. There was no difference found between boys and girls in regard to communication and word processing but significant differences in the case of games and programming. In general, boys use computers more often than girls to play games, but also to look up information. Downloading music or software is far more frequent among boys in all countries and boys more often use graphics programs. Boys said that they mainly learned to use the computer alone or with a friend, while girls report they have mainly done so at school or with their family. For full report see
www.eurydice.org

Finally I would like to invite readers to reflect on the following question:

Can a sound knowledge of learning styles change technology-driven teaching (which e-learning often is) into REAL learning?

Integration of VATK and MI in a Learning Cycle (Tapanui Primary, NZ)

Learning Outcomes   **Activities**

- identify, describe different jobs workers do
  { 1. CLASS TRIP – look for –   What jobs people do   Video
    2. VIEW VIDEO – what jobs did we see workers doing?   What they use/need   digital camera
                                                           Why they use this
                                                           – do this
                                                           – need this

- sequence activities that make up a system
  { 3. DIGITAL PHOTOS – in small groups
         ✆ what is happening
         ✆ how it is being done
         ✆ why it is being done

- suggest reasons why it is done this way
    4. PUT PHOTOS/CAPTIONS IN SEQUENCE What do you think happens next? Cut and paste activity to form flow chart

    5. POTS FOR BLUBS – newsprint papier mâché pots
       – torn magazine paper and colour
       – cut flower/leaf outlines
       – stick around pot
       – varnish

                                                                          PLANT
                                                                          BULBS IN
                                                                          POTS
- identify parts of bulb plants
- describe needs of bulb plants and how they grow
  { 6. NEEDS OF PLANTS – Clearfile in big book ─────────►
       Active/Passive concert – sunlight
                              – food (soil)
                              – water

    7. SHOW WHAT YOU KNOW – about bulbs and bulb plants
       – draw pictures with labels
       – make a mind map
       – write a story
       – make a flow chart
       – make a model
       – match captions/story
       – question cards – reporters in pairs

Multiple Intelligences and V–A–T–K:

Kinesthetic:	field trip
Visual:	Learning tools – Photo/drawing Complete caption sequence/captions match
Audio:	Learning tool – reporters activity/class book
Tactile:	Learning tool – wheel/bulb pot making
Linguistic:	Write thank you letters/captions/story
Musical:	Create a rap or song about planting bulbs
Vis/Spatial:	Workers drawings
Math/Logical:	Measurement – plant growth
Bodily/Kines:	Field trip/learning tool activities/bulb pots
Intrapersonal:	Reflecting on whole unit
Interpersonal:	Reporting back session/small group captioning
Naturalist:	Field trip/study of plants–bulbs

Chapter 17

How to integrate LS and multiple intelligences

Before a discussion about the integration of LS and multiple intelligences (MI), it is necessary to clarify a few misunderstandings that have surrounded these two concepts ever since MI were introduced by Howard Gardner in the early 1980s. This has led to widespread confusion among educators who were keen to achieve better learning outcomes from their students but at the same time were struggling with the notion of intelligence in multiple forms as well as the concept of style diversity and different learning needs in the classroom.

Although in many references, and particularly on many websites, LS and MI are being described as one and the same or at least 'interchangeable', the informed educator will be aware that this is far from reality and will agree that the differences between LS and MI are very pronounced.

Following are the points of distinction:

a) MI is a theoretical framework for defining, understanding, assessing and developing people's different intelligence factors.

b) MI does not give information about the specific learning needs a student has during the information intake process (that is, how the classroom environment needs to be set up for making learning successful; which time of day is best for concentrating; which physical needs will enhance or diminish study success).

c) MI does not give insight into students' analytic/holistic thinking styles and brain dominance.

d) MI does not provide an in-depth understanding of students' learning attitudes and how they respond to authority, which is very important for successful learning processes.

e) The learning style analysis (LSA) gives a diagnosis about someone's best way of learning (personal preferences during the process of information intake) and provides guidelines (also called 'prescriptions') for improving academic achievement.

f) Knowledge about a certain combination of preferred LS elements can predict school success or failure and identify underachievement in traditional school systems.

g) LSA reveals flexibilities, preferences and non-preferences in 49 different areas that can significantly contribute to a student's success or failure in learning.

h) Students with similar intelligence factors in the MI framework can have vastly different learning styles, based on their personal biological make-up and their individual conditioning.

i) LSA results can be divided into *biological or natural* and *learned or conditioned* style elements (which can change over time in contrast to biological ones which have a tendency to remain fairly stable over a lifetime); this is an important feature that the MI framework does not have because no one knows for sure what 'intelligence' really is and how it develops in human beings. There is also more research-

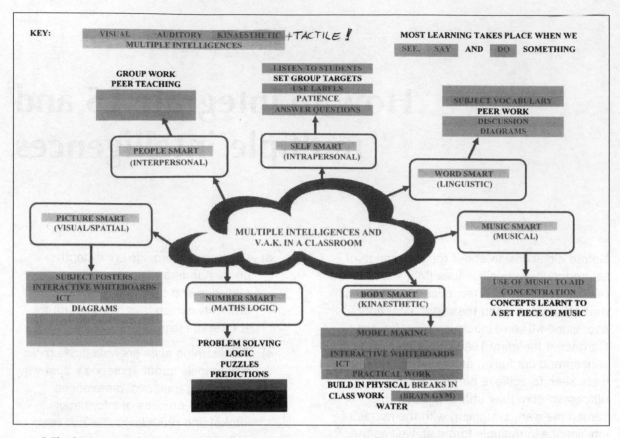

Mind map used as overview for teachers at Broughton Hall High School, Liverpool

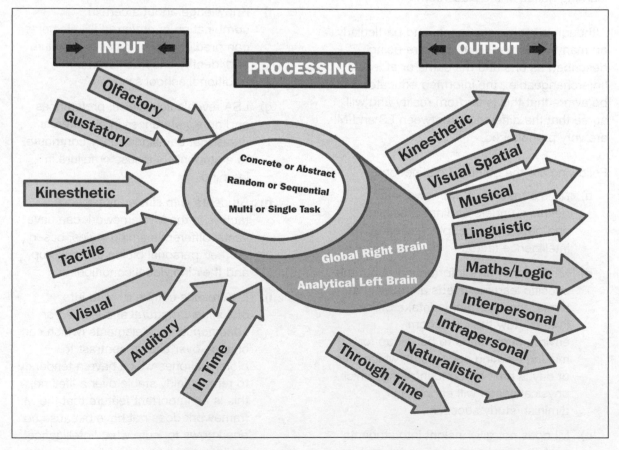

Information processing showing input through senses and output via MI, based on course handout from M. Scaddan, Auckland

based information available about LS but it would be interesting to find out if a certain combination of LS features correlates with a certain combination of MI factors. If readers are interested to carry out such research, I would be prepared to contribute with my knowledge and our various LSA instruments. Please contact me at barbara.prashnig@clc.co.nz for more details.

j) MI has more to do with the OUTPUT of information – maths, musical, linguistic 'talent' combined with skills and special 'gifts' – whereas LS reveal information on INTAKE/INPUT capabilities in human beings, which cannot be described as 'intelligence' but as 'personal preferences'. It is therefore no longer appropriate to say a student who learns/reads/works better in dim light with music in the background while moving around and chewing or fiddling with something is less intelligent than a student who concentrates better in bright light and silence, by sitting still and eating/drinking/chewing only before or after a learning session. Regrettably, many gifted students who do not fit the norm and have an 'unfortunate' or 'strange' learning style have been misjudged by their teachers, not only these days but also, or even more so, in the past. There are many historic reports about so-called school failures and 'uneducatable' students who later became geniuses after leaving behind the constraints of formal education, intellectually surpassing their teachers on many levels.

Once the difference between LS and MI is understood and accepted, it will not be hard for teachers to combine these two concepts as the classroom work of many of the graduates of my 'Diploma in Holistic Education' course shows in the samples presented opposite.

A good guideline for personalizing learning is to always remember that a profound knowledge of learning styles is invaluable for information intake and reinforcing curriculum content. Multiple intelligences, however, can be applied for practising, demonstrating and enhancing content that has been learned in various ways and is best used to show how 'smart' students are.

The most important aspect for a successful integration is that the combined application of LS and MI starts with the lesson planning and needs to be considered in every lesson of every teaching unit to do justice to the learning diversity and developmental potential of students' intelligence factors. Whenever teachers plan to deliver curriculum content, they have to ask themselves if they are catering for their students' different learning styles, particularly when content is new and/or difficult. It is most important to plan for multisensory delivery, to build movement into the learning process whenever possible, to allow fiddling and chewing without causing disruption and to use music for those who need it and when it is appropriate to enhance learning. When classroom environments are set up to cater for students' LS preferences at the beginning of a school year, they do not need to be considered in planning any longer because such classrooms will in any case enhance the learning process.

Teaching with matched instructions to students' learning styles will allow teachers to cater for those who need their help most and will free them to incorporate MI approaches in the form of different 'learning stations', which will enable students to practise their skills in many different ways (with words or music, with numbers, visually or with their body, by themselves or with others).

Encouraging students to show their skills in many different ways will certainly help in developing different intelligence factors, particularly during the early years in education. Combined with personalized instructions, it will not only increase their learning motivation and enrich their classroom experiences but also create long-term memory and guarantee school success.

Marvellous Me Unit Outline (traditional lesson planning)

Level 4	Y8	8 lessons

Overview: A human biology unit on the main body systems and special emphasis on the brain and how it learns.

Assessment:
- Bookwork
- TechnoBody task – set as homework for the duration of the unit. No other homework set.
- (IG Processing, Reporting, Technology application)

Lesson overview:
1. Intro – Vital statistics, calculating averages...
2. Who am I? What am I made of? Cells-tissues-organs-systems
   Main systems...
   Skeleton
   Muscles and movement
3. Circulatory system – heart, blood and vessels – immune system
4. Respiratory system – lungs and breathing, gas exchange – CV link
5. Digestive system – eating to pooing – provision of energy
6. Excretory system – skin, fighting disease, urine and sweating, sebaceous glands, lymph system, etc + Immune system
7. Nervous system – the brain as master computer, nerves, stimulus and response, impulses, the senses and organs associated.
8. The brain and how it learns – learning theory – holistic approach – L/R brain dominance

H Beamish 04/02

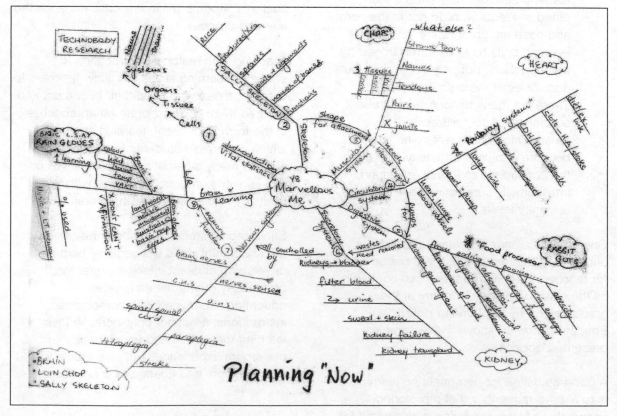

Lesson planning for a learning cycle with a mind map

Chapter 18

How to fit LS into a full learning cycle

Repackaging teaching content

The reflections of the 'Unit on the Brain' (see overleaf) by Pam Shand, a primary school teacher in Glenorchie, NZ, show clearly that it takes time to 're-package' teaching content into a fully integrated learning cycle.

For several days before we actually started I mentioned to the children that this unit would be beginning. There was mixed eagerness as we had done work on this topic last year…

My teaching assistant, Marian, could not actually be with us during the delivery and my children and I started alone. We spent the first morning (about an hour and fifteen minutes) setting the scene and doing the Prelude (or Overview as part of Houston Model lesson planning). For this the children moved all the tables back and sat in a circle. As we went through the exercises there was some restlessness, inattention and calling out – what I might expect from this group of fairly immature, self-conscious children. Nevertheless, some excellent attention was observed – and with it some good learning.

My question is: Was this restlessness generated by the new topic and especially the new format? Or was it more to do with my inexpert delivery? It will be interesting to notice what happens in the next cycle. In the next topic I will also include more visual charts – I only used the whiteboard this time.

On day two we had a brief review and did both concerts. We have included three different versions of the concert script. Marian did a wonderful job of writing the initial script but I found, as I rehearsed it, I needed to make changes for my voice, the way I read, and my own sense of information flow.

Re-writing this script into Suggestopedic style (as requested by Barbara Prashnig) was too difficult for the time available so I asked my husband to help out (the computer whiz!). He edited further and included diagrams. The concerts went well with a surprising amount of co-operation from the children (unfortunately there were three who were positively silly in the corner, which distracted my attention terribly … most of the others were relaxed and focused. I believe I had the music in the passive concert too low, and my voice too loud … perhaps part of the problem?). After the concerts we took a short break, and came back into stations where all our self-made learning tools were set up.

As the children worked with materials I realized that I had not planned sufficiently for this stage. Some of the exercises required only a couple of minutes to finish, where others required ten minutes or more. So I was calling for a rotation long before some were ready, and long after others had got bored and restless.

Next time I would spot these difficulties and extend easy exercises with reading material and questions for discussion; or I would simply ensure that the materials used in the rotation required much the same time.

For more information on the Suggestopedic learning cycle see the CLC website:
🖱 www.creativelearningcentre.com

Learning Activities (by Pam Shand)

Learning Activities (by Pam Shand)	Learning Styles Tools	Content	Primary Activators
Introduction: (25-30 mins) Welcome to topic Expectations – During topic Brain Gym® – centring exercise What I know about the brain… sharing circle Vocabulary Display the SLOs Discuss use of music	(1 hour initial ongoing on following days) Jigsaw Task cards (Videos Posters (with labels) Flip chute Peg activity Synaptic tag	Parts of the brain & location Parts and function Parts, function & anatomy Parts and function Parts and function Parts and function synapse	T T A/V V/T/K T T/V K
Instructions (10 mins)	Hand-link synaptic tag PowerPoint presentation	Synapse function Parts and function	K V/T
Prelude (30-40 mins) Introduction of teaching content Why the brain is important Reptilian/ Mammalian brain/Neo cortex	**Reporting back**		**Secondary Activators** (Max 1 week)
BIG PICTURE: the first delivery of information Delivered by CONCERT **Active Concert** Vivaldi: Spring (5 mins) Parts of the brain (hemispheres, lobes, rep/mamm/cortex) Function of these parts Brain waves Neurons	The children will select options from a contract and choose their own mode of reporting what they have learned. The modes for reporting are linked to multiple intelligences		
Relaxation 2 minutes no talking			
Passive Concert Pachelbel: Canon (5 mins) Children relaxed and lying/sitting comfortably			
Activation (2 x 30 mins) ACTIVITIES Swim cap – draw parts of the brain Songs – neuron parts, function, how it works Team relay message game Reflex game with ruler	Songs Audio taped information Models Colouring-in Learning Styles Tools Interactive use	Parts and function Parts and function Parts and function Parts and function	A A/K V/T V/T

A different focus

Robyn Sinclair, a primary support teacher, reflects on her teaching unit about a volcanic eruption:

- The first session involved giving the big picture of what they were expected to do for the next few weeks. I tried to give positive messages about the skills they had learned in the action learning unit last term with regards to research skills. I also talked about the PowerPoint presentation they did previously. As they had all these skills, the learning now would be easy! Rules were revised to ensure all the students knew the expectations of the teacher and that the learning environment was conducive for all learning styles.

- To create a mental map, children drew on their existing knowledge and drew a mind map. Using inspirations, students were able to add visual stimuli for remembering and organizing their information in a personal and fun way. Before the students started I modelled the use of the software and reminded them of appropriate search items when researching, especially helpful when searching the internet, setting them up for success. Posters were displayed to help students. Using the computer to mind map motivated and interested the students.

- Using a puppet for tactile learners, students talked about what they already knew. The concert reading (as an information storing exercise) had already taken place and this gave a good basis for existing knowledge. This session worked well as the students were able to focus on the task ahead.

- During the research session, students were able to move freely between the computer and library rooms. They were able to sit at tables of various heights, sit on cushions and on the floor. There were opportunities to sit by the window for natural light or fresh air, sit under heaters or in low light. A water fountain is close by the library. The students were able to access information from books, posters, CD-ROMs and websites. Cordless headphones gave the students opportunities to listen. Students then added new information to their existing mind map. Learning style tools were available to help students consolidate learning on the Mt Tarawera disaster. The PowerPoint quiz also appealed to all students and was a great success.

- Students presented their information using PowerPoint – a highly visual and auditory tool. Students could add voice-over and pictures, as well as words to communicate their knowledge. The learning styles game on PowerPoint tools helped the tactile learners to remember what each button did.

- As I was not the classroom teacher, I did not conduct the active and passive concert reading exercise although I was fully involved in the writing of the concert. My role was to support the learning cycle within my one-hour session with the class each week.

- Overall, the unit was a great success, students learned a lot and we had fun.

Improving students' learning

The following short evaluation of learning cycles used in teaching units is from Pat Whyte and Ngahuia Hana from Hawera Primary in NZ:

Learning tools are used at every stage in the learning process, to transfer content to long-term memory, reinforce concepts, for self-assessment, to review previous learning and to raise interest. Most units have students creating LS tools as a learning task. One of the greatest outcomes for us from your Diploma and the new teaching was the activation of learning within ourselves. We are now constantly reviewing our teaching to be in line with the needs of our students, and so our teaching practices are ever evolving. The growth in our students this year has been incredible. We have some students who came to us with a reading age of eight years and below. Most of these are now reading at above their chronological age, 11–12 years. Our maths class, one of the lowest achieving

PERIOD	CONCEPT/ACTIVITY	VISUAL AIDS/ TEACHING MATERIALS	MUSIC	V – A – K – T	MULTIPLE INTELLIGENCE 1 – 2 – 3 – 4 – 5 – 6 – 7
1/2	• Introduction mind map/ list of learning objectives	Poster/ visual display	Introductory		
	• Revision of meanings	Cut & match sheet	Baroque		
	• Periodic table familiarisation	Periodic table poster Periodic table blanks	Baroque		
	• Element flip cards	Chutes	Baroque		
	• Element Bingo	Bingo set	None		
3	• Lesson introduction mind map/ list	Poster/ visual display	Introductory		
	• Make up mixture of $CuCO_3$ and water. Separate by filtering. Complete write-up sheet	Chemicals and equipment available	Bright and bouncy eg beatles on strings		
	• Make up solution of $CuCl_2$ and water. Separate by evaporation. Complete write up sheet		Star wars themes		
4	• Lesson introduction mind map/ list	Poster/ visual display	Introductory		
	• Melt and solidify wax. Write up	materials and equipment available	Bright and bouncy		
	• Evaporate and condense water. Write up.				
5	• Lesson introduction mind map/ list	Poster/ visual display	Introductory		
	• Heat potassium permanganate, check with glowing splint Write up	materials and equipment available	Bright and bouncy		
	• React calcium with water. Write				
6	• Lesson introduction mind map/ list	Poster/ visual display	Introductory		
	• React carbonate with acid. Bubble gas through lime water. Write up	materials and equipment available	Bright and bouncy		
	• React Magnesium with acid. Do pop test. Write up.				
	• Active/ passive concert		Romantic/ baroque ↓		
7	• Revision with learning tools	Electro-board Cards Learning wheels	Romantic.		
8	• test				

Multiple Intelligence
1 Interpersonal
2 Intrapersonal
3 Bodily kinesthetic
4 Verbal linguistic
5 Logical mathematical
6 Rythmic – musical
7 Visual spatial.

Jeannette Vos
Learning Cycle

Lesson plan for chemistry combining MI and VATK by Brain Waller, Taradale High School, NZ

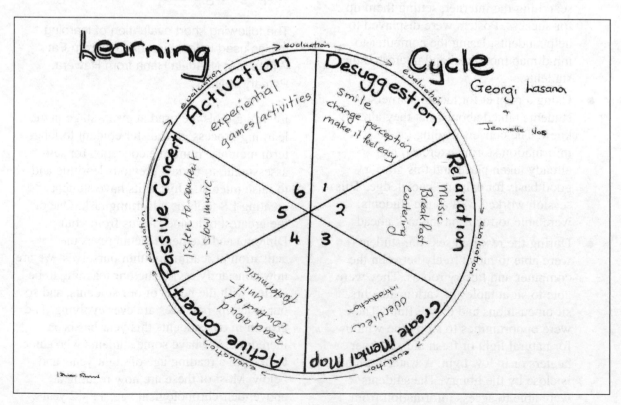

Lesson plan following G. Lozanor's Suggestopedic learning cycle by Pam Shand

(our school streams for maths) is now operating at a level where other teachers are questioning our assessment levels.

Golf and LS

Even in golf coaching a learning cycle with considerations of LS can be applied as Wayne Thomas, professional golf coach, Melbourne, Australia, describes:

Everything begins with a thought, notion or concept. I find most golfers are unknowingly working from unworkable concepts. They can put these unworkable concepts to action but they do not produce the kind of results they anticipate and learn a false sense of what they think themselves capable of. It is important to clear all unworkable concepts and then put in place concepts that are workable, test them, observe the outcomes, refine and do the process all over again until a workable repeatable swing motion is in place and becomes second nature. Most students are amazed at what they can achieve and produce with their golf in a very small space of time when workable concepts are in place.

I use a specific learning cycle every lesson:

1 **Introduction** for new students involves taking down personal details and discussing where they are at with their golf and ascertaining what they would like to achieve short term and long term. With students who are having ongoing lessons the introduction takes the form of a review from the last lesson and what progress has been made.

2 **Preparation** to ascertain what subject the student wishes to address, what their expectations are for this lesson and what outcomes they wish to achieve and then to do some warm-up exercises.

3 **Clearing** any unworkable concepts and what impact they are having on a learner's playing success is most important at that point: identifying what the student believes is the problem, what they have done in the past to rectify it and what results were achieved doing this.

4 **Information** is the instruction using sensory-rich material in many forms and has the student able to demonstrate what they have learned using any means they need. It could be a physical demonstration, they may verbalize the material or they may write it down in word or picture form.

5 **Application** is the doing, self-assessing and making appropriate corrections under guidance until desirable results are achieved.

6 **Review** is a summary of the lesson, what was achieved, and students demonstrate certainty on how to follow the pattern of the lesson in their practice.

7 **Celebration** is very important in anchoring the positive results achieved with an emotion that serves the person well assisting with recall.

In every lesson I use many visual aids and assist to retrain the many visual illusions a golfer experiences and interprets. I also notice these visual interpretations will then be processed into a tactile or kinesthetic sense and that this needs to be trained or retrained.

A syndicate evaluation of the clothing unit at Glendowie Primary, Auckland, NZ is provided below.

This unit was very successful in that it catered for many of the children's different learning styles. During the introduction to the unit children could respond both orally and with the use of koosh balls for those tactile learners. It was interesting to note the different responses to the koosh ball, from constant fiddling, holding still or preferring not to hold it while responding with their ideas.

The instruction part of the unit provided the opportunity to discuss how the unit would be taught and the variety of learning experiences the children would partake in. The class also used this time to revise class rules for working in groups, book work and so on. This enabled the analytic learners to have a good understanding of what was expected of them, while allowing the holistic learner an overview of the learning experiences.

The content of the lesson was taught using a wide range of learning experiences allowing children to use their different learning styles.

Activation-Learning Style Activities

Auditory Learners	Students	
Make their own tape that explains Anzac Day What When Why Share tape recording with the class	Luke Melissa Robert Sharna	Bijay Megan Aaron Leah
Visual Learners	**Students**	
Create a postcard from Gallipoli Write a letter home	Hayden Rawinia Frances Samara Elizabeth	Jared Alesha Charlene Danetta
Tactile Learners	**Students**	
Question/Answer puzzle-self correcting Flip chute cards Electroboard	Kiri Cameron Jordan P Michael	Bevan Paniora Jamie Jade
Kinesthetic		
Make Anzac biscuits Wrap the biscuits with a thought or feeling about Anzac Look up web site for anecdotes	Tyro Jorda Fom	

Sharing Circles

We have a sharing time most days before or after braingym.

The children use a speaking token- either a wand, a koosh ball or a small puppet.

Every Monday morning, we use our sharing circle to talk about our weekends and our sporting achievements. Other sharing circles are used for "I feel like saying..."

Activities ranged from group-work to individual, written to tactile activities, with the use of both visual and auditory stimuli. Children were allowed to select a number of activities based on their preferred learning style.

The concert reading exercises provided the opportunity for knowledge to be revised. This is an area that is new to both the children and ourselves and certainly one which will be involved in the writing of the concerts, especially looking at turning them into poems or songs. As we become more familiar with the different sources of music available we believe we will gain greater confidence with using the concerts.

Our planned technology unit about clothing provided an ideal way for the children to evaluate their learning from the fabric and fibres unit. By designing and labelling their own protective clothing they showed that they understood the different materials that make up different types of clothing and the different properties of fabrics.

Another teacher at Glendowie Primary describes how learning styles have helped in various ways.

Since completing the holistic learning styles course I have made some changes to my programme. It has made me more aware of how my children learn and what they need to learn best. It has also highlighted my particular learning style, which has greatly benefited me in completing my Bachelor of Teaching studies this year.

I believe that teachers who teach in junior classrooms already have a good grasp of the basic philosophies behind learning styles. I have always had a bright, stimulating and 'hands on' classroom. Hopefully one that encourages a range of learning and enthusiasm from the children I teach.

There are aspects of my teaching style that are learning styles friendly and other more traditional attitudes/methods that were learned from my days at Teachers Training College. I believe that my teaching style enables me to accept ideas and, where necessary, implement them into my classroom programme. Below are some ways I have implemented learning styles into my classroom, some of which I have always used.

Mobility: The children are given times during the day where they can move about and times when they need to be stationary. I have moved furniture around the room to create areas with more space to allow more freedom of movement.

Intake: The children are allowed to get a drink when necessary during the day, although because of the age of the children, I don't allow them to have food or drink in the classroom. We have 'drink breaks' where the children have five minutes to eat or drink before continuing with their work.

Sound: We have quiet times and busy times in the classroom depending on what we are doing. I have used music in the classroom during SSR, writing and handwriting. Jeff Clarkson's 'Soft Focus' has been very useful.

Light and temperature: Obviously this is very reliant on the set-up of the classroom. These are the two areas of learning styles I personally struggle with. I need to work in an environment that is well lit and warm and realize that this will not always suit all my students.

Study area: My hobby tables and cushions allow the children to choose where they would work best (where possible). This also allows children to also choose who they would like to work with (when possible).

Social: I have begun to give the children more choice in the person they would like to work with. The emphasis being on making 'good choices' about the people we work best with.

Sensory modalities: I have tried to make resources or plan programmes that better cater for the learning style needs of the children – particularly being aware of the kinesthetic learners and their need to be moving and physically involved. I have tried using some quick games to assist with this and found it helps all the children with their concentration when they have a short break between activities.

'Learning-Scapes' in Kindergarten Settings

David Spraggs, Teaching Services Manager,
Tauranga Regional Free Kindergarten Association, NZ

When I began the Diploma of Holistic Education with Barbara Prashnig, I was hoping for some further insights into learners and the learning process. This was achieved within Barbara's programme.

In my current work I support kindergarten teachers with their programmes for 3- to 5-year-old children. One of the things we hold dear to ourselves as kindergarten teachers is a focus on how children learn (the learning process) rather than curriculum content (knowledge). This means that for someone in my role, who is charged with provocation so that practitioner work is enhanced, I need to be extremely clear and articulate in what could constitute a barrier for the learning process. Through the insights that Barbara shared, I have been able to continue to get teachers to reflect on what could be happening for children in their care.

A particular focus I have used within the last couple of years is to get practitioners to think about the 'learning-scapes'. They are made up of various elements and these elements have been used for room set-up in numerous reports back to my teachers and have included:

■ The Lightscape

This has included discussion about the qualities of light being provided in the kindergarten and the impact this can have of various children's thinking processes. We have talked about separate light switching so that banks of lights can be switched off. We have also talked about the types of light being used and the possibilities of replacing some 'fluorescents' with 'incandescents'.

■ The Soundscape

It focuses on the sound that children have that envelops them throughout the processes of learning within a play environment. Attention has been focused on teachers making specific decisions about the music they use within the programme and why these specific pieces of music. We have also focused on what qualities of sound should be available for children and whether small portable sound systems have the quality of sound reproduction to allow the sound to be useful for children. Speaker placement has also been a focus in many kindergartens with discussions centring around switches to turn on and off speakers positioned on the ceiling to face the floor so that sound is limited to areas within the environment rather than 'blaring across' the play environment. Teachers are being very thoughtful about choices they now make in regard to the types of music they utilize with children and the power that music can have to settle a group or 'wind a group up'.

■ The Scentscape

Scent or smell within the environment is something that has been tackled in a number of environments. Some kindergartens are now thinking about the smells that they can utilize to support children and adults in their environment. Some are utilizing oil burners and so on to produce the range of scents that support learning within the kindergarten.

continued on page 152

Chapter 19

Examples of LS use in different educational settings

LS in preparatory schools

Jim Boyd, Head of Year 8 and Head of English, Millfield Preparatory School, UK

To say that I had been searching for LS for almost 20 years is only a slight exaggeration. Early in my teaching career I wanted to know why some lessons worked well with one group and not with another. Why could a higher set take longer to grasp certain concepts than a much lower set? I had a hunch that there must be a deeper explanation than the 'time of day', 'mood of pupils' that was often given. Learning styles are not the complete answer but they are a huge leap forward.

I have presented them at Millfield as a buoyancy aid. That is how I see them. They enable children to stay afloat and then their energies can be directed at moving through the water, reaching each island of knowledge and understanding in turn. They become more effective learners and far less stressful and stressed-out pupils.

As I was the co-coordinator of our 'gifted and talented' pupils I decided to try the approach initially on them. The top scholars were introduced to the concept and completed the questionnaire. The findings and recommendations were presented and discussed with parents. The class took to it immediately, making their own koosh balls and standing, kneeling, sitting or lying to complete tasks. Their feeling was that they were, as one pupil said, 'learning without even realizing it'. One pupil's parents were very resistant to my suggestions. They

insisted that their 13-year-old daughter study at her desk, in silence in her bedroom. Her profile indicated that she preferred background noise and possibly company. She was crying out for a different approach. I suggested that they allow their daughter one week without restraint and to check the results. The following week she completed her work lying behind the sofa with the TV on for background noise. The parents were surprised at the improvement in her work but mainly the immediate cessation of the need to 'nag' her to complete it. Their daughter was awarded a top academic scholarship to Millfield and her parents are converts. All the pupils' levels of attainment improved, not a single child underperformed.

After this success I moved on to other groups with overall general success and individual cases of dramatic success. One highly analytical boy used to drive teachers and his parents to distraction with his seemingly irrelevant questions. His parents were convinced that he was asking these questions to avoid getting down to his work. When I explained that their boy needed to clear away this clutter and that these things were important, they agreed to spend five minutes at the start of 'home/own work' answering all his questions. They were delighted with the change and even called me a genius! I am convinced that all pupils and parents who approached the concept with an open mind benefited enormously and their homes were certainly more peaceful. One set of houseparents in one of our boarding houses now has two rooms set aside for prep – one a quiet, formal area and the other an informal area. Conflict has not arisen because the

■ The Texturescape

This aspect is focused around what it is that children can access that is supporting the tactile learner. Is there a range of surfaces and materials that allow for differing sensations through the body and skin? In my opinion we, as teachers, have been very good at this over the years but with little in the way of cognitive thought about it. My focus has been to bring this back into the current thinking base for our teachers.

■ Learning styles

This has supported my beliefs around teachers teaching the way they best learn. We have many conversations after observing in our various kindergartens about the learning styles of children and there is observable evidence that teachers are supporting all the combinations of learning styles and modalities within their programme. We have also supported teachers in thinking about and identifying their own learning styles and what this means for their teaching. This has also meant that as a senior teacher I have had to be clear about my learning style and model how this can impact on teacher learning as much as the teacher's learning style/modality can impact on the child. Parents have appreciated some of the information that our teachers have shared with them through learning portfolios about possible preferences that their children have been exhibiting, which can then be used to have conversations between the parent and the school their child may attend in the future. Learning modalities and styles have also made our teachers more aware of the fact that there are many ways that children can learn.

Other interesting facets have been the discussions with teachers about the 'bad behaviour' they sometimes have to deal with, and whether in fact this behaviour is different to their expectations and could it be alluding to the child's preferred learning style.

Experiential learning for young ones

children have to produce the goods; their work has to improve and it does. By using the pupils' learning styles as a negotiating tool, prep time has become more productive and peaceful.

Staff have been encouraged to embrace little concepts one at a time and see the difference. At the very least there is a greater understanding of why children fiddle, draw, fidget. More positive staff have begun to have certain areas of their classroom divided and are consulting individual profiles whenever difficulties arise. Learning tools have been popular with children especially the wrap-around as an aid to revision. There does, however, continue to be a hard core of staff, mercifully in single figures, who refuse to alter something that has 'worked' for years.

I personally have a greater understanding of children as learners, it has removed stress from my teaching, they are no longer fiddling because they can't be bothered to listen, they are fiddling in order to listen. My classroom is far less stressful because students know that as long as their style does not adversely affect anyone else, they can relax and start to perform and learn efficiently and happily. What more can I say except thank you, Barbara.

LS in primary/elementary schools

The following reflections of LS teacher Keshena Mallouhi from Rivergum Primary School, Melbourne, Australia, show that the long road of implementing LS is not always easy but certainly worth every effort.

Learning styles was presented to me as a new methodology of teaching that altered HOW to teach but not WHAT to teach. By this I mean that the curriculum itself remained the same; however, the form that each lesson took was different. Initially, I was daunted yet excited by the process. I was overwhelmed with questions about how LS and hands-on components could be implemented in the upper years of our primary school. How on earth could I make division learning styles-friendly? How could I make my classroom bright, energized and positive without making

it look like a prep classroom? Since these initial questions, LS has become integral to my teaching and I am proud of the deliberate and conscious decisions to cater for all learning styles of my students.

The challenges of integrating LS into a classroom and the broader school community have been numerous. Initially, I believed that the greatest opposition to LS formatted classrooms would in fact come from the parents of students as they would worry that their children would be disadvantaged by a lesser amount of 'chalk and talk' traditional teaching. I also believed that they would be concerned about increased practicalities (hands-on activities) and this would therefore create an over-dependency on hands-on learning. To some small degree I found that this was in fact the case. However, the greatest opposition to learning styles was in fact coming from other fellow teachers who had not received the training and remained negative.

Colleagues were in fact surprisingly hostile to the whole philosophy. Comments such as 'all LS in the senior school is merely finger painting' and 'you're no longer a real teacher' were directed at the teachers involved. Issues arose as LS had been introduced to only two of the eight Grade 5 and 6 classes and thus a strong feeling of 'us vs them' began to cause a rift. Planning was therefore a point of contention also, as the LS teachers were forced to complete the regular team planning as well as adapting their schedules to ensure that all four modalities were covered (visual, auditory, kinesthetic and tactile).

Rising tension was observable as LS increased in popularity among the student body and broader school community. Children in LS classrooms were voicing new and increased enthusiasm to be at school and bragged to other students that they were learning 'better'. This triggered parents to enquire why their students who were in non-LS classrooms were not permitted to learn with the same diversity of activities. Thus, a competition resulted between LS and non-LS classrooms and further caused a sense of disunity among the Grade 5 and 6 team.

Introductory Sessions: Personal Profile

by Bob Ayliffe

Basic assumption: the more that students can discover about themselves, the higher the chance of success. Finding out how they learn best reassures them, and dispels many of the negative self-beliefs that accompany adult learners and 'school failures' who enrol in second-chance courses/institutions. (The writer's experience in this area has included: Post Secondary Education; Adult Education Centre; Correctional Institution; Indigenous Education Unit.)

Therefore, it has been my practice for the last decade to run ALL students/classes through the following programme for the fist two two-hour sessions, regardless of course type or module name. (Note: LSA is only a recent inclusion in this.)

1. Course Outline
Overview of course proper. Ask students to re-create this as a 'road map'. From start to finish, 'places' (topics) on the way. Reassure that teacher is the navigator, rather than the driver.

2. Me
Personal profile. OHP (no overlay) directed onto whiteboard. Ask each student to stand in front of board, thus casting a shadow of their profile. Trace around this on A3 paper. Allow students to 'beautify' if desired. Cut and paste onto coloured cardboard sheet.

3. My Brain
Give each student a round balloon (let them choose colour). Ask students to blow up and tie off balloon to size of their brain. Explain hemisphericity. Ask students to draw the hemispheres onto their 'brain' with felt pen, and write in functions of each. Ask students to compare Brain Dominance results in their LSAs, let them label their balloons accordingly.

4. Crossovers
Demonstrate, explain the relevance of crossover exercises. Class perform a number of crossovers to music. Anything upbeat. 'Piki Mai' (Kiri Te Kanawa: *Kiri: Maori Songs*; EMI Classics has excellent beat for this).

5. How Do I Learn?
Ask class to recite 'Incy Wincy Spider' (perhaps uniquely Australian? Taught in kindergarten). Teacher lead with hand movements. Amazing to so many students that they remember this, word and action perfect, from anything up to 30 years ago. Discuss WHY? WHY do they remember this insignificant little song? Eventually class will deduce the reasons. Explain concept of VATK: use exaggerated illustrations (oversize ears, eyes, mouth, hands). Practical illustration: teach class 1–10 Memory Pegs, or Morse Code in 20 Minutes (this uses colour, sound, gestures, humour, visualization – covers all bases). Ask class to compare their VATK results in their LSA profiles; look at group results to find out what their preferences are and how they learn best.

6. What I'm Good At
Explain concept of multiple intelligences. Ask students to self-assess on basic MI bar graph.

7. The Jigsaw Me
Bring all components together on cardboard sheet. Profile pasted in centre; surround with:
- Balloon brain taped in one corner
- VATK summary (illustrated) in another
- MI graph (cut and pasted coloured bars) in third corner

8. The Real Me
Run LSA on each student, and explain individually. Run Group Profile, Teacher LSA and TSA.

9. The Sum of Us
Paste reduced photocopy of individual's LSA graphs in fourth corner of cardboard sheet. Discuss with class the significance of – individuality, individual needs, range and similarities within the group, correlations and mismatches with teacher profile. Brainstorm potential problems. Decide how to deal with such diversity. Determine the 'rules of engagement' for the semester. Completed profiles (with student permission) posted about the room, as ongoing reminder of individuality, and for student and teacher reference. Within a week or so, texta markings will cause balloon brains to begin to lose air and shrivel. Handy teaching strategy 'Use it or lose it'. Can be a link to a lesson later on metacognition; memory aids etc.

At a classroom level the challenges and the rewards were numerous. Children were exceptionally receptive to hands-on learning activities and thus teachers were forced to work a great deal harder to 'hands-on-ify' the curriculum. Questions arose, such as 'How can I make long multiplications kinesthetic?' or 'How can I make spelling tactile?' Resources also became vital and yet scarce. Teachers were coerced to be more creative, more innovative and more open-minded than ever before.

And thus, within several months teachers became effective and efficient at 'hands-on-ifying' almost any topic. Thus, long multiplication was taught outside on the basketball courts before students wrote it in their books.

Spelling was equally a challenge. Watching TV sometimes gives you great ideas. While watching a TV ad advertising a bakery, the baker wrote the slogan in flour. That started the wheels churning and thus we used tubs filled with approximately an inch of flour and asked the children to write the weekly spelling words with their fingers in flour. Although the children were upper primary school, they loved the opportunity to work with flour. Likewise, we also created SPUGGLE, a combination of spelling and juggling. Each child is given a small bean bag and asked to throw the bag vertically as they spell a word. Each throw of the bag corresponded with a spoken letter.

Learning styles has breathed new enthusiasm into myself as a teacher. Children are treated as complex individuals who are all capable learners when given the opportunity. One of the most satisfying situations was with a challenging student (teacher's code for impossible pupil with a severe learning disability) called Andrew. Andrew started the year with continuous complaints of 'I'm dumb', 'I hate school', 'I can't do English'. There were constant voicings of can't, won't, didn't and don't from Andrew. As the year progressed and the children undertook countless LS activities and surveys regarding their LS, Andrew soon discovered that in a learning styles environment he was actually an exceptional tactile and kinesthetic learner.

One memorable day Andrew stood up, and in a moment of revelation he stated: 'I'm not dumb, I'm just tactile!' Wow, what a moment. Humorously, this backfired when an emergency teacher arrived in the classroom and Andrew explained that he is a tactile learner and therefore he wouldn't do a boring writing task because it was visual and didn't cater for him.

The satisfaction of a teacher is heightened in a LS classroom as children begin to own their learning and understand their personal strengths as well as their shortcomings. They know which is their preferred learning style modality, whether they like dim lighting, whether they need fruit snacks and what time of day they work best. Children become active participants in the classroom and actually begin to suggest methods and activities. This was a mind-opening realization that indeed students want to be involved in the organization and planning of the classroom.

LS in high schools

Michelle Hayward reports about the implementation of LS in Broughton Hall High School, Liverpool.

Welcome to Broughton Hall! We're an 11–18 girls' high school in Liverpool, UK. For some years now we've been on a journey towards understanding what makes our students perform best and get the most out of their school experiences. We've drawn heavily on the work of Barbara Prashnig and her research into learning styles to inform our approach. We certainly don't have all the answers, in fact we probably haven't asked many of the questions yet – but we are making an impact on the way our students learn across the whole school.

The keys, we find, are knowledge, awareness and enthusiasm. As you walk round the school, there are numerous posters and displays highlighting learning styles and multiple intelligences (MI). The pupils are aware of their learning styles and MI through the SMART card system, which gives them all a pocket-sized card detailing their

Bernhard Schrag, a past tutor at Waikato Polytechnic in Hamilton, NZ, received the following student comments after he had been using alternative learning and teaching styles. He is now teaching in Denver, Colorado, and continues to use these methods.

✻ Having music in practicals is really good. However, the radio would be better than classical. We have had the radio a few times and it has worked well.

✻ Great improvement in teaching style compared to last year – with music (has really helped; sets rhythm to work to). He told us about mind mapping on the first lesson for easy recall for studying.

✻ Music in class – except for the fact that anything other than classical music is detrimental to us.

✻ I liked the way he introduced us to listening to music during theory tests and practicals. He obviously thinks of the students first.

✻ I like the way the tutor has taken the time to learn how to teach (i.e. music, mind maps and visual learning). It was a pity he was not able to teach us for the whole eight weeks.

✻ He's experimental in his approach to teaching, and showing new learning techniques. Has a genuine concern for how his students are doing on the course. Always willing to help students when necessary.

✻ He knows what he's talking about and is also usually a good, concise tutor. In most of the subjects he has a really thorough knowledge of, he also likes to have the class bouncing ideas off each other in order for us to learn off each other's knowledge.

✻ Letting us listen to classical music, I found that it does help a lot, and I wish we were able to listen to it for Trade Certificate as well, everything flows smoothly and it relaxes you. He was a lot of fun, sometimes until you get him angry, but then he's still fine.

✻ His idea of music in the class during practical and tests is a great idea. It relaxes you and lets you concentrate on what you are doing. He has planned lessons well and covers the content well. The classical music is also productive in classes. He has great new ideas like flow diagrams and music and makes points very clear and teaches well as opposed to telling students what to do and how to do it.

✻ He allows us to listen to music in classes which is good because it saves the dead silence when we are working, which when we are at home or work is generally the way it goes. Quite good how he didn't insist on us knowing an answer in theory. If we didn't know, we would pass on the question with no embarrassment.

✻ Excellent method of teaching. Good way in which he gets across information (i.e. cards, drawing, maps). More tutors should follow him.

✻ Enjoyed his classes, some of them were fun and different. He uses alternative teaching methods like charts, mind maps, music, student participation). Students have to think. The music is pretty good, it was really helpful.

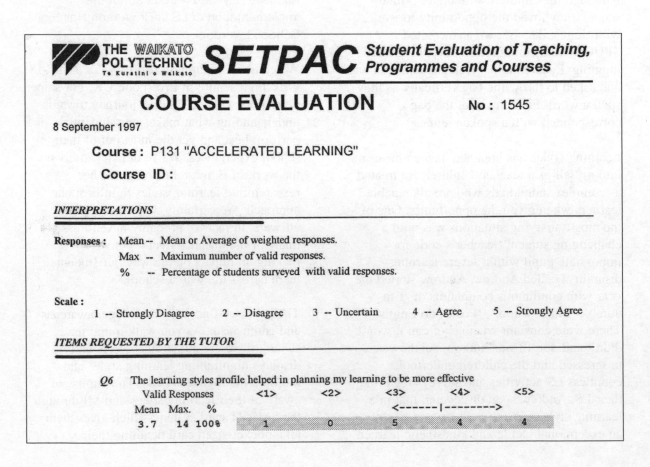

THE WAIKATO POLYTECHNIC Te Kuratini o Waikato **SETPAC** *Student Evaluation of Teaching, Programmes and Courses*

COURSE EVALUATION
No : 1545

8 September 1997

Course : P131 "ACCELERATED LEARNING"

Course ID :

INTERPRETATIONS

Responses : Mean -- Mean or Average of weighted responses.
Max -- Maximum number of valid responses.
% -- Percentage of students surveyed with valid responses.

Scale :
1 -- Strongly Disagree   2 -- Disagree   3 -- Uncertain   4 -- Agree   5 -- Strongly Agree

ITEMS REQUESTED BY THE TUTOR

Q6   The learning styles profile helped in planning my learning to be more effective

		<1>	<2>	<3>	<4>	<5>
Valid Responses						
Mean	Max.	%		<------	------->	
3.7	14	100%	1	0	5	4	4

preferences. Pupil awareness has been fundamental to our approach, and sessions explaining learning styles are built into the PSHE (personal, social and health education) calendar to promote understanding of individual learning preferences. We have found that care needs to be taken not to 'pigeon-hole' students and impose a method of learning on them. Rather, teachers are now more aware of the need to provide a 'balanced diet' of approaches to learning, and we are working towards ways of giving students more ownership of their learning self-knowledge and encouraging them to act on it individually, especially for revision, homework and research tasks. It has become apparent to us that learning styles are about how a person does things, NOT has things done to them! This applies to staff, too. There are teaching methods that individual teachers' may not feel comfortable using, especially if forced to. The answer seems to be to use a 'buffer' approach, allowing teachers' enthusiasm to be sparked by techniques and strategies they have found out about themselves and that they feel might benefit the learning that goes on in their classrooms.

We do find that there are certain aspects to a traditional school environment that can impede an approach that embraces the diversity of learning styles. This is tricky – unfortunately you can't just knock down all your old classrooms to make way for fantastic new learning rooms of the future. Our school is in the process of preparing a room designed for various methods of learning and teaching, which takes account of Prashnig's findings on the educational benefits of the 'comfort zone'. The idea is to make the room available to teachers to book on a week by week basis so they can take advantage of space, a water fountain, comfortable seating, flexibility and exciting resources and see the effect on their students' learning. This is just the next step – we are a changing school.

LS in adult education / vocational training

LS is particularly beneficial in tertiary education institutions where practical subjects are taught. The big problem there is

that the majority of these students are 'non-academic learners' who find it very hard to study theoretical content in traditional ways.

Tanya Berryman, tutor at the Bay of Plenty Polytechnic, Tauranga, NZ reflects on why her students resisted the introduction of learning styles and teaching tools.

I experienced that an integration of new ideas into the classroom, in this case creative teaching, can meet with some resistance. For me this came as a real shock. 'Why aren't the students as excited about this as I am?' It seemed that they just didn't know what would work better for them and the fact that they had not attended the training with me really emphasized this. I personally was sold on the new ways of creative learning, LSA, style diversity, teaching tools and development of a classroom culture to reflect these.

So why weren't my students as excited as I was? The students that I teach are here to study a very practical subject, 'Beauty Therapy'. However, as with all practical tasks, there is significant underpinning knowledge required that is delivered in theory classes. Just imagine how some naive students feel, when having enrolled on a Beauty Therapy course (not having done their course research in advance!) and then suddenly having to learn theory about cells and tissues to level 5. It is a huge shock for some of them.

In the meantime, during my own learning curve with holistic education, I began to see great ways to introduce creative teaching techniques into theory subjects. However, my enthusiasm overflowed and turned classes into total confusion for the students. As we are aware, change is often unsettling and having a tutor suddenly arrive in a class and throwing all the conventional practices (reliably set in their comfort zones after years of traditional learning) out the window was, I believe, a bit too much for these adult learners.

As I was searching for a solution, I asked myself the question: 'How can I get the students to take this new learning style concept on board?' The obvious first step was to have the students complete and then receive a copy of their own LSA-Adult profile

The following description is an extract from Kim's LS testimonial in which she describes how an understanding of learning styles has changed the way her children do homework and how this has influenced their family life. I hope that Kim's experience will help many parents who are fighting a never-ending battle over their children's homework.

Last year was a huge learning curve for us all. Reeling from the death of my husband, Scott – we were all trying to find our way in a whole new world. Our youngest son, Dale, had the hardest time adjusting to this life. I personally feel that the school didn't give him a chance to do this. After what was considered to be an accepted amount of time to 'get over' this, Dale was expected to conform to 'normal' behaviour. When Dale failed to do this he became labelled as a problem child and treated accordingly. As such his learning suffered greatly. I feel that if they had taken into consideration what my little boy was experiencing and given him the time to adjust, his schooling may have not suffered and he wouldn't have been labelled as a child with 'severe behavioural problems'. I believe that if they had applied LSA with Dale last year, both parties would have been able to come to an understanding instead of a constant battle of wills.

Over the Christmas break I watched my son visibly transform from a child full of angst to one who finally has an inner peace. He has now come to terms with the loss of his father. This is even evident now to his teacher – who, coincidentally, is the same as last year. Dale now approaches school with enthusiasm and has found it an enjoyable experience. After a recent conversation with his teacher, who now has an understanding of LSA and is implementing it into the classroom, she realizes that Dale is a tactile and kinesthetic learner and understands his behaviour, which she previously tried to put a stop to. She also has a better understanding of the Irlen Syndrome and the connection to LSA. Dale will finally be receiving his work on blue paper and is allowed to use his tactile methods of reading. I have found at home that Dale reads well and actually comprehends more if he can touch the words with his fingers. Previously his teacher was only allowing him to use a ruler to track his reading, but this doesn't work for him. He needs to touch it, feel it, to know what it is. His teacher had told him 'You're not in kindergarten anymore and shouldn't be doing this; you're too old to read this way.'

Dale found this very conflicting as I encouraged him to read this way and his teacher was telling him not to. However, now that his teacher has a better understanding of LSA she now makes allowances for his methods. The teacher now is making his learning experience a holistic one, instead of making him conform to the traditional learning behaviour expected. Dale has an area in his classroom where he can go for time out without disturbing other class members. We are working together to make learning a fun and enjoyable experience for him – which is what it should be. I was implementing LSA at home and then having it all undone at school. This was very frustrating, and I felt I was fighting a losing battle.

Dale now has a homework pattern that is successful. I have found that if we leave his homework until after tea at night his attention span is longer, he is more co-operative and he accomplishes more. I was trying to get him to sit down and do his work at designated times; this was stressful for him and me. He would end up in tears and I would be pulling my hair out. This is wrong, homework and learning shouldn't be like this. I have my best times and they work for me – why shouldn't it work for him? Dale has benefited the most from LSA. I've been able to use it far more with him than I have with my older two sons.

Dan and Troy are very flexible in the way that they learn, so having to conform at school and then become holistic at home comes easy for them. However, they have their preference. They have a class now called 'Learn to Learn' where some LSA is used. We are still ever hopeful that the high school section becomes more supportive of this programme and implements more holistic methods as well. Together we are working out ways to get

continued on page 160

and give them the chance to process this information. This led to some great class discussions and significantly improved understanding from the students as to why things were changing. I also went back over my notes to find other strategies to put into place, many of which Barbara had outlined during her training, but which had been overlooked by my enthusiastic approach.

The creative teaching itself is very much based on brain-based theories and accelerated learning; however, I believe the implementation of the learning style tools leads to the experiential learning theory that gets students involved in the development of their learning. The experiential learning cycle is encouraged as an approach for group facilitating, and the introduction of learning style tools into the class requires more of a facilitative approach. It encourages the students to take some ownership of what is learned not only of content within the class but also their own personal process of learning. The importance of such a multi-reflective process cannot be overlooked for its genuine inclusion of students' learning.

So what impact has the introduction of LS and teaching tools had on the students? The best way to indicate this is by sharing with you some of the feedback I have received from the personal teaching evaluations the students completed in 2004:

'It's good because she makes sure we all learn in our own styles.'
'Tania teaches in all learning styles so everyone can understand.'
'Very good with learning styles.'
'She makes a stable happy work environment.'
'I wish I had a teacher like her at school, she understands my learning style.'

My enthusiasm is no longer the issue, now it is a lack of time for resourcing and developing more teaching tools for use in the classroom.

My recommendation to teachers

If you ever meet resistance to the introduction of the changes that you are inspired by during your LS training and creative learning

experiences, please do not give up! I found it was a change in my approach that was the solution, not the idea itself.

LS at university or college

Dr Christine Woods at Auckland University, NZ, describes how she uses the working style analysis with owner-managers at the Small and Medium Enterprises department.

Over the past five years I have been involved in a business growth course targeted at small and medium-sized business owner-managers. The purpose of the course is to assist them to grow an already successful business. The focus is not to tell them 'how to' run a business; rather the course is designed to enable like-minded people to come together to share ideas, find new knowledge and perhaps regain some of the energy they had when the business first started. Each course has 20 participants and takes place over five three-day residential blocks spread over five months.

While some participants left school without qualifications and have always been self-employed, others have university degrees and corporate experience. But one thing they do share is the knowledge that they are both the main inhibitor to growth and the most significant enabler of growth in their business. Understanding and reflecting on who they are is vitally important. One means of working effectively with these people is through assessing and sharing their learning and working style analysis (WSA). For most of them the WSA is a revelation. Very little time has been spent on considering the fact that they have a unique working style and way of learning. Giving them the time to reflect on this reminds them of why they enjoy doing certain things in a certain way and why they avoid other tasks like the plague!!

The penny seems to drop particularly hard when they consider the one staff member that is giving them the most trouble – why is it that they clash regularly and consistently over the smallest of things? Here are some of the comments that have been shared: 'Why does Jo struggle to come in each week for the regular early morning meeting?', 'So what's

around any problems they may be experiencing at school by referring back to their LSA and seeing how we can effectively apply some of its recommendations and they can study independently. I have found that the boys understand their assignments and homework better, when they come home and explain to me what they have to do. As they are both external auditory learners, this clarifies in their minds what should be done.

Music has become our constant accompaniment at homework times, which are staggered to suit our learning styles. My eldest boy, Dan, supports 'The Mozart Effect' and actually puts the CDs on when studying or doing research. It's amazing the difference music makes. I was taught, at school and in the home, that music was distracting and that there was no way you could study with 'that racket' going on. So I was naturally dubious and sceptical that music enhances the learning experience until I began to put it into practice at home and then watched the effect it had on my children. Dale's whole mood and approach to work is much calmer and clearer with classical or soothing music softly going in the background. Dan and Troy are more willing to sit down and tackle their homework and they accomplish more with it going. On a personal note, I am able to get through my weakest subjects of science and maths with Mozart playing in the background. I don't get as caught up by formulas or lost in how to accomplish these tasks!!!!

In all honesty I would not have believed this if I didn't experience it for myself and then see the proof right in front of me with my children. Not only does music assist with our studies, I have found that having soothing music going in the background when they arrive home from school reduces the tension and aggravation and they are more relaxed – less fights as they clamour to tell me about their day. So the age-old adage that 'Music soothes the savage breast' really rings true in this household.

One of the greatest tools I was taught last year was mind mapping. This has become my way of tackling all my tasks now. It helps me to stay focused and I find when I do this that I don't lose direction. When I don't do it I become so lost and gather way too much information. I get overwhelmed and the task then becomes so much harder than what it actually is!!! Troy also uses this; he mind maps his assignments. He then expands this map with information and uses it as a form of presentation. To Troy this is the most logical way of doing everything, as he says 'It's all there for everyone to see and understand.' Troy is such an impulsive thinker that he often just jumps into tasks without considering all the facts or consequences. Mind mapping allows him to stay on track and to actually stop and think about what it is he is doing or required to do.

Brain Gym® is used at home as well. Most times, before Dan and Troy begin their study we do some of the energizing movements. We have found that it helps us all to concentrate longer. I usually do this with them and they get a good laugh at my expense and at my lack of co-ordination. I don't mind as this lightens their moods and they approach their homework happy and relaxed. I also use this with Dale when he becomes frustrated, uptight, aggravated and upset with his homework. Getting him to do some Brain Gym, with left and right crossovers and also a few of the energizing movements, gives him the break he needs and removes him from the stressful situation. More times than not this helps him to relax and approach his homework from a different angle. He then understands and accomplishes what he couldn't do before.

LSA not only taught me things about myself, but about my children as well. After doing the LSA I realized how much I imposed onto them my perceived ideas of learning and homework. I realized that I was making them conform to the traditional way, without considering their individuality. LSA has not just been my journey but my boys have been swept along for the ride. I don't know how to find the words to describe what this household is like at times – chaotic is one that comes to mind – as we try to incorporate four different learning styles.

so wrong with a noisy office – I've worked in one for years?' and the perennial favourite 'If I've TOLD them once, I've told them a thousand times!!!' – and once we have gone through the analysis, the suggestion to SHOW them instead doesn't come from me but from other participants in the course. By considering the uniqueness of each person's learning and working style – not just their own, but those of their staff members – new insight can be found that enables the team to work together more effectively. And this will result in an improved bottom line for the business.

Working and learning styles do not provide the answer for owner–managers seeking to grow their business. But that's because there is no one question. Rather it serves as a useful framework for them to reflect on their own abilities and gain new insight into team dynamics within their organizations, but it also helps them with their academic studies.

LS in self-study

When students have to study by themselves, they often use study techniques they acquired at school, no matter if they work for them or not. To avoid unnecessary learning difficulties in formal education, it is most important to know one's LS and use them for best outcomes. The LSA-Adult profile and report provide valuable information about the best study practices, particularly when a student has to learn something new and/or difficult. Closely following these recommendations has helped many adult learners in coping with demanding study situations, improving their exam results and, most importantly, often keeping them on their courses. The more students know about their personal learning style, the more they can be flexible, utilize their strengths and avoid learning strategies that cause them stress and frustration. Kim's story is a moving tribute to a teacher who was daring enough to introduce the LSA to his adult learners and how understanding her own and her children's learning style has changed Kim's life (see 'Dear Bob' letter on page 16).

LS in sports training and coaching

Wayne Thomas, a professional golf coach near Melbourne, Australia, describes how he is using LS in sports coaching.

I have designed and presented training seminars for fellow PGA golf professionals on a variety of subjects related to identifying and understanding human mental and physical patterns, golf swing, club fitting and introducing learning styles into their coaching and regularly present seminars and golf schools to amateurs.

I have always recognized there is something missing with coaching, despite the excellent results many of my students reported receiving; what concerns me most is a person's inability to sustain new levels of performance and continually falling back into old patterns. My continued pursuit of knowledge about golf swing, human movement, mental approach to oneself, equipment and communication skills wasn't providing the key that would open the gate to the amazing potential we all possess, sustain it and continue expanding.

When I first met Barbara Prashnig and she put forward the notion HOW PEOPLE LEARN is more important than what people learn, it sparked for me a new era in coaching; I immediately began changing my coaching styles and the learning environment to match the students' learning styles as opposed to expecting my students to adapt to my way of coaching.

There must be a starting point, with the creation of the thoughts and belief system that each person uses when they begin something new, including an introduction to golf. How people visually perceive the golf swing, their belief system in their ability to perform the task of hitting the ball to a satisfactory outcome and how to play the game are all factors influencing performance. The unsuspecting novice can easily be influenced by what other golfers say and many unworkable concepts are passed from one person to the next. What fascinates me about

Project:
Engaging the school community in learning
Mary Brell, Keys to Success, Orange, NSW, Australia (January 2005)

Purpose
To ensure that teachers, parents and students are able to:
Understand their own learning
Understand the learning of each other
Establish action plans for school and home learning

Process
Jodie Russell, principal, saw the need to introduce the work and philosophy of Barbara Prashnig to her school community. She had been doing a lot of work on learning and this work was going to support and enhance the work that had already been done.

Jodie employed an external consultant, Mary Brell from 'Keys To Success' to support the process at the school. Three days were set aside for the whole project. Mary's background in learning and particularly the work that she had already done with Barbara would enhance the learning and the task that Jodie had in mind.

Stage 1
On day one, parents and students were introduced to the notion of LS by being placed into different situations so that they could experience the learning environments.
The activities included giving the participants reading tasks while placing them in:
a warm room / a cool room / with formal, upright seating / sitting on bean bags,
in silence / with music playing in the background.

The participants experienced other environments that are used in LS teaching. At the end of the day the participants were asked in which environments they preferred to be. This was their practical introduction to learning styles.

Parents and students were separated and Mary worked with the parents while Jodie worked with the students and they all completed the LSA instrument.

Stage 2
On the second day, Mary once again worked with the parents and Jodie worked with the students interpreting their profiles. Later that day, the parents spent some time with their children sharing the information from their profiles. It was during this time that parents were able to realize that their child, at times, learned differently to them and had different learning requirements. At the end of the day, both parents and students set simple goals for learning which would be explored further in the final session.

Stage 3
Day three was the day where activities were decided upon for both the parents and the students. Mary once again worked with the parents and Jodie with the students.

Comment
The process was one that empowered both students and parents. Jodie, as the teacher, is now able to direct her class in such a way that will enable the students to take control of their own learning and the environments that they require to support their learning.

Parents found the process and the information very enlightening; they are now able and willing to understand their child's learning needs and can support that learning in a more satisfactory environment at home.

this is most people take for granted that what they are told is truth and attempt to apply this information almost without question.

To begin with I thought this was a form of laziness, a lack of exercising their powers of observation and reasoning, but I now believe it is a more complex issue. The majority of people I believe are not aware of their learning styles, and combining the emotional content with not knowing how to learn makes progress very slow for most people. I believe we have been so conditioned to fear failure it's like a disease and crippling our capacity to learn. There is no success or failure there is only learning through experiencing and observing outcomes, and then refining what we have learned to achieve new levels of performance.

The sensory modalities or what I call 'The Four Senses' (see Chapter 9) influences how material is presented to the student and what kind of teaching tools and aids the student responds best to. In my new coaching I use an array of teaching and learning tools to provide a sensory-rich learning experience.

Golf is a game that will never be mastered fully as it is an eternal learning experience; there are many, many facets to take into account. As a golfer's level improves, more things are unconcealed that must be taken into account. Both the analytic and the holistic learner needs assistance with structures; however, because of the diversity of learning styles, these structures can vary greatly from player to player and often structures need to be reviewed, modified and adjusted to find the right mix that produces rewarding results.

LS in the workplace

When people have to learn something new and/or difficult at work or have to solve problems, they will always try to do that through their style preferences first. If these techniques do not lead to success, they will then try a different approach and by doing so have to use their flexibilities. Being flexible is much easier when someone knows their learning or working style and yet many employers do not consider this valuable information, missing out on improved training and increased productivity.

LSA and WSA results can be used for team building, conflict resolution, workplace set-up, training, staff selection, enhancing meetings and career planning.

One interesting aspect I have seen in my training with people in the workplace has also been observed in Finland by Raija Leskinen who describes it as follows.

I have worked very much with small business owners and I have noticed that they are very often strongly kinesthetic as learners. They also very often have a low level educational background. There is also a clear need for renewal of their skills in order to stay competitive. It has been quite a challenge to get these people to study and/or to develop themselves and their business.

LS with parents and the community

Engaging a whole-school community in learning was the aim of a project created and supervised by Mary Brell, our partner and LS consultant in New South Wales, Australia. She collaborated with a principal to ensure that teachers, parents and students were able to understand their own learning, to understand the learning of each other and to establish action plans for school and home learning. Details about the project and its success are described opposite.

The comment from one of our business associates about his nine-year-old daughter's LSA profile expresses what so many parents have told us after receiving their children's profiles: 'When we read Samantha's LSA report we could instantly see that everything it said was completely accurate. It was an exact match of her personality and learning style. Of course it is necessary to see this written down by an independent source, in order for us to make affirmative action. Thanks for making such an innovative service available.'

Parent working bee day: making resources to improve classroom environments at Tumbarumba High, Australia

💻 For full report see online appendix 14.

Sharing cooked lunch with their teacher in their own classroom is very common for students in Scandinavia

Linda MacRae-Campbell / How to Start a Revolution at Your School

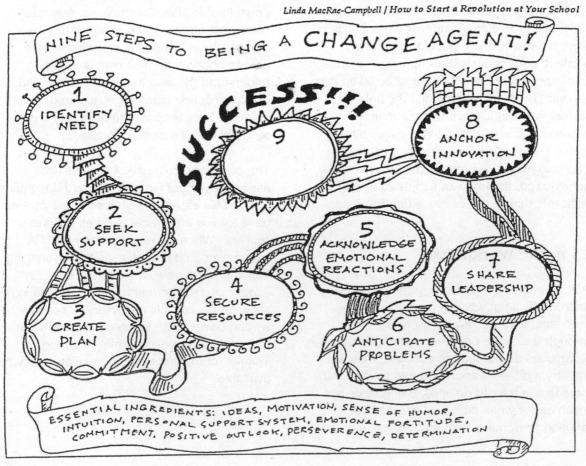

NINE STEPS TO BEING A CHANGE AGENT!

1 IDENTIFY NEED

2 SEEK SUPPORT

3 CREATE PLAN

4 SECURE RESOURCES

5 ACKNOWLEDGE EMOTIONAL REACTIONS

6 ANTICIPATE PROBLEMS

7 SHARE LEADERSHIP

8 ANCHOR INNOVATION

9 SUCCESS!!!

ESSENTIAL INGREDIENTS: IDEAS, MOTIVATION, SENSE OF HUMOR, INTUITION, PERSONAL SUPPORT SYSTEM, EMOTIONAL FORTITUDE, COMMITMENT, POSITIVE OUTLOOK, PERSEVERENCE, DETERMINATION

Chapter 20

Do's and don'ts with learning styles

The following pieces of advice and cautionary notes come from practitioners and have been collated in no particular order of importance but should give teachers some good ideas about what to do in applying LS in their daily work and what to avoid. Feel free to add your own do's and don'ts and share them with colleagues interested in style diversity who will be grateful for such insights.

Do always emphasize to students that the LSA is not a test and therefore nobody can pass or fail; explain to parents that there is no such thing as a correct or better LS profile. Make sure that parents and students understand that all the profiles are unique and everybody has strengths they can use for better learning.

Don't use an assessment such as LSA in school (in regular classes) without explaining to teachers that they also have a teaching style that they must know in order to match their teaching to their students' learning styles.

Do involve pupils in creating the best possible learning environment. Explain why you are doing it, let them help design and implement quiet areas, relaxing dens and darker corners for reading, watching educational videos or working on computers.

Don't forget that each learning style classroom must have a comfortable area where students can learn informally on soft furniture or on the floor.

Don't ever remove all desks from a classroom as there will always be some students who need to sit upright at a desk.

Do accept that attitudes are learned style features, that they will change through the schooling years and that this process is often accompanied by confusion. Honest discussions and interpretation of their LSA results will help most of the time.

Don't hesitate to engage the additional help of a person the student trusts when a situation gets difficult, particularly in matters of discipline.

Don't overwhelm holistic students with factual questions or with questions that require outlines, sequence of events, details and structure.

Do ask holistic students for the general theme, the big picture, an overview or the main idea. Ask 'what-if' questions and questions requiring idea synthesis and encourage imaginative and creative replies.

Don't give analytic students open-ended questions, or questions with no 'right' or 'wrong' answers.

Don't expect that all students in your class have the same or similar learning styles – consult the group profile and you will see the style differences but also similarities that will guide you in subgrouping your students.

Do NOT label students according to their preferences in the sensory modalities. Since the 'accelerated learning' movement has swept the UK in several schools I have seen students given different coloured labels with VAK to indicate their preferred learning style. This is a very bad practice because it does

Pilot study at Sanquhar Primary School, Scotland
April–June 2005

'The practical implementation of a learning styles approach within the classroom and its impact'

Suzanne E. George

Our pilot study was based in the Primary 4 class consisting of 30 pupils aged between seven and eight years. We felt it necessary to consult with children as the changes proposed were in stark contrast to their traditionally organized classroom. We also wanted children to understand the concept that we all learn differently and emphasize how important it is for them to find their own preferred working environment rather than sit with their friends.

Class Organization:

In the Primary 4 class, the classroom was organized to allow children the flexibility to choose where to sit to complete work tasks. These included:

Workstations – Using cardboard partitions we were able to create single workstations for those children wishing to work on their own.

Listening table – A group table was set up to allow the children to have their own headsets to listen to classical/baroque music while they learn.

Group tables – This allows children to work alongside peers in a group situation. (Prior to the class reorganization all desks were grouped in this manner.)

Bright/low light areas – For children who prefer brightly lit areas tables have been set up along the windows. The use of lighting and blinds in some areas of the classroom had also been adjusted to create bright and low light areas.

Floor space – Through the reorganization of the tables a large area of floor space has been left to create an alternative work area. Children have the option to sit or lie on the floor using clipboards to complete work tasks and they were also encouraged to bring in cushions and pillows for chairs or for use on the floor. This links to the idea of uncomfortable settings causing fatigue and lack of concentration.

Early results were very positive. We found that children very quickly organized themselves into their preferred area. Once organized, the children were focused on their tasks. Through working with the class on previous occasions it was fascinating to discover that the children seemed more focused and that the class had a very busy, learning environment. The atmosphere was one of calm. The children seemed more independent and were surprisingly less distracted than in the previous class layout.

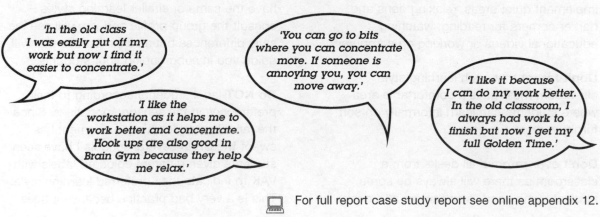

For full report case study report see online appendix 12.

not leave room for flexibility and does not take into account style combinations and sub-modalities.

Do subgroup students according to their sensory preferences in addition to matching their other learning needs, particularly when they have to learn something new and difficult. Once they understand, they need to switch groups to continue learning through their other senses to reinforce content and become more flexible.

Do find out your own teaching style – it will help you to become more flexible and accommodate students' learning needs much better.

What NOT to do in LS application

Never focus on non-preferences of students

Non-preferences need to be avoided whenever possible because they become weaknesses over time if students have to learn in a way that is not their preferred style; accept them and focus on preferences and flexibilities – there is plenty to choose from in everyone's profile.

Never label students according to their sensory modalities

There are no so-called 'visual' or 'kinesthetic' students because they all have combinations of at least two sensory preferences (some have six and more!), they have internal modalities and possess flexibilities that can become preferences when students are very interested in a subject topic.

Never underestimate students' ability to KNOW their LS

Even young students know deep down how they want to learn and how they can do it best, often against their teachers' and parents' opinion; it is always the learner who knows HOW they want to do it, even if they are not allowed to do so.

Never assume all students can learn the same way as you do

What makes sense for you in learning (such as step-by-step approaches) might be very

confusing for students who have a different thinking style. If you as a teacher need quiet to concentrate, this does not mean your students can learn well in quiet classrooms. For many, quiet learning environments are unbearable and their behaviour will become disruptive.

Never switch on the lights in a classroom because you need them

Many students, particularly younger ones, need much less light than adults do and get agitated under fluorescent lights. They will not tell you, because you are the authority in the class but they will get restless and you will encounter more discipline problems, particularly with underachievers. It might be harder for you getting used to dimmer light levels but discipline will be better!

Never assume you fully know the style features of a student

Many aspects of LS cannot be observed and remain hidden until the student is exposed to severe pressure (whatever that might mean for them). Only LSA assessments can provide an accurate picture of the true learning needs of a child. No matter how well you know your students, there will always be surprises in their learning abilities.

Never give up on underachievers

They can become very successful learners once their non-traditional learning style combination is understood and matched accordingly in teaching. They will fly!

Using learning styles in social studies

Mary Greenland

A number of years ago Nayland College, Nelson, NZ recognized a need to build a twenty-first-century learning culture, aiming to become an 'intentional school' where effective teaching creates positive learning with engaged students.

The 'Effective Learning Programme' (ELP) was introduced into Year 9 several years ago to help deal with behavioural and disciplinary issues. It has been run by the Social Studies (SS) over the last few years. The programme aims to encourage and motivate students to become responsible for their own learning. It seeks to help students develop effective learning strategies, identify their preferred LS so that they become more self-motivated and positive about learning, and develop time management and self-management (goal setting) skills.

Recognizing and catering for diversity in the classroom has been a key feature of ELP. Identifying the preferred learning styles of disaffected and less engaged students and allowing them to use these in their class and assignment work was seen as a step towards increasing their enjoyment of school.

In the first few weeks of the school year all Year 9 students completed the LSA. (In 2004/05 this was done online.) Students and their parents got a printout of their results. Copies are kept in the staff workroom for access by all staff. As the LSA report is quite complicated, SS teachers work through the results with each student and students produce a simplified version. Students keep this in their working folders and teachers also have access to copies. Then teachers create group profiles for each of their classes. These are used to gain insight into the grouped preferences within the class, to create teams for co-operative work and to encourage students to acknowledge the diversity within the classroom and use it to broaden their discussions and tolerance. SS teachers share these group profiles in Form Group Conferences held once a term with other teachers of the class. With the LSA now being online it is possible for other teachers to get group profiles of their classes which are organized in ways other than by form (for example, graphics, outdoor education, creative foods).

Within Social Studies teaching programmes the use of LSA has meant great changes:

- Acknowledging the importance of LS to the engagement of students has meant rewriting our assignments to cater for the diversity in styles. When being issued with an assignment students are able to follow the instructions as listed steps (for analytics) or as graphics (for holistics). This has proven to be very effective in getting students on task more quickly and staying motivated.

- Presentation of their research findings has been opened up to allow students to communicate in their preferred style. This has made reporting back much more interesting and kept students more interested in the findings of their peers.

- Students are also encouraged to work in teams with other students who have different LS preferences. This has generated more discussion of issues and topics. Engagement in tasks has improved as students recognize the different strengths and abilities of their peers and are able to work within these. They have also become more tolerant.

- Commenting on one student with a fractured attendance record, whom no one used to want to work with, two students were overheard saying: 'She can work in our group – she just needs to know exactly what she has to do, then she does it one step at a time – it just takes her a bit longer.'

- At times students are instructed to use a learning style that is not their preference in order to increase their tolerance towards others' styles.

Some quotes from students:

'Like for the "global" people, he'll say "This is what the finished thing looks like" and for the "analytical" people, he'll go through the stages step by step.'

'If we hadn't done the LSA, the teacher probably would have done things the way he does it, but now that he knows how we are, he does it how we learn best.'

continued on page 170

Chapter 21

How to sustain a learning styles programme

LS in preparatory schools

In Chapter 19, Jim Boyd, Head of Year 8 and Head of English, Millfield Preparatory School, UK, describes how the introduction of LS has changed learning and teaching at his school and in this second part of his report he suggests ways of starting and continuing with LS.

I believe that there are two approaches to introduce learning styles. One is the start from scratch with 100 per cent involvement. The alternative is a 'drip, drip' approach that lets things filter down and lets the results speak for themselves. I now have children asking me to persuade other teachers to take more notice of their learning styles. It's a difficult position to be in but I will keep promoting and proving. On the positive side we are now about to start our second induction of pupils and the senior Millfield has decided to test all their new pupils, approximately 250 boys and girls. What I often have to stress to teachers, pupils and parents is that I see it as an aid, a facilitator that can have dramatic benefits but it is not a miracle cure or a quick fix. However, I am certain that everyone who has approached LS with an open mind has seen the benefits and has changed the way they teach and learn.

LS at high school level

Andrea Wilson reports the following for Christchurch Girls' High School.

For the past three years Christchurch Girls' High School in NZ has provided the opportunity for Year 13 students to complete a LSA-Senior at the beginning of the school year. In conjunction with this, the girls attend a workshop to discuss the different learning styles. The profiles are available to staff and copies are taken home by the students. The majority of students report on the accuracy of the profile and the usefulness in helping to understand the best way they can learn. It has been particularly useful around exam time to help refocus students. Some staff have expressed a greater understanding of their students overall having read this information. Comments from parents indicate their enlightenment on reading their daughter's profile.

Sheila Ayliffe, the principal at Tumbarumba High School, NSW, Australia took the lead in introducing LS to a very traditional, rural high school and part of this journey is described here.

LSAs have been completed for Years 7/8 and at a follow-up meeting, group profiles were presented to staff, with explanations of how to use the Interpretation Manual and profile data to enhance classroom practice. In addition, our Year 11 students have now completed their LSAs, which are being used to assist students to develop an appropriate study schedule by incorporating strategies that cater for their strong preferences.

As part of our literacy strategy we operate a special reading group where targeted Year 7 students are buddied up with an older student mentor. This group reads together each morning when the whole school starts the day with DEAR – Drop Everything And Read.

'Like, if it's not fun for us, it's probably fun for someone else in our class ... one day we have fun, another we don't but somebody else has fun, so we keep quiet.'

'I could have just done a poster, but I like making things that are "different", so I put it on a T-shirt.'

In becoming more aware of their students' LS the teachers also become aware of their own. Often they recognize their style of learning is a mismatch with how the students learn. So they change as my own example shows:

Mary Greenland

as a learner – result from LSA:	as a teacher – quote from TSA:
strongly analytical, sequential, reflective,	'very holistic, favouring intuitive emotion
prefers listening, reading, working alone,	and feelings which you encourage to flow
likes external reassurance	through social interaction among your students'

All SS teachers have completed their own LSA and TSA. They are now aware of their preferences and how these can be utilized in their classrooms.

Case Study   'Andrew'

In Year 9
Andrew was a quiet student. A minimalist – not particularly motivated to achieve beyond the minimum requirements. There was little participation in group-work.

Assignment 1 –   Limited output, no extra effort evident, low achievement (traditional)

Introduction to learning styles analysis
Assignment 2 –   produced a booklet (analytical/sequential) and also produced a mobile (visual, tactile). He did double the work; couldn't always do it in his preferred style but could expand on his work by using another method.
Assignment 3 –   a group activity – full participation, confident team member.
End of year
examination   –   Andrew gained three excellence and two merit grades.

In Year 10
Individual recognition of his learning style was so important for Andrew that when this was removed he was 'lost' as a learner. When his preferred LS was not being utilized he lost interest, reduced his output, and his behaviour deteriorated.

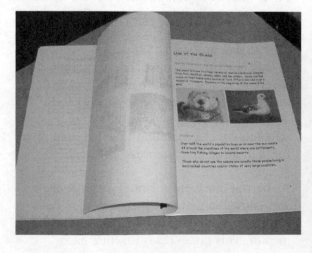   

Andrew's work (Nayland College, Nelson, NZ)

Following our learning styles seminar with Barbara Prashnig at which we were introduced to Brain Gym®, we now have the students complete a series of crossovers to music before they begin reading. The students have reported that they find this activity has increased their alertness for the rest of the day and the co-ordinating teacher has reported significant increases in the students' reading performance.

Another benefit of our LSA training has been its use to help individual students from outside the target group. When students are referred to me with particularly challenging behaviour, or in need of a study programme, I always begin with their LSA. This then forms the basis of advice I provide the classroom teachers with, about how to better engage the student, or to the students to help them better understand their learning needs and thus develop more positive attitudes.

Establishing a future plan

Term four is a time when we develop our programmes for the new year. Through the collegial group we evaluate the success of the teaching/learning plans we have implemented, asking both teachers and students for feedback to determine whether our goal of improved student engagement has been achieved, albeit on a small scale. We can then share our experiences with our colleagues and encourage them to adopt the LSA approach to student learning with some of their classes in the new year. We will also explore the development of lesson planning software that links learning style profiles to the New South Wales Quality Teaching Program.

Following our successful working bee to manufacture the soft furnishings for some of our classrooms, we hope to conduct another, this time to construct a selection of learning tools for use in classrooms.

Finally, it is our hope that we are again successful in gaining CAP district funding to undertake additional modules of the Diploma in Holistic Education course in future. Then the cycle will begin again

For full report see online appendix 14.

LS in adult education settings

My late husband Armin and his colleague Ralf Schmidt, both lecturers at the School of Baking and Patisserie at Manukau Institute of Technology (MIT) in Auckland, NZ, describe how they have been using LS over the past few years in vocational training.

Both of us are teaching at Manukau Institute of Technology, one of the largest polytechnic institutions in New Zealand, in the subject areas of baking and pastry cooking. The use of the LSA-Adult instrument was introduced into the baking courses first in 2002. Initially we applied the LSA for selection of students into the full-time baking course. This was really helpful, particularly in view of having applicants from up to 15 different nations and cultural backgrounds. The results showed that the majority of applicants were 'hands-on' people and later we found out that most of them were challenged by traditional teaching methods in academic learning. Here the LSA results gave us the opportunity to individualize our delivery of academic back-up information for practical aspects of the course.

For these new and diverse ways of delivery to be accepted by all students it was necessary to introduce them thoroughly to the concepts of LS. Even though there was occasional resistance among more adult persons, ultimately all students agreed to give it a try. After only a few weeks of having a choice of studying theory in 'their' style they have taken on the concept enthusiastically. There is still the odd grumbling of 'that's childish' or 'primary school teaching', but once that was overcome these students became the most ardent supporters of the LSA concept. They found that they are not 'stupid' when it comes to academic learning and they can remember and process even more challenging data if they are allowed to learn in their way. For the first time in their life they were in control of their own learning and were prepared to take responsibility for it. This also boosted students' self-confidence, the results of which were high attendance, punctuality and a positive attitude among all participants in the baking programmes.

LS tools for pastry course at MIT

Theory lessons at MIT with LS tools make learning difficult content easier

Display of students' final exam products from Pastry and Bakery course at MIT, Auckland, NZ

After three years we can say that particularly helpful was the introduction of LS tools, which the majority of students like to handle and manipulate. Equally important is the playing of appropriate 'learning' music while working in the bakery kitchen and during written assessments. A revamp of the classroom setting has worked very well, with the introduction of bean bags, individual desks and low- and bright-light areas. Our LSA classroom also features peripheral posters relating to the subject. With the introduction of koosh balls and squeaky toys and noise instruments, we encourage our students to participate in their learning in a light-hearted and fun way. As each student is allowed to learn in their own style (as long as they do not disturb others), even older participants from more structured and serene cultures find a way to participate successfully.

While we still have a long way to go and keep learning much more about the diversity of learners, we are totally excited by the improvements of outcomes for our students since the introduction of LS. We are currently looking at improving the flexibility for change in our classroom settings to accommodate as many different learners as possible in all our programmes. By the time of the start of the next academic year in 2005 we attempt to have all modules of our full-time course converted into learning style mode.

After one year of using this concept, we can say that LS has definitely brought back the excitement and fun to our own learning and teaching and all this in spite of more and more restrictive, time-consuming requirements asked of us by the system.

Keep going!

Ralf Schmidt, who had a very difficult teaching year after having to take over Armin's classes following his sudden death, sent me the following final report.

Another school year has passed and on reflection I have to say that ... the students have come a very long way in a short time. Ten months ago the group of 18 students had no concept of baking or even an idea what to expect in this course. Fourteen students made it to the final assessment and completed all successfully.

And what a result it was – fantastic artworks and baked goods of the highest standard – all done without further instructions from me (see pictures on page 172).

How was that possible?

I guess that the use of learning style techniques played a large role in this amazing development of the students. They could learn and work on their own, in pairs or in a larger group. The learning was often self-guided, mostly student-centred and took place in their own time during the day; this was a chance for students who otherwise would have fallen through the cracks.

We utilized music for learning, koosh ball sessions, different light levels in classrooms, water and food when needed, visual stimulation and lots of hands-on practice. Throughout the school year I checked the recall of theoretical content every session to verify where the students were and nearly all of them were always on task. The students are all delighted about their exam success and it will be an amazing new start for many in an industry where quality standards and creative ability are vital ... there are no boundaries to achieve excellence.

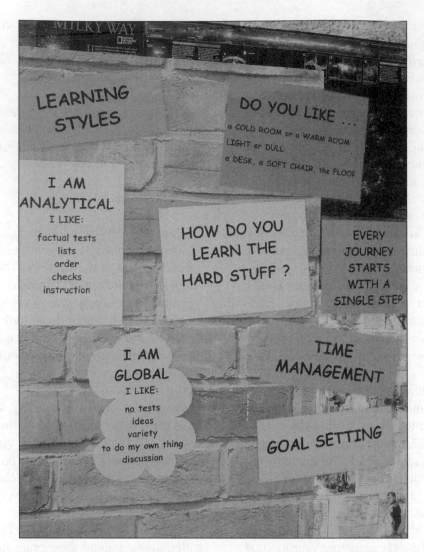

The Learning Styles Wall at Nayland College, Nelson, NZ

NAVIGATING UNIQUE PATHWAYS IN LEARNING

Chapter 22

What about testing and exams?

There is strong consensus among educators that no matter how we teach our students, ultimately they need to be capable of taking tests and sit exams successfully. I do not contest these aspirations for a minute, particularly as long as we have systems in place that measure students' learning success in prescribed tests, assessments and exams. To be successful in such a system based on assessment for learning such as in the UK (i.e. dependent on testing), students need to be well prepared and confident to achieve desired outcomes. As long as such systems are in place, teachers and parents will do their utmost to help their children achieve the best possible results.

Since the LS concept has been introduced on a large scale in various countries, I have met many progressive teachers who have embraced the diversity concept wholeheartedly and with great success, more so in primary schools than in high schools; but even if such educators are very much in favour of learning styles and personalized instructions, many of them (particularly in high schools) cannot see how LS would be beneficial for test-taking as it is impossible to accommodate individual needs during such activities. I fully agree. However, such reasoning contains a profound misconception about LS and it needs to be clarified under which circumstances learning style approaches are most beneficial for students.

Considering the complexity of learning processes, we have to distinguish between information intake and information output. Curriculum delivery, skills acquisition and increasing understanding about subject areas are all variations of information intake, during which personalizing learning through LS applications can make all the difference between learning success or failure. This is particularly the case when students have to learn something new and/or difficult.

Exams and tests are situations where information output is required, during which students show what they know, what they have learned and how well they understand curriculum content. They are not taking in new information but demonstrating their knowledge under time pressure, and generally students find such situations quite stressful.

The point of difference is:

a) during the presentation of new and/or difficult information learning styles need to be accommodated to ensure the best possible learning outcome.

b) that during tests and exams LS applications are not so crucial because most students have enough flexibilities to cope with adverse situations; this is especially true when the learning process preceding the exam has been accomplished with teaching methods matching their personal learning styles. When students are allowed to learn in their best way, they understand and remember better and are much more confident in showing what they know in an exam situation, even when their personal learning styles are not being matched during the exam. Yet they are less prone to failure or having memory lapses because with LS based study techniques, curriculum content is more readily available, even under pressure.

What is Learning Style?

INTAKE – Processing – Storage of...

NEW and/or DIFFICULT information

What is Multiple Intelligences?

OUTPUT of information through personal Skills, Talents, Gifts...

www.clc.co.nz (2005)   1

What happens at Exams?

= OUTPUT of information not necessarily through one's personal learning style.

Once information is learned through one's personal learning style (INTAKE),

confident OUTPUT happens in many different ways - even under exam pressure.

www.clc.co.nz (2005)   2

What you do think of your classroom?

- It's big and I like the displays on the wall.
- Colourful and warm.
- I think it is very nice to have our own classroom.
- The chairs are really comfy.
- I think it is wonderful because we have comfortable seats and other brand new furniture.
- The classroom is new and its got lots of new facilities. Top of the range chairs with cushions on our chairs.
- Teacher is thoughtful and kind. The classroom is 'wicked'.

Is there anything you would like to see differently in your classroom?

- I don't think so because the classroom looks great.
- No! Not really! I would like to sit by Abbey!
- Curtains because the sun gets in my eyes.
- I'd like music to be on.

What do you like best about your new school?

- The day goes quickly because the break times are different from my primary school.

- My registration class is really warm. The seats are that comfy I could fall asleep.

- I like the teachers also art, RE and English.

- That we learn different languages.

Feedback from students after introducing LS to these classes at Trevethin, UK

We know that from research on the original LS instruments as well as from anecdotal evidence and practical experience with our LSA instruments. Therefore this important conclusion can be drawn:

Exam results improve when students have been allowed to learn and prepare themselves in their own best way, based on their personal learning style. In short: LS teaching improves grades and test results.

Case Studies

Trevethin School Year 7 Project

This study from the Torfean County Borough Council near Cardiff, UK is kindly provided by Gareth Bucklands, Adviser.

Three classes of approximately 24 children were created, the LEA liaised with the school to draw up a training programme including critical skills, first steps and whiteboard training, preferred learning styles were analysed and parents were informed and involved.

There is conclusive evidence that the project has had a significant and positive impact on standards in terms of improved achievement and attainment. To achieve this in such a short space of time is remarkable and has pleasantly surprised many of the people involved.

The quality of the curriculum has improved both in terms of the delivery, methodology and the content. Also the learning environment has been considerably enhanced. There is enthusiasm among all concerned for a continuation of the project in Year 7 and an extension in to Year 8. There is a growing awareness among staff and pupils about preferred learning styles.

There has been a dramatic endorsement of the project from the teachers involved, and while they were never sceptical, they are now immensely strong advocates of the approaches developed. They saw how this has impacted on their teaching and acknowledge the professional development opportunities received.

Outcomes from this cohort were the best ever for a Year 7 in this school in all aspects: performance, attendance and behaviour. Not a bad start!

For a full report see online appendix 9.

LS pilot project in Ontario, Canada

Sonia Pouyat, the project leader, reports that in the first year there were seven schools involved, from three cities and surrounding rural areas with 1,000 students from Grades 3 to 11, and 50 teachers. Two special education programmes were included: one for students who had been expelled from their community schools and a school for students with emotional and behavioural challenges that the community schools could not accommodate. The purpose of the project was to implement the LSA and its accompanying teaching style analysis (TSA) tool and demonstrate its value as a resource for teachers that contributes to improved student performance, as well as to determine what is involved in its broad application. All schools voluntarily entered the project with the agreement of their principals, encouraged by enthusiastic teachers who had prior introductory training in the approach to learning styles. Key goals were to implement the LSA in a variety of classrooms and determine its impact on students' study skills, self-knowledge and self-esteem, learning attitudes, behaviour in classroom, parent co-operation regarding student learning and teachers management of classrooms, teachers feeling better equipped to teach a diverse group of students.

One key result was that the project raised teachers' awareness of their teaching styles and stimulated a process of questioning and discussing teaching methods in relation to students' learning styles in an unprecedented way. This was the main benefit of the first year for most of the schools involved. Positive impact on students' self-esteem and interest in learning was observed in the Expulsion Program, where the project was fully implemented within the timeframes by teachers with the privilege of small classes.

For a full report see online appendix 8.

School leaders of the future

	Roles	New management skills
1	Visionary	**Developing the right vision** How do you share your vision to the organization? Are you making it clear enough to be communicated to all members of your school? Can you access leading-edge thinking?
2	Empowerer	**Providing frameworks and directions vs giving independence to staff** How do you trust people and communicate it? How is everyone assessed for professional performance as well as the values of your school?
3	Learner	**Having a personal/professional development plan** How can you continuously learn about the future of education and business? Are you aware of changes in the educational market? How do you learn as a manager, as a human being? Do you know what are the core competencies for education in future?
4	Coach	**Practising role-modelling** How do you provide staff and associates with capabilities and opportunities that help them to achieve their goals? How does the sharing of goals and the sharing of learning happen at your school?
5	Team player	**Actively becoming part of a functioning team** How do you participate in professional groups? Are you encouraging team building at your school? Can you be a leader as well as a team member?
6	Mentor	**Providing guidance and wisdom** Do you ask the right questions, share your expertise? Do give enough, but not too much, guidance to those you are mentoring?
7	Risk taker	**Taking the utmost business and performance risk** How do you encourage experiments, learn about failures? How do you invest in developing people with the right skills for the future? How do you put people into new positions and how do you give them new responsibilities?
8	Collaborator	**Creating a network of contacts** Do you know where capabilities exist and how to transfer them? How do you manage alliances and joint-ventures, different kinds of working contacts and contracts?

Adapted from conference handout by L.M. Otala, Helsinki

Chapter 23

New roles for school leaders during change and beyond

When working with principals, deputies and management teams in schools, I have often encountered the need for a new definition of leadership and the wish for a better understanding of the many roles educators in leading positions have to fulfil in an ever more complicated organization still called school these days. During my seminars for school leaders, 'Creating the School of the Future', the material opposite has been very useful for these people, has given them a deeper understanding of the complexity of their roles and has helped them in planning future developments for their schools.

The Forbury success story in the deep south of NZ

One of the principals who has taken on and very successfully fulfilled this role is Ms Janice Tofia, Principal of Forbury Primary School in Dunedin, NZ. I respect her greatly and admire how she had the courage to take on a failing school, believing in the learning styles concept and preventing the school from being closed down because of underperformance. Here is her report from December 2004.

After working for the Education Review Office for a number of years (this involved also evaluations of the quality of the education provided at Forbury School) in October 2001 I took up the position of relieving principal of that school. This school was experiencing a high level of dysfunction as the Board of Trustees (BOT) had resigned at the end of 1999 and after some operating difficulties, a Commissioner was appointed,

and early in 2001 the principal resigned. A retired principal filled the position for over a term. When I applied, I knew this was a significant challenge but I underestimated how much of a challenge it would be.

The previous two years had certainly been very difficult. There were many significant events that impacted on people young and old with long-lasting effects. There had been little involvement from the school with the outside world. While the final events were the resignation of the BOT, the appointment of a Commissioner, the resignation of the principal, there were other longer lasting issues that included a rapid drop in the school roll, very severe and challenging student behaviours, a lack of parent involvement, and increasing levels of stress among staff.

This first term was a challenge. It was my first experience as a principal and I had to learn about the logistics of being one including coping with the demands of 'Payroll' at the end of a busy day. A classroom block in the school grounds had recently been demolished and an exposed floor area with nails, glass, bottles, rocks and sticks was a haven for many of our boys ... and a management nightmare.

The many changes at school had taken their toll on staff and students. Students acted out their stresses by bullying each other physically and emotionally, were abusive to staff, destroyed each others' work, and did not know how to accept or handle praise. They were angry about anything and everything, and their behaviours were a long and loud cry for help. It was not possible to implement a

Learning Styles Implementation at Tumbarumba High School

Tumbarumba High School is a small isolated school situated in the foothills of the New South Wales Snowy Mountains in Australia. It receives federal government funding through the Country Area Program (CAP) - an equity programme designed to help overcome the potential problems of isolation and to support students to maximize their learning outcomes. All CAP schools are required to develop programmes which address three criteria: Quality Improvement, Quality Teaching and Learning, and Quality Technology in Teaching and Learning.

The following is a summary of the school's journey to date, written by the principal, Sheila Ayliffe:

As part of our planning for 2004 our school successfully submitted a proposal to the CAP District Committee for additional funding to conduct a learning styles seminar for teachers from a number of small schools. This was facilitated by Barbara Prashnig and a parent evening was also organized to introduce the LS concept to parents. They were excited about these new approaches and became great supporters because they understood that LS also helps their children at home when doing homework.

Being an isolated community, we are experiencing the countrywide decline in the rural sector, and in particular falling employment opportunities, and the size of our school population is gradually decreasing. In order to maintain our curriculum the decision was made to establish a vertical structure for students in Years 7 and 8. This had not been done at our school in the past, so presented staff with new challenges. Our theory for improvement was, therefore, to conduct the initial learning style analysis (LSA) training for all staff and, in conjunction, an information session for parents to help them understand how they could use their child's learning profile to provide support in the home context.

As part of our Literacy strategy we operate a special reading group where targeted Year 7 students are buddied with an older student mentor. This group reads together each morning when the whole school starts the day with DEAR — Drop Everything And Read. Following our learning styles seminar at which we were introduced to Brain Gym®, we now have the students complete a series of crossovers to music before they begin reading. The students have reported that they find this activity has increased their alertness for the rest of the day and the co-ordinating teacher has reported significant increases in the students' reading performance.

Another benefit of our LSA training has been its use to help individual students from outside the target group. When students are referred to me with particularly challenging behaviour, or in need of a study programme, I always begin with an LSA. This then forms the basis of advice I provide the classroom teachers about how to better engage the student or to the students to help them better understand their learning needs and thus develop more positive attitudes.

See page 100 for our lesson planning using learning styles approaches.

In our collegial group we decided that we would initially concentrate on the group's strong preference until teachers were more confident about adopting a full learning styles approach to their lesson development. We have members whose Year 7/8 classes show the follow strong preference profiles, that is, approximately 60 per cent or over:

continued on page 182

Learning Styles in Action

workable behaviour management programme as the children would not accept any consequences for their actions. I spent much of my days managing the fallout from the classrooms, and learning about the depth of poverty, hopelessness, the lack of experiences, the anger, the low self-esteem and lack of confidence that existed in our students.

We could not display work anywhere in the school or in classes as it got torn from the walls, and eyes were scratched out of photographs. Teachers continued to extinguish the small and large bush fires that regularly erupted. Although this sapped the energy of staff, teachers and ancillary staff remained committed to the children of Forbury School. They knew that it should and could be better and their high level of professionalism and support for me was a critical factor in effecting change. Until this day I greatly appreciate what all my teachers do during their working day.

The Commissioner continued with his duties and responsibilities, and his term of governance was extended to the end of November 2001. I also had my leave extended until the end of 2001. The Commissioner's task was to provide the Ministry of Education with a report setting out the future options for Forbury School. These ranged from closure to further resourcing. The longer the Commissioner stayed at Forbury School, the more evident it became that something special was needed to improve the lot for our children. A visit from the Minister of Education, Trevor Mallard, left us with a challenge to develop a plan that included something creative and radical. He wasn't interested in a sticking plaster approach.

Around that time, Emeritus Professor Barbara Prashnig had delivered her first two learning styles seminars in Alexandra, Central Otago. The media report caught our eye as the implementation of a 'learning styles' approach to teaching and learning appeared to be creative and was certainly a radical starting point. After exploring the possibilities of implementing such an LS programme, we made a clear statement about the significant needs of our students: academic, emotional,

social and behavioural, physical and health, family and home based. Together with a monitoring component, the Commissioner's report was submitted to the Ministry of Education, and, with some amendments, was accepted as a 'pilot project' with NZ $387,000 school support funding over three years with the right of termination after one year if the approach was not supporting student achievement.

What was included in the project?

The Forbury School–School Support project was quite complex and far reaching. The components included strategies involving health, home, learning, self-esteem, staffing and accountability such as:

➤ team building with staff and trustees

➤ staff training in LS teaching

➤ setting up LS classrooms with furniture, fittings and resources

➤ screening students for Irlen Syndrome (Scotopic, Sensitivity Syndrome – SSS)

➤ assessing all students with the LSA

➤ providing parents with useful parenting skills through the 'Parenting with Confidence' programme and 'Tool Box' sessions

➤ providing me with principal release from teaching

➤ testing all students in reading, writing and number each six months over three years

➤ introducing the 'Kiwi Can' programme in Term 3 and onwards.

How much of this did we achieve?

■ We all participated in team building activities and development involving all staff and trustees. This meant all participants completing a personal style analysis (DISC) and a working style analysis (WSA). The profiles of various groups – BOT; BOT and staff; staff; principal and staff and so on were very interesting.

■ All teaching and ancillary staff have completed their Diploma of Holistic Education so that they can deliver programmes that cater for students' preferred learning styles.

LSA Results at Tumbarumba High School, NSW, Australia

Group 1	Group 2
AUDITORY (external) 33% – talking/discussing AUDITORY (internal) 66% – self-talk/inner dialogue	AUDITORY (external) 64% – talking/discussing AUDITORY (internal) 78% – self-talk/inner dialogue
VISUAL (words) 58% – reading VISUAL (external) 66% – seeing/watching VISUAL (internal) 41% – visualizing/imagination	VISUAL (words) 71% – reading VISUAL (external) 85% – seeing/watching VISUAL (internal) 71% – visualizing/imagination
TACTILE (touching) 66% – manipulating/handling	TACTILE (touching) 100% – manipulating/handling
KINESTHETIC (external) 58% – experiencing/doing KINESTHETIC (internal) 75% – feeling/intuition	KINESTHETIC (external) 92% – experiencing/doing KINESTHETIC (internal) 92% – feeling/intuition
INTAKE 50% – needed	INTAKE 78% – needed
MOBILITY 75% – movement needed	MOBILITY 50% – movement needed
TEMPERATURE 66% – cool	TEMPERATURE 64% – cool
MOTIVATION 83% – self-starting CONFORMITY 66% – conforming	MOTIVATION 78% – self-starting CONFORMITY 42% – conforming
RESPONSIBILITY 75% – high/strong	RESPONSIBILITY 78% – high/strong
VARIETY 58% – change-oriented	VARIETY 35% – change-oriented

Christine Easterbrook and Belinda Henderson, the authors of this report, were surprised at the variation in the two groups, when the students had been randomly allocated to their year groups. One member of our group who teaches both classes commented that she finds one easier to work with than the other.

This led us to complete the teaching style analysis (TSA) and examine reasons for the teacher's finding one group easier than the other. Needless to say, one group better matches the teacher's profile. We are now debating whether to complete LSAs before we allocate our incoming students to classes and trying to match TSAs to class profiles.

Through the collegial group we are evaluating the success of the teaching/learning plans we have implemented, asking both teachers and students for feedback, to determine whether our goal of improved student engagement has been achieved, albeit on a small scale. We then share our experiences with our colleagues and encourage them to adopt the LSA approach to student learning with some of their classes in the new year. We would also like to explore the development of lesson planning software which links learning style profiles to the New South Wales Quality Teaching Program.

Following our successful working bee to manufacture the soft furnishings for some of our classrooms, we hope to conduct another training, this time to construct a selection of learning tools for use in classrooms.

Finally, it is our hope that we are again successful in gaining CAP district funding to undertake additional modules of the Diploma in Holistic Education course in 2006 to continue the training we did in 2005. Then the cycle will begin again!

■ The project initially provided for the setting up of three classrooms. Since the approval of the project we have had a roll increase (69 on 1 July 2001 and 132 at the end of Term 4 2004) consequently we had to set up six classrooms. In creating 'brain friendly' LS classrooms with the appropriate furniture, fittings and resources, we have cleaned out, reorganized, planned for work flow, reused equipment, created colour schemes and changed existing bits and pieces. We set up areas for specific curriculum content; established an area for the teacher's things so that there is organization, no time lost with searching for things. We bought sofas, bean bags, junior furniture and storage equipment. There are now curtains in each classroom so that teachers and students have greater control over light levels (limited use of fluorescent light and true light tubes ordered).

■ Twenty-eight students were screened for the eye condition SSS, also called Irlen Syndrome after its discoverer Helen Irlen. This syndrome is also called colour dyslexia and some of the symptoms are: moving words, white 'rivers' down the page, words spilling over, moving letters, lights in words when reading.

■ Parenting skills were taught through the 'Parenting With Confidence Programme' with a series of 'Tool Box' sessions. With that we had limited success – we are not sure why – possibly it was introduced a little soon – too much information at once maybe – or it is possibly easier not to get involved in this difficult area.

■ Although I was provided with principal release from teaching to manage the project and other issues, I spent a high proportion of my time on social and behavioural issues – but have noted that the frequency and severity of the challenging behaviours is now decreasing.

■ We have trained staff and implemented the 'Kiwi Can' programme that aims to build students' self-esteem and confidence as a result of the programme. A strength of this programme is the setting of a school focus to meet identified needs, and the built-in accountability.

■ The sixth and final testing was completed at the end of 2004 measuring the progress of students in literacy and numeracy. The literacy testing included skills and knowledge in reading and writing, and students' numeracy development. These assessments indicate some very good gains, particularly in reading. Despite not teaching the strategies needed to progress along the stages of the number framework, some students have also made significant gains in mathematics.

■ All students' learning styles have been analysed with emphasis on the ways they like to work and learn including their preferred sensory modalities A, V, T, K, and other aspects.

■ All classrooms have easy listening 'Soundfield' systems – these are wonderful and should be in every classroom. They surround the children with sound, making listening much easier.

■ Teachers have been trained in the effective use of music to settle and focus students, and to enhance learning. This is working very well.

■ We have changed the school day with hourly learning blocks.

■ We have implemented various literacy support programmes like Jolly Phonics and Smart Phonics, HPP, tape assisted reading programmes (TARP), Perceptual Motor programmes, reading CDs. There is much more to be done such as sensory processing and integration to fill the gaps.

■ We feed children several times every day – breakfast, break food, and lunch. We transport children to and from school.

What problems have we experienced?

The sayings that 'Hindsight is 20/20 vision' and 'if I had my time over again knowing what I know now' are true and things would have been easier, had we known…

■ Going into the unknown – somewhat blind. Still coming to grips with the whole concept and also having to manage it. While we have had a good level of support from Professor Barbara Prashnig and our adviser Frances Hill from Te

A large component of our learning time takes place outside the classroom - the best hands on text book available.

Outdoor adventures, Waterwise, MERC, Goat Island, Rangitoto Island, aid in developing self confidence, initiative, cooperation and self esteem

We use our "Ladder to Success" to guide us with organising, planning and presenting our discoveries and investigations.

Interaction with global organisations and schools establish an awareness for international concerns and build empathy towards other cultures.

A major component of the childrens learning is Inquiry Learning - investigations in the 'real world' working with and alongside professional people. We have designed our own business cards, fax and letter headers and are treated as professionals.

Inquiry is a method of learning where the students:

- **are encouraged to recognise and state problems**
- ask questions about these problems in a matter that allows them to pursue answers
- recognise answers are both the final product and the starting point for further study.

Our 'ladder' enables us to follow a series of steps. This learning style stimulates creative thinking and curiosity, promotes the development of interpersonal skills, increases students motivation and self esteem because students have more control over their own learning.

Our carefully balanced programme covers all the New Zealand Curriculum areas and also includes: Japanese, Spanish and an extensive inclass Information and Communication Technology programme

Stepping into the future with

ROOM 14

Sharyn Hay -1999

The Classroom of the Future created by Sharyn Hay at Devonport Primary, Auckland, NZ

My personal teaching style has become a major interest to educationalists. I have an extremely full intinery on the national and international level to key note at Conferences, and provide seminars and professional development to teaching professionals. I am an enthusiastic classroom teacher and therefore have declined to go out on a consultant level. This is where I am proud to say the children come first and any extras come second. The children do feel proud to hear that their work has been displayed and modelled in an exotic location over the holidays!

So what's so special about the Room 14 programme!

A new style of teaching derived from Inquiry Learning, Whole Brain Learning, Information and Communication Technology and Individualised learning styles. This provides a stimulating learning environment where the children take control over their own learning and I act as the tour guide

"Don't wait for your boat to come, swim out to greet it!"

Our quote for 1999 enables us to focus on using our initiative in a safe, caring environment in preparation for facing challenges in the 'wider world'. The children are encouraged to take a risk and grasp new challenges thus going beyond their horizon.

Monitoring and self assessment play an important part in our learning. Each child creates a portfolio which includes an audio tape and a video so that they can listen to or observe their progress depending on their preferred learning style

Homework is crucial to the Year 8 programme. As well as 20 minutes of reading I am expecting the children to complete an hour of quality learning time each night covering topics that are applicable to the weekly class work. The work caters for a wide range of abilities learning styles.

Acceleration learning techniques are scattered throughout the programme to maximise our learning potential. We meditate regularly, listen to music suited to specific learning tasks, burn aromatherapy therapy oils to suit learning needs, recite GLP's, and exercise our brain through brain gym

Higher level thinking skills play a major role in my programme. We investigate De Bono's theory of 'Six Thinking Hats' to complement our investigation work. We utilise a wide range of thinking tools to classify, organise and present our thoughts and discoveries.

Sharyn Hay -1999

Moana School in Geraldine, there is no one in the near vicinity to call on and for staff to observe brain-friendly classrooms in action.

- The huge commitment to training – out of school time – weekends, holidays, or often after a busy day.
- The training of new staff so that they are quickly up to speed with the practices in place.
- The workload in delivering programmes based on National Curriculum requirements as well as meeting students' individual learning styles requirements through innovated teaching approaches.
- The availability of resources – many needed to be made as one cannot buy the self-correcting LS tools.
- The ongoing severe and challenging behaviours of a small group of students. Each week brings horror stories about children's social behaviours, deprivation, and varied care and protection issues. Children staying away, children dragged out in the night, not protected from drugs and alcohol, huge anger issues, sexual awareness at a young age, lack of experiencing family activities.
- The well intentioned various community groups who wish to assist – initially these were very time consuming. It needed a community liaison person to manage these projects – I feel the time was not right for community involvement.
- We did not begin until term 2 of 2002 because of the need to have the initial performance assessments completed before any interventions could begin.

What changes have we noticed?

Apparently, with the conditions right, a big change was evident from the implementation of approaches involving teaching and learning styles in only 6–8 weeks.

When we continue to deal with some very difficult behaviours we know the time-frame will be longer. Despite the fact that an LS approach to teaching and learning cannot resolve extreme behavioural issues, we have noticed some significant changes.

Changes in students

- much improved playground behaviour with children hurrying back to class after breaks;
- much more settled class environments;
- much greater respect for the school property, and the property and work efforts of others;
- most behaviours are managed in the classrooms now – much less overflow to the principal;
- able to accept consequences for their actions;
- improved tolerance levels of others' differences;
- the emergence of a culture where the children are taking more responsibility for their learning – a greater involvement and higher level of engagement in learning tasks;
- making the most of opportunities offered and available – these include:
  - taking golf lessons that resulted in a group promoted to the elite group and one student winning a set of golf clubs;
  - performing in the hip-hop dance group on national television, in a live performance with invited adult artists, and in school dance performances;
  - being part of the Heartland Music programme for gifted and talented students where children are given individual tuition on piano, guitar, drums, percussion and singing (we have 12 students in this programme);
  - helping in the school edible garden;
  - singing in the choir at the local music festival and the neighbouring retirement homes;
  - participating in sports events such as the triathlon, cross country and athletics where children have had individual successes;
  - entering art competitions and having success;
  - performing in the school Kapahaka group with pride;
  - running school assemblies where two students are responsible for organizing and directing proceedings;

Figure 7 indicates the number of levels students have moved through since the initial testing conducted in March 2002. Six students are achieving at the same level they were recorded at in March of 2002. Twenty-six students have moved up either one or two levels. One student has moved forward twenty-two levels. Thirty-eight students have moved up three or more reading levels.

Figure 7: Extent of change in Reading Levels, March 2002–May 2003

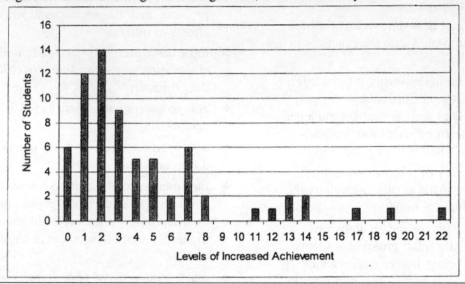

Table 18: Year 1–4 students' attitudes towards mathematics (expressed as percentages)

		☺	☺	☹	☹	Don't Know
1.	Would you like to do more maths or less maths at school?	70	7	5	14	4
2.	How much do you like doing maths at school?	62	24	5	4	5
3.	How good do you think you are at maths?	78	12	3	2	5
4.	How good does your teacher think you are at maths?	60	14	4	2	20
6.	How do you feel about doing things in maths that you haven't tried before?	60	14	2	17	7
7.	How much do you like doing maths in your own time (not at school)?	52	24	6	9	9
8.	Do you want to keep learning maths when you grow up?	76	16	0	7	1

Table 19: Year 5–8 students' attitudes towards mathematics (expressed as percentages)

		☺	☺	☹	☹	Don't Know
1.	Would you like to do more maths or less maths at school?	41	18	18	16	7
2.	How much do you like doing maths at school?	55	20	12	8	5
3.	How good do you think you are at maths?	37	25	25	6	7
4.	How good does your teacher think you are at maths?	39	20	8	6	27
6.	How do you feel about doing things in maths that you haven't tried before?	35	30	14	8	13
7.	How much do you like doing maths in your own time (not at school)?	33	18	23	20	6
8.	Do you want to keep learning maths when you grow up?	51	20	10	12	7

Results taken from 'Report of Student Achievement' Forbury School, May 2003, Dunedin College of Education, pp 8 and 21

- ❏ helping design and paint the school space mural;
- ❏ fundraising for the new school playground.

All of the above is recognized at the end of year celebrations where our traditional school cups are presented and 22 miniatures are presented to worthy recipients.

Changes in teachers

- ❖ A strong collegial bond has formed between staff members who support and protect each other, celebrate each others' successes, share tasks to be done, plan together.
- ❖ Increasing knowledge and confidence to experiment with new approaches such as the use of music at the beginning of the day throughout, sessions with Brain Gym®, using relaxation techniques, state changers, refocusing activities, and taking time to reflect on practices that work.
- ❖ Learning about and implementing a Perceptual Motor Programme (PMP) to increase children's motor skills, balance, memory, sequencing.
- ❖ Currently learning about sensory awareness, processing and sensory integration.
- ❖ Planning an integrated curriculum as well as considering students' preferred learning styles. There have been many fine examples where teachers have delivered new and difficult information in ways that the students can best take up the information in their preferred way. They then have opportunities to present what they know and have learned in a way they choose.

Parents/caregivers

- ❖ We have a significant group of parents/caregivers who are involved in daily school life – making breakfast and lunches, helping in classrooms, with swimming, and with general tasks.
- ❖ The school corridors now buzz with adults before and after school – years ago few adults came into the school building.
- ❖ Parents/caregivers have joined the Board of Trustees which is still ministerial

appointed, and have formed a Parent Teacher Association.
- ❖ Parents/caregivers are much more ready to bring anything to school to talk about it.
- ❖ An adult literacy group has conducted weekly sessions that involved a reasonably sized group of parents.
- ❖ A number of parents have helped with the garden planting vegetables and harvesting these, planting sunflower seeds with their children, planting garlic on the shortest day, and weeding the garden.
- ❖ A large number of parents attend goal setting with the teacher of their child and their child.
- ❖ Helping daily with the implementation of the PMP programme.
- ❖ Spending many hours helping with the addition of the many books to the library that were provided by the Rotary Club Dunedin East.
- ❖ Training and taking individual students for reading activities.
- ❖ Support sports groups with transport and uniforms.

Community interest

- ❖ Gifts of resources (for example, cushions, CD player and CDs, raw resources, sipper bottles).
- ❖ Volunteers to help with many activities.
- ❖ Donations of food and clothing from various service and church groups.
- ❖ Sponsorship of students to camp, and sports activities.
- ❖ Actual help with the beautification of the school grounds by building a windbreak, constructing seating, building gardens, planting flowers and vegetables, painting a mural, raising funds for the new school playground and a garage for the van.
- ❖ Financial sponsorship from Mainfreight for the Duffy books in homes programme.
- ❖ Sponsorship from Masonic Lodge for Perceptual Motor Programme equipment.

For further reports see online appendices 4 and 5.

A Case Study of Representative Youth Soccer and Learning Styles Application

Andrew J Martin

Massey University, Palmerston North, New Zealand

The purpose of this case study was to review how learning styles research can be applied to meet the holistic (physical, mental, social and emotional) needs of representative male youth soccer players, aged 13–16. Traditionally, soccer coaches tend to focus on players' physical (skill and fitness) development without careful consideration of their holistic needs. The coaching session focus tends to involve a series of 'drills' and exercises, with a small-sided game being played at the end of the practice. Consequently, players' participation experiences can vary enormously in degrees of enjoyment and learning, and motivation for further involvement. The development of an effective approach to coaching soccer becomes more complex when not only elements of the game are considered, but also differences in individual players' learning styles and sensory modes.

Playing soccer favours kinesthetic or experiential approaches to teaching and learning. The experiential cycle involves reflection on game experiences and leads to increased self-awareness, improved skills and game performance. However, it should be recognized that players with visual preferences may respond better to instructions being drawn on a whiteboard using pin figures or for the learners to see themselves on a video playback. Similarly, a learner with an auditory preference may respond better to keywords when learning a specific skill. Children and teenagers not only learn in a variety of ways, they are at different stages of learning and progress at different rates. This diversity requires the coach to implement a wide range of learning strategies to provide a balance of challenging experiences for the team, while enabling individuals to develop a broad set of their skills related to their level of ability.

The coach

My own coaching styles analysis (CSA) which is similar to the TSA (teaching style analysis) indicated that my current coaching methods were spread between traditional/analytic and individual/holistic approaches in the sensory areas, but I was aware that there was a need to be more flexible in my session planning and management. My coaching philosophy is based on the belief that the success and challenge of my teaching depends on more than just achieving results, but providing and developing an environment and activities that give a positive learning experience, while improving the players' knowledge. The players' enjoyment and development is not just about the skills of soccer, but involves a number of other factors, such as social and team involvement. This social aspect and feeling of belonging are often more important factors in sustaining players' interest and involvement, than the sport itself. It is my role to develop a positive learning environment using a variety of facilitation methods that aim to enhance the learning process for the individual players. For example, my awareness of a player's left/right eye dominance led to switching the player from the right to the left side of the pitch. With that the players' performance improved dramatically, as did their enjoyment of the game.

Summary

This case study has illustrated how a holistic experiential approach and linking of learning styles research can be used to develop a positive learning environment and enhance the enjoyment and skill development for youth soccer players. Session planning that involves placing emphasis on understanding tactical aspects of the game, rather than focusing on technique, caters for all ability levels and coaches with limited technique and experience. The management of the group is easier as the players love to play games, have fun and are involved all the time. However, rather than just presenting a series of drills the good coach needs to utilize these modified games to enhance the players' understanding of specific aspects of the game. This is particularly important in soccer as players do not have access to the coach during a game and, as a consequence, are required to make decisions for themselves.

For the full case study including observations about the players, the learning environment, improving decision making and game understanding, questioning, playing games, modified game examples, playing games and a bibliography, see online appendix 11.

Chapter 24

A look into the future: LS utopia or personalized learning for all?

In my work with educators, students and parents I often come across extreme reactions when style diversity in learning is discussed, be it at home or at school. Initially, it is unimaginable for many educators (particularly for high school teachers or teachers at college level) to allow their students to learn in less formal, non-traditional ways. Matching individual learning needs seems impossible in classrooms that are too small, have too many students and inadequate resources. It all seems too utopian to be workable.

Despite resistance, scepticism, denial and often ridicule of style diversity, I can now say that thousands of educators around the world are practising LS methods with successful outcomes.

School culture as a celebration of diversity

The following contribution by Alan Wagstaff of RAW Education in Swanson, near Auckland, NZ gives a glimpse of what the future can hold for schools when diversity becomes the basis for a new awareness and is implemented in a planned fashion.

Schools need a raft of fundamental strategies in order to foster a culture that celebrates diversity. Responding appropriately to students' learning styles is an important part of this 'celebration'. However, LS works best when supported by other fundamental structures to ensure it is 'do-able' and sustainable. There are many pressures on today's teachers. When LS strategies are the product of an entire school ethos devoted to the celebration of diversity, teachers more readily embrace and sustain them.

Five areas, in particular, contribute to an ethos promoting diversity in school life. They are:

1 When a school's *day-to-day operation* is run in a decentralized, shared decision-making way that encourages the different working styles of participants, a culture of diversity is set up at the most fundamental level. Students realize that teachers and staff 'walk the talk', staff realize that the culture of diversity is authentic.

2 An *LS-friendly curriculum* that provides for (at least) left- and right-brain responses in all subject areas, the clear identification of a continuum of core skills (across all year groups) so that individualized programmes can easily be created, especially in the core subjects of mathematics and English (mother tongue) and supports teachers in their efforts to respond to different learning styles.

3 A *timetable structure* that ensures teaching is to be approached in a number of frames – for example, integrative, differentiated and peer-grouped – gives confidence and clarity to teachers. This impacts on LS work by making it clear that this mode of teaching is to occur at certain times of the day – but not at all times. Other, useful teaching strategies are therefore encouraged as well.

4 Especially in *mathematics and English* (mother tongue), it is vital that an easy-to-use system is in place that rapidly identifies any gaps in the matrix of knowledge individual learners have –

In an email to the principal of Wellington High School, Mr Col Feather, the itinerant behavioural teacher, Denis Graham, urged the school to consider applying the LSA to all 65 students:

You may recall my enthusiasm about the Prashnig workshop that I attended late last year in Dubbo. I have to say again that this was the most significant T and D programme I have undertaken in 27 years of teaching! ... I believe that Prashnig's most powerful tool is offering teachers a programme called 'Learning Style Analysis'. In a nutshell, the Student LSA challenges us as teachers to programme our lessons according to the learning style of our students. I think it has outstanding potential for both the way your teachers teach and importantly as to how your students learn. I have trialled the learning style analysis, and the results were spot on. I believe the analysis has particularly strong application to many of your boys. The itinerant Behaviour Team will soon be using this analysis as part of our functional assessment instruments across the Dubbo and Warrumbungles schools.

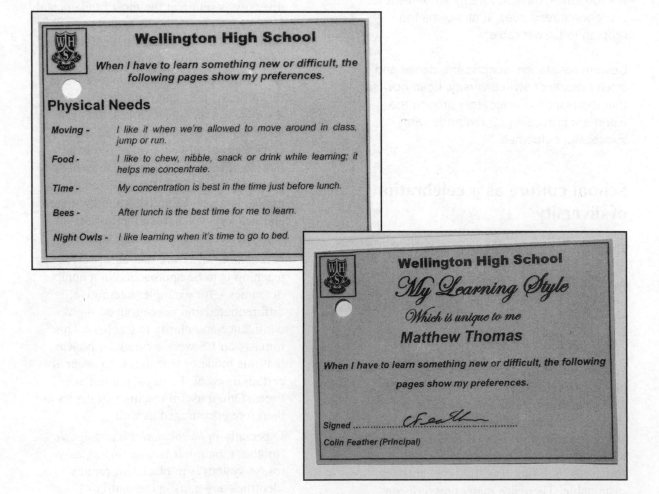

Every student receives a personal LS card based on their LSA results

going as far into the learning history as necessary. Such a system would first have to decide which objectives were core out of all possible maths and English objectives. The system would also need to provide a simple assessment tool and a set of teaching materials so that individually targeted programmes were easy to set up and operate in a mixed needs class. Then, as well as taking LS into account, the level of learning experience being offered would also be appropriate.

5 *Health and physical education* can make a major contribution to the celebration of diversity in a school by going beyond the tradition 'games' and 'agilities' boundaries and including 'social skills' in the learning programmes. Issues such as the differences brought about by culture, society, gender and sexual orientation can be explored in healthy ways. Co-operative learning and 'values' can be taught proactively. These matters cultivate the soil in which LS can take root.

In summary, we suggest LS strategies flourish best when they are a consequence of an entire school culture devoted to the celebration of diversity. In order for such a culture to be established some fundamental and detailed structures need to be in place. These detailed support systems have been developed and schools that have taken them up have experienced profound and positive changes.

No learning styles utopia but LS diversity applied

When I began introducing the LS concept to teachers all those years ago, first in NZ, then in Sweden, I was aware that implementation would be easier in primary schools because high school teachers told me it will never work at that level. They said it was an idealistic, utopian dream that would be best forgotten. I accepted their reservations, worked extensively with primary school teachers and saw the successes they had with their children. But I never forgot what I really wanted: to see LS used in high schools, particularly for students who

struggled academically. I knew it was not utopia, and slowly, over the past five years, more and more high schools have been using LS, not without scepticism, but always with successful outcomes. The report I received from Denis Graham, about LS implementation at Wellington High in NSW, Australia, is proof that LS application is a workable reality to improve teaching and learning in high schools. They also developed a very interesting and innovative way of introducing the LS concept to their students.

By mid-2005 the enthusiastic team of Year 7 teachers struck upon the idea of running a Student Learning Styles Awareness Day as a follow-up to the online LSAs that the students had completed. An innovative set of 'credit cards' were produced for each student based on results from their LSA report. These are easy to read, portable and published in a 'cool' format (see page 190).

The students had a full day in the school library where they were first introduced to their LS cards and then able to move through a series of mini classrooms experiencing different learning styles. The day's learning theme was 'flowers'. Students undertook sequential activities that involved auditory, visual, tactile and kinesthetic activities based on the flower theme. At the end of each activity students were asked to match what was on their cards with the activity they just completed to find their comfort and suitability with that particular learning activity. In addition there were trials with the use of food, working alone, in pairs and groups, using bright and dimly lit areas, as well as experiencing warm and colder environments. Teachers worked in close proximity with students for some activities and allowed total autonomy in others. Each of these settings was later evaluated by the students and compared with their LS cards.

After this successful introduction, the challenge now is for the innovations at Wellington HS to roll on into 2006 and beyond. Teachers are keen to trial new ways of classroom management and teaching is now much more collaborative, and learning is also more engaging and fun!

No LS Utopia at Wellington High School, NSW

Denis Graham commenced work at Wellington High School in Central NSW, Australia, as an itinerant behaviour teacher in late 2004 and his work on LS formed part of his action research with NSW Dep. of Ed. Schools' Leadership Directorate. His initial brief was to assist an innovative and committed group consisting of Year 7 adviser and 14 classroom teachers and a career adviser on transition issues from primary to secondary schooling. Within the group of 65 new students there were a small number with both emotionally disturbed behaviours and mild intellectual disabilities. Levels of disengagement from learning were of concern to the teachers and students' motivation to study (especially among boys) was very low. Suspension data and reports of negative behaviours were high. (See graphs below.) The school decided to use special priority funding provided by the Commonwealth for Schools from low socio-economic communities to employ Professor Barbara Prashnig (New Zealand) and Mary Brell to run LS workshops. Their presentation fitted in with the school plan with its focus on quality teaching. The school had already had three teachers attending Barbara's workshop and the Year 7 teachers were keen to embrace the use of the LSA for all their students.

In late term 2 Denis spoke individually to the majority of Year 7 teachers as a follow-up to Barbara's workshop. All teachers reported making some changes/adjustments to their classroom practices as a result of the workshop and had noticed some anecdotal improvement both in learning and behaviour. Some of these changes/adjustments included:

- Introducing more **tactile** and **kinesthetic** activities into lessons. (Time consuming in preparation, but some wonderful learning outcomes)
- Using various forms of **lighting** in the room. (All reported success with this)
- Introduction of a variety of **seating plans** including individual and small group designs. Cushions have already been used very successfully in one room and informal seating had been tried in two other rooms
- Allowances being made for **intake** of water and a variety of food in class time. Dried fruit, fruit, snack bars and water bottles were the most common being experimented with. (Most teachers reported responsibility with the disposal of rubbish and more settled students)
- 'Koosh' balls and other tactile objects have been trialled in two classes

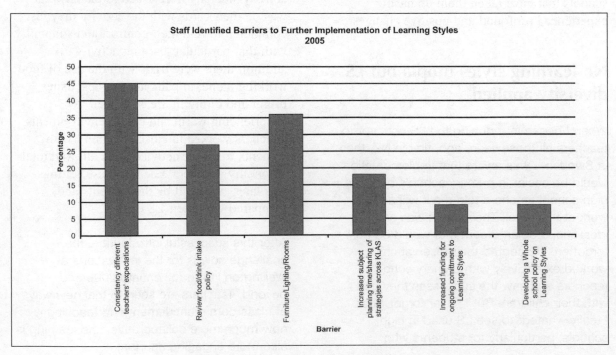

Results from Wellington High, NSW, Australia

Conclusion

In writing this book I have also followed a learning cycle, taking the reader from a broad overview through to the underlying theories of style diversity, to the assessment instruments, our 'tools of the trade', into practical applications contributed by practitioners in many different educational settings, and onto a final look into the future of personalized learning.

The question now arises: Do learning styles work and do we need to implement them in our daily work as educators? On all accounts it can be stated that yes, LS do work, that yes, this is the new way of learning and yes, knowledge of style diversity is helping to educate those who have so far failed in the system because current systems are failing students who cannot learn in traditional ways.

I am delighted by the overwhelming evidence gathered from practitioners around the world, some of whom I have not even met as yet. I admire and deeply appreciate their work, their dedication to their chosen profession and, most of all, their love for students in their charge and their unwavering belief that everyone CAN learn, if we just know how to teach them.

As requested by many educators who wanted to take the LS approach further but did not quite know how, I hope the experiences described by practitioners as well as the tips and explanations will give sufficient information so that they cannot wait to use and implement what is appropriate in their daily classroom work. However, only by consistent application will it be possible to gain experience and build courage for doing more with learning styles and personalized learning, particularly with students who struggle in the current system.

When I began to work with the diversity concept, I was so fascinated with the potential it could have for teaching in general and classroom work specifically that I wanted this to become not an alternative but the new standard in education. 'Fat chance', many said when I shared my dreams with them, because 'the system will never change', they believed. To a point that is true, but every system is made up of people: people who create it, people who control it and people who work within it, and also people who work against it, circumvent it, undermine it, and build systems within a system. These are the ones who have been courageous enough to trust my suggestions, brave enough to go against resistance and ridicule from colleagues, parents and supervisors, who have not given up, and who by their sheer perseverance are bringing about changes to teaching practices unimaginable ten years ago.

It has been a long ten years and sometimes it felt like a lifetime, but my journey to this point was worth every single day, even at times when resistance to this concept and academic arrogance made me sad and furious, and my concern about legions of struggling students, lost for learning, became nearly unbearable. I never lost faith that slowly, slowly the diversity concept combined with creative learning would spread, and when I was about to despair about the 'fossilization' particularly in high schools and higher education, an email or letter arrived, telling me what incredible results teachers had when using LS and how they are encouraged to continue with this work. Such feedback gives me strength to continue with what has become like a crusade for me and many like-minded educators around the world and we know a change for the better is on its way.

To everyone working with LS once again a heartfelt thanks and I urge you to keep up the good work. You are making a difference and our future generations need you.

Useful websites

http://web.sfn.org	scientific brain facts
www.21learn.org	21st Century Learning Initiative
www.6seconds.org	Emotional Intelligence Network
www.accelerated-learning.com	general learning
www.allianceforchildhood.net	young children's education
www.ascd.org	professional development, books
www.brainconnection.com	brain science and learning
www.brainconnection.com	scientific learning
www.brainexpo.com	brain-based learning and teaching
www.braingym.org	brain integration
www.brainstore.co.uk	making learning fun
www.buildinglearningpower.co.uk	learning strategies
www.cdipage.com	parenting information and child development
www.colourtest.ue-foundation.org	Luescher colour test
www.creativelearningcentre.com	LSA and TSA assessment instruments
www.drhuggiebear.com	ADHD and other learning problems
www.epic.co.uk	blended learning
www.ericec.org	myths about gifted students
www.esteemplus.com	personal and professional growth
www.eurydice.org	information network on education in Europe
www.findarticles.com	underachievers
www.fishpond.co.nz	book info, LS
www.funteaching.it	professional development
www.glidden.com	colours and emotions
www.hoagiesgifted.org	gifted underachievers
www.howtolearn.com	learning, reading, LS
www.irlen.com	visual distortion problems, Irlen Syndrome
www.kidsource.com	gifted underachieving
www.k-l-s.co.uk	Kaleidoscope Learning Solutions
www.ldpride.net	learning styles
www.learningnetwork.ac.nz	general education info
www.marvinmarshall.com	discipline without stress
www.mckergow.com	research on music and learning
www.mind.org.uk	mental health, stress and well-being
www.narva-bel.de	full-spectrum fluorescent light tubes
www.naturallighting.com	healthy lighting
www.networkcontinuum.co.uk	education books
www.readingandwriting.ab.ca	Irlen Syndrome
www.rockymountainprinting.com	information about colours and their quality
www.scilearn.com	scientific learning
www.skyscapes.biz	panels for diffusing light
www.smartkids.co.nz	self-correcting, hands-on learning tools
www.smartkids.co.uk	self-correcting, hands-on learning tools
www.songsforteaching.com	music and learning
www.sylviarimm.com	parenting

Further reading

Abbott, John and Ryan, Terry (2003), *The Unfinished Revolution*, Network Educational Press, Stafford.

Angelo, Simon (2004), *Study Success: How Students get Top Results in School*, Accelerated Learning Institute, Auckland.

Barth, Roland S. (1990), *Improving Schools from Within*, Jossey-Bass, San Francisco.

Brown, Don and Thomson, Charlotte (2000) *Co-operative Learning in New Zealand Schools*, Dunmore Press, Palmerston North, NZ.

Claxton, Guy (2002), *Building Learning Power*, TLO, Bristol.

Dunn, Rita and Griggs, Shirley (2003), *Synthesis of the Dunn and Dunn Learning-Style Model Research: Who, What, When, Where, and So What?*, St John's University, New York.

Gilbert, Ian (2002), *Essential Motivation in the Classroom*, Routledge/Falmer, London.

Glasser, William (1986), *Control Theory in the Classroom*, HarperCollins, New York.

Hood, David (1998), *Our Secondary Schools Don't Work Anymore*, Profile Books, London.

Hughes, Mike (1999), *Closing the Learning Gap*, Network Educational Press, Stafford.

Jensen, Eric (1998), *Teaching With the Brain in Mind*, Association for Supervision & Curriculum Development, Alexandria, VA.

Mandel, Harvey P. and Sander, I. Marcus (1996), *Could Do Better: Why Children Underachieve and What to Do About It*, Jossey-Bass, San Francisco.

Prashnig, Barbara (2004) *The Power of Diversity*, Network Educational Press, Stafford.

Rimm, Sylvia (2004), *Why Bright Kids Get Poor Grades: And What You Can Do About It*, Random House, New York.

Schargel, Franklin P. (2003), *Dropout Prevention Tools*, Eye on Education, Larchmont, NY.

Spevak, Peter A. and Karinch, Maryann (2004), *Empowering Underachievers: How to Guide Failing Kids (8–18) to Personal Excellence*, New Horizon Press, Fall Hills, NJ.

Sterling, Stephen (2002), *Sustainable Education: Re-visioning Learning and Change*, Green Books, Dartington.

Teachers' Pocketbooks (2001–05), Laurel House, Arlesford.

The Mind Gym (2005), Time Warner Books, London.

Whitley, Michael D. (2001), *Bright Minds, Poor Grades: Understanding and Motivating Your Underachieving Child*, Perigree Books (Putnam Publishing), New York.

Index

Learning Styles in Action

Index of contributors

Other titles from Network Continuum Education

ACCELERATED LEARNING SERIES

Accelerated Learning: A User's Guide by Alistair Smith, Mark Lovatt & Derek Wise
Accelerated Learning in the Classroom by Alistair Smith
Accelerated Learning in Practice by Alistair Smith
The ALPS Approach: Accelerated learning in primary schools by Alistair Smith & Nicola Call
The ALPS Approach Resource Book by Alistair Smith & Nicola Call
MapWise by Oliver Caviglioli & Ian Harris
Creating an Accelerated Learning School by Mark Lovatt & Derek Wise
Thinking for Learning by Mel Rockett & Simon Percival
Reaching out to all learners by Cheshire LEA
Move It: Physical movement and learning by Alistair Smith
Coaching Solutions by Will Thomas & Alistair Smith
Coaching Solutions Resource Book by Will Thomas

ABLE AND TALENTED CHILDREN COLLECTION

Effective Provision for Able and Talented Children by Barry Teare
Effective Resources for Able and Talented Children by Barry Teare
More Effective Resources for Able and Talented Children by Barry Teare
Challenging Resources for Able and Talented Children by Barry Teare
Enrichment Activities for Able and Talented Children by Barry Teare
Parents' and Carers' Guide for Able and Talented Children by Barry Teare

LEARNING TO LEARN

The Practical Guide to Revision Techniques by Simon Percival
Let's Learn How to Learn: Workshops for Key Stage 2 by UFA National Team
Brain Friendly Revision by UFA National Team
Learning to Learn for Life: Research and practical examples for Foundation Stage and Key
    Stage 1 by Rebecca Goodbourn, Susie Parsons, Julia Wright, Steve Higgins & Kate Wall
Creating a Learning to Learn School by Toby Greany & Jill Rodd
Teaching Pupils How to Learn by Bill Lucas, Toby Greany, Jill Rodd & Ray Wicks

EXCITING ICT

New Tools for Learning: Accelerated learning meets ICT by John Davitt
Creative ICT in the Classroom: Using new tools for learning by the Learning Discovery Centre Team
Exciting ICT in Maths by Alison Clark-Jeavons
Exciting ICT in English by Tony Archdeacon
Exciting ICT in History by Ben Walsh

PRIMARY RESOURCES

Foundations of Literacy by Sue Palmer & Ros Bayley
Flying Start with Literacy by Ros Bayley
The Thinking Child by Nicola Call with Sally Featherstone
The Thinking Child Resource Book by Nicola Call with Sally Featherstone
Critical Skills in the Early Years by Vicki Charlesworth

Towards Successful Learning by Diana Pardoe
But Why? Developing philosophical thinking in the classroom by Sara Stanley with Steve Bowkett
Help Your Child To Succeed by Bill Lucas & Alistair Smith
Help Your Child To Succeed – Toolkit by Bill Lucas & Alistair Smith
Promoting Children's Well-Being in the Primary Years:
    The Right from the Start handbook edited by Andrew Burrell & Jeni Riley
Numeracy Activities Key Stage 2 by Afzal Ahmed & Honor Williams
Numeracy Activities Key Stage 3 by Afzal Ahmed, Honor Williams & George Wickham

LEARNING THROUGH SONGS

That's English! Learning English through songs (Key Stage 2) by Tim Harding
That's Maths! Learning maths through songs (Key Stage 2) by Tim Harding
Maths in Action! Learning maths through music & animation – interactive CD-ROM
    (Key Stage 2) by Tim Harding
That's Science! Learning science through songs (Key Stage 2) by Tim Harding
This is Science! Learning science through songs and stories (Key Stage 1) by Tim Harding

VISUAL LEARNING

Seeing History: Visual learning strategies & resources for Key Stage 3 by Tom Haward
Reaching out to all thinkers by Ian Harris & Oliver Caviglioli
Think it–Map it! by Ian Harris & Oliver Caviglioli
Thinking Skills & Eye Q by Oliver Caviglioli, Ian Harris & Bill Tindall

DISPLAY MATERIAL

Bright Sparks by Alistair Smith
More Bright Sparks by Alistair Smith
Leading Learning by Alistair Smith
Move It Posters: Physical movement and learning by Alistair Smith
Multiple Intelligence Posters (KS1 and KS2–4) edited by Alistair Smith
Emotional Intelligence Posters (KS1 and KS2–4) edited by Alistair Smith
Thinking Skills & Eye Q Posters by Oliver Caviglioli, Ian Harris & Bill Tindall

EMOTIONAL INTELLIGENCE

Multiple Intelligences in Practice: Enhancing self-esteem and learning in the classroom
    by Mike Fleetham
Moving to Secondary School by Lynda Measor with Mike Fleetham
Future Directions by Diane Carrington & Helen Whitten
Tooncards: A multi-purpose resource for developing communication skills by Chris Terrell
Becoming Emotionally Intelligent by Catherine Corrie
Lend Us Your Ears by Rosemary Sage
Class Talk by Rosemary Sage
A World of Difference by Rosemary Sage
Best behaviour and Best behaviour FIRST AID by Peter Relf, Rod Hirst, Jan Richardson & Georgina Youdell
    Best behaviour FIRST AID also available separately
Self-Intelligence by Stephen Bowkett
Imagine That... by Stephen Bowkett
ALPS StoryMaker by Stephen Bowkett
StoryMaker Catch Pack by Stephen Bowkett
With Drama in Mind by Patrice Baldwin

PERSONALIZING LEARNING

Personalizing Learning: Transforming education for every child
by John West-Burnham & Max Coates

Transforming Education for Every Child: A practical handbook
by John West-Burnham & Max Coates

Personalizing Learning in the 21st Century edited by Sara de Freitas & Chris Yapp

The Power of Diversity by Barbara Prashnig

EFFECTIVE LEARNING & LEADERSHIP

Effective Heads of Department by Phil Jones & Nick Sparks

Leading the Learning School by Colin Weatherley

Transforming Teaching & Learning by Colin Weatherley with Bruce Bonney, John Kerr & Jo Morrison

Classroom Management by Philip Waterhouse & Chris Dickinson

Effective Learning Activities by Chris Dickinson

Making Pupil Data Powerful by Maggie Pringle & Tony Cobb

Raising Boys' Achievement by Jon Pickering

Getting Started by Henry Liebling

Closing the Learning Gap by Mike Hughes

Strategies for Closing the Learning Gap by Mike Hughes with Andy Vass

Tweak to Transform by Mike Hughes

Lessons are for Learning by Mike Hughes

Nurturing Independent Thinkers edited by Mike Bosher & Patrick Hazlewood

Effective Teachers by Tony Swainston

Effective Teachers in Primary Schools by Tony Swainston

Effective Leadership in Schools by Tony Swainston

Leading Change in Schools: A Practical Handbook by Sian Case

VISIONS OF EDUCATION SERIES

Discover Your Hidden Talents: The essential guide to lifelong learning by Bill Lucas

The Brain's Behind It by Alistair Smith

Wise Up by Guy Claxton

The Unfinished Revolution by John Abbott & Terry Ryan

The Learning Revolution by Gordon Dryden & Jeannette Vos

SCHOOL GOVERNORS

Questions School Governors Ask by Joan Sallis

Basics for School Governors by Joan Sallis

The Effective School Governor by David Marriott (including audio tape)

For more information and ordering details, please consult our website
www.networkpress.co.uk

Network Continuum Education – much more than publishing...

Network Continuum Education Conferences – Invigorate your teaching

Each term NCE runs a wide range of conferences on cutting edge issues in teaching and learning at venues around the UK. The emphasis is always highly practical. Regular presenters include some of our top-selling authors such as Sue Palmer, Mike Hughes and Steve Bowkett. Dates and venues for our current programme of conferences can be found on our website www.networkcontinuum.co.uk.

NCE online Learning Style Analysis – Find out how your students prefer to learn

Discovering what makes your students tick is the key to personalizing learning. NCE's Learning Style Analysis is a 50-question online evaluation that can give an immediate and thorough learning profile for every student in your class. It reveals how, when and where they learn best, whether they are right brain or left brain dominant, analytic or holistic, whether they are strongly auditory, visual, kinesthetic or tactile... and a great deal more. And for teachers who'd like to take the next step, LSA enables you to create a whole-class profile for precision lesson planning.

Developed by The Creative Learning Company in New Zealand and based on the work of Learning Styles expert Barbara Prashnig, this powerful tool allows you to analyse your own and your students' learning preferences in a more detailed way than any other product we have ever seen. To find out more about Learning Style Analysis or to order profiles visit www.networkcontinuum.co.uk/lsa.

Also available: Teaching Style Analysis and Working Style Analysis.

NCE's Critical Skills Programme – Teach your students skills for lifelong learning

The Critical Skills Programme puts pupils at the heart of learning, by providing the skills required to be successful in school and life. Classrooms are developed into effective learning environments, where pupils work collaboratively and feel safe enough to take 'learning risks'. Pupils have more ownership of their learning across the whole curriculum and are encouraged to develop not only subject knowledge but the fundamental skills of:

- problem solving
- creative thinking
- decision making
- communication
- management
- organization

- leadership
- self-direction
- quality working
- collaboration
- enterprise
- community involvement

'*The Critical Skills Programme... energizes students to think in an enterprising way. CSP gets students to think for themselves, solve problems in teams, think outside the box, to work in a structured manner. CSP is the ideal way to forge an enterprising student culture.*'

Rick Lee, Deputy Director, Barrow Community Learning Partnership

To find out more about CSP training visit the Critical Skills Programme website at www.criticalskills.co.uk

Learning Styles in Action